DANNEMORA

DANNEMORA

Two Escaped Killers, Three Weeks of Terror, and the

Largest Manhunt Ever in New York State

CHARLES A. GARDNER

CITADEL PRESS

Kensington Publishing Corp.

www.kensingtonbooks.com

CITADEL PRESS BOOKS are published by

Kensington Publishing Corp.
119 West 40th Street
New York, NY 10018

All Kensington titles, imprints, and distributed lines are available at special quantity discounts for bulk purchases for sales promotions, premiums, fund-raising, educational, or institutional use.

Special book excerpts or customized printings can also be created to fit specific needs. For details, write or phone the office of the Kensington sales manager: Kensington Publishing Corp., 119 West 40th Street, New York, NY 10018, attn: Sales Department; phone 1-800-221-2647.

CITADEL PRESS and the Citadel logo are Reg. U.S. Pat. & TM Off.

ISBN-13: 978-0-8065-3924-9
ISBN-10: 0-8065-3924-0

First Citadel hardcover printing: March 2019

10 9 8 7 6 5 4 3 2 1

Printed in the United States of America

Electronic edition: March 2019

ISBN-13: 978-0-8065-3926-3
ISBN-10: 0-8065-3926-7

Dedicated to all law enforcement

CONTENTS

PROLOGUE
INSIDE HONOR BLOCK

As the weekend began, the two killers returned to the top tier of Cell Block A, finished with Friday's work in the prison tailor shops. But instead of joining the other inmates for evening recreation, they stayed behind in their cells. This didn't attract much notice; both were in the habit of skipping recreation. In fact, it had been months since either of them had joined in the card games or clustered around one of the TVs down on the block's first level.

Like most nights, they were busy, taking advantage of their neighbors' absence for a few hours. But tonight was different. Tonight it was time to pack.

In cell A-6-23, the balding blond thirty-four-year-old cop-killer was stuffing clothing, a pair of hiking boots, and a stash of food into a cloth guitar case. Next door, in A-6-22, the burly forty-eight-year-old double murderer—the jailhouse artist the other inmates called "Hacksaw"—was loading up a backpack he'd stitched together from stolen fabric on one of the prison's sewing machines. He had a new pair of boots, too, which he set on the floor along with his backpack.

By a quarter to ten, they were done, and the packed bags tucked out of sight. That's when the other inmates filed past on the way back to their own cells.

Instead of eating earlier in Clinton prison's mess hall, they waited until after recreation and prepared their own suppers in their cells. This wasn't unusual, either. Tonight's dinner was chicken and salad, and plenty of it. Enough to share with the guy in A-6-21. The same guy that Hacksaw had presented with a TV set just that morning. A guy who now had more than one reason to be grateful to his neighbor. And, along with his neighbor's morbid but well-deserved nickname, another reason to keep his mouth shut about anything he might hear going on next door that night.

When eleven o'clock arrived, the cop-killer in A-6-23 laughed to himself. He didn't like the guard who would be making the midnight-shift count; he was one of those sticklers who wouldn't let the little things slide. He'd shine a flashlight into each cell and make each man show himself, instead of just taking for granted that somebody was under every pile of blankets. But before tonight's guard shift was over, the inmate assured himself, that uniformed prick would finally get his. And hard.

The count was finished a few minutes after eleven, and the cells went dark. As soon as the guards' footsteps receded down the stairs from the third tier, the two inmates quickly re-made their beds. Stuffed bundles of clothing made it look like somebody was in each bunk. Hacksaw took the time to write a couple of notes that he'd leave behind. One of those he wrote with a black Sharpie marker on a painting of Tony Soprano. He'd painted it himself; he was as skilled with a brush as he was with a saw. The note said, "Time to go Kid 6/5/15."

Soon it would be midnight. But for now, it was still June 5, 2015. In less than an hour, he hoped, he and his friend would be climbing into a Jeep on one of the back streets of Dannemora, New York, and on their way to Mexico. First, though, he had to remove another of his paintings, revealing the hole he'd sawed in his cell's steel back wall. After slipping through onto a dimly lit catwalk in the utility space behind the cells, he reached back through the hole and returned the artwork to its place, securing it to the steel wall with magnets. Next to him, his younger friend was doing much the same, pulling his guitar case through the steel wall, camouflaging the hole behind him.

As they'd done on so many other nights, both inmates quietly slid into a gap between the catwalk and the steel walls, using pipes and conduits as rungs to climb down into the prison's subterranean guts. There they threaded their way through what was now a familiar maze of tunnels. Well before midnight, they squirmed through a stretch of eighteen-inch pipe under Clinton Correctional Facility's thirty-foot-high perimeter wall. A few minutes and a few hundred yards later, they arrived at a manhole that led up to the street. They were early.

Now it was just a matter of waiting the few minutes until midnight, when the Jeep that would complete their escape was due to arrive. The young cop-killer worried about this and said so. But Hacksaw reassured him. Don't worry, he told his partner, as they crouched under the manhole cover. Lifting it to take a peek outside. Checking the time. Almost twelve.

Don't worry, Hacksaw said. She'd promised him she'd be here.

PART I
THE SETTING

CHAPTER 1
DAY ONE

THAT SATURDAY STARTED LIKE ANY OTHER. It was the first weekend in June, a peaceful summer day in the Adirondacks. Sunny but with a cool breeze out of the north; a nice day to be out and about.

June 6, 2015. It was Mom's birthday. At eighty-two, she was still plenty active, and we had no reason not to follow our long-standing tradition. We'd made plans to pick her up and take her for lunch at a little joint in Huntingdon, Quebec, just across the Canadian border. Haute cuisine this was not; it was just something we had been doing every year, a silly, simple ritual. "International dining," Mom likes to call it.

I was getting organized for the day when the phone rang. I checked the clock: Just after nine. Was something up with Mom? I grabbed for the hand-set. I'll admit I felt a bit of relief to hear it was one of my neighbors, but my relief quickly turned to concern. This particular neighbor worked in the state prison in Dannemora, just a forty-minute drive from here over two-lane mountain roads. The call was to warn me that something very big was going down.

It seems that two inmates had broken out. The news hit me right in the gut. See, I knew all about this place, properly called the Clinton Correctional Facility. It's where I'd started my career as a prison guard, twenty-seven years before.

I thanked my friend for the heads-up and put down the phone.

Damn. Something like 2,600 of New York State's most violent prison inmates were locked up in Dannemora, and now they were two short. All the experience I'd gained—much of it the hard way—from a quarter century in the Department of Corrections told me: nothing good could come from this.

Even so, I wasn't about to let this spoil our day. Penny, my wife, had already walked the dogs and was back in the house. I told her what I'd heard. She took this in stride; after all, she'd worked in the prison system herself. It's where we met. Even after she left Corrections to go to work for the local school district, she'd been listening to the stories about my adventures inside the prisons.

So the day was going to be business as usual as far as we both were concerned. I'm not intimidated, worried, or scared by inmates, inside or outside the walls. Here's the thing: in my opinion, inmates are like a pack of wolves. In a group, they are deadly. However, if you only have one or two of them to deal with, the odds are in your favor, especially if you're the bigger dog.

Mom lives near downtown Malone, and even though it's the biggest town in this end of the Adirondacks, that's not saying much. It took Penny and me just a couple of minutes to get to Mom's house. We headed out around 10:30, picked up Mom, and then took State Route 30 as we'd done thousands of times before, due north. I barely slowed down through a couple of tiny crossroads burgs, Constable and Trout River, and in just fifteen minutes we were at the border. That's where today's harsh reality struck us. At the normally sleepy Trout River border crossing, we saw spike strips on the pavement. A "fleet white" Ford Explorer with the blue stripes of U.S. Customs and Border Protection was blocking both lanes of Route 30, and the way into Canada.

That triggered my professional instincts—retired or not—and I took a closer look. It wasn't just a roadblock; turns out we were down-range from a posse of border agents wearing bullet-proof vests and carrying military style M-4 rifles. Looking up the business end of a high-powered semi-automatic weapon is never good. But in our peaceful neck of the woods, this would quickly become our new normal.

The officers indulged me for a couple of minutes of tense conversation that confirmed what I'd figured. High alert. Two escaped inmates. Could be anywhere. And so, naturally, they were watching the border. Very closely. Penny, Mom, and I waited in the truck for the few minutes it took an officer to open the back doors, pop open the cap's rear window, and give our Ford F-350 truck a careful inspection. A second officer moved the official vehicle and spike strip a few feet, opening up the northbound lane. A third man lowered his M-4 and waved us through to Canadian customs.

That was our first real snapshot of what was going on.

What we didn't know then, couldn't know, was that this drama would stretch out for three long, tense weeks, and come to an end just a short distance from where we were.

A few minutes after crossing the border and passing a sign that read "Montreal 63," we were sitting in LeBlanc Patate in Huntingdon, also known as Pivans to the locals. The place is just across the road from a dam and a picturesque old stone mill on the Trout River. We ordered our usual, slaw-covered dogs and fries. In my opinion, this is the very best food you can get in a cardboard box. But the menu is limited, as you might expect at a joint named for a white potato. So dessert would come from somewhere else.

It's our custom, on Mom's birthday, to take her for ice cream. For that, we drove back into the United States. This time, we used the Chateaugay, New York, crossing. Here, just like at Trout River, we ran into watchful, heavily armed customs officers. Normally they're warm and relaxed. Today, though, they were all business: not just alert, but aggravated, too. One officer explained why he was frustrated. Nobody had been able to give them a good timeline of when the inmates had escaped. And that, of course, had everything to do with how far they might have gotten by now. Not far into United States territory, at U.S. Route 11, we came to the first of several roadblocks we'd have to pass on our short drive home. Just like at the border, we were stopped and the truck was searched by state troopers carrying assault weapons. Their tactics were familiar to me. During my years in uniform, I'd been through many a drill myself on how to conduct a roadblock and search a vehicle.

This roadblock is where I first saw what would be in everybody's faces for weeks: these escaped inmates' mug shots.

Their names were David Sweat and Richard Matt. These guys, the troopers told us, were both convicted murderers. Not too surprising, considering that the great majority of inmates at Clinton had committed violent crimes. Both of these characters were considered extremely dangerous. And these officers, like the customs agents at the border, were unhappy that they didn't have better information about when the two had broken out.

From the troopers at the roadblocks, I learned a bit about who they were looking for. Richard Matt had been in prison for the kidnapping, torture, and murder of a seventy-six-year-old businessman. Matt had been in his employ. His victim's body was cut into pieces and thrown into a river. David Sweat had been convicted of murdering a deputy sheriff by shooting him and running him over with a car.

Despite this sobering news, I was determined to carry on with the second course of Mom's annual birthday celebration. By the time we got to Harrigan's ice cream stand just past the four corners at Brainardsville, we'd been through a second roadblock and were only twenty-five miles from Clinton Correctional Facility. Delicious as Harrigan's soft-serve is, after all we'd been through that day, we just didn't have our hearts in this simple and sacred tradition. I told myself, this is no joke. We need to get Mom home where she'll be safe.

Mom was happy to get back to her place in Malone. She told me she wasn't going to let this business scare her. She's no stranger to the prison system; she'd worked in the Department of Corrections herself, as a nurse.

But when we got home, we went right to the TV. For the rest of the day we flipped obsessively from channel to channel, getting snippets of the story from both local and national media. We didn't know this yet, but we were in the middle of what was quickly shaping up to be New York State's biggest and most elaborate manhunt ever.

On day one, I thought about this from my perspective as a retired corrections lieutenant. But how this could change all of our lives, I had no idea. And as it unfolded, it became more than a cops-and-robbers story—or cops and murderers. Through the weeks leading to its bloody conclusion, it would prove to be an example of law enforcement at its best. But it also turned out to be a tale of treachery, lust, and betrayal. At least two prison workers had betrayed their professional trust and the state's public safety. A veteran guard had let inmates get the better of him, turning him into an unwitting conduit for tools they would use in their breakout. And a married woman had cheated with two vicious killers, conspired with them to kill her husband, and planned to run off with them after they escaped. At the end, even the escapees would turn on each other, one of them abandoning the other to his fate.

And at the very top of New York State's government, powerful men behind desks found scapegoats among the prison's staff. When somebody had to take the fall for the conditions in Clinton prison, those at the top paid no penalty—even though their own decisions had made those conditions inevitable.

What happened in the Clinton prison was the predictable result of twenty-plus years of relentless cost-cutting pressure from the state. This left the Corrections staff with no choice but to set priorities among conflicting rules—rules that couldn't all be followed to the letter. Unless guards substituted time-saving alternatives for certain required security steps, the prison's routines would come to a halt. Unmentioned when it came time to parcel out the blame was one essential fact. By skimping on resources for so many years, the state had made full compliance with its own requirements impossible.

CHAPTER 2
IRON MINES AND IRON BARS

WHEN TOURISTS DRIVE INTO NORTHERN NEW YORK'S Adirondack Park, they're entering a paradise. At each of the dozens of entrance roads stand unique welcome signs in the shape of the park.

It's hard to describe that shape. You might say it's something like a potato. That's fitting; potatoes are one of the few things our region's farmers can grow in our short summers and rocky soil. I've also heard the park's shape compared to a heart. Not a Valentine's heart, but a real, beating human heart. I won't overdo things by forcing some kind of metaphor out of the shape. But whatever the park's outlines look like to you, inside a squarish corner up near the top of the map you'll find Dannemora. Just outside the park's boundaries is Malone, thirty miles away as the crow flies. More like forty by road.

The drama began in Dannemora and unfolded through some of the park's roughest country. It ended just northeast of Malone. And that's my home.

Something visitors quickly notice is the Adirondack Park's vast size, more than six million acres that long ago were declared "forever wild."

It's a state park, but it's bigger than most national parks. It's bigger than the state of New Hampshire. And while its hundreds of miles of roads are sprinkled with little settlements, it remains one of the wildest parts of the eastern United States.

To locals like me—I was born and raised in Malone—it's just "The Park." Within its boundaries are thousands of enchanting lakes, ponds, rivers, and streams; thousands of miles of serene, picturesque hiking trails; scented wildflowers and pine trees; and a vast diversity of wildlife. A visitor to the Adirondacks soon notices a certain smell that can't be duplicated. Nature combines the scents of pine trees, flowers, water—yes, water has a smell—and fresh air. That mixture of aromas creates something unique to The Park.

But unlike most state parks elsewhere, this isn't entirely public property. Much of the park's land remains in private hands, some of it owned by timber companies. That land, in turn, is often leased to local families or little hunting clubs, who post "no trespassing" and "no hunting" signs along many of the park's remote roads and trails. Each of these hunting camps usually includes a cabin. Some of those cabins would play a crucial part in the drama.

Between the park and the Canadian border is a smaller swath of land that also figures into this story. It's a mix of farms, woods, and little towns that wasn't settled until well after most of the rest of New York. It's a place where the economy once depended on iron. Now it's more about iron bars, stone and concrete walls, and razor wire.

Lake Champlain, which separates New York from Vermont, defines the eastern edge of what we locals call The North Country. Back in the 1700s, in two wars, French and British and American armies fought over the lake. Then, like now, it was part of the direct route between New York City and Montreal. But it wasn't until well after the Revolution that settlers began to push west from the lakeshore into what's now Clinton and Franklin Counties.

Some came to farm, despite the cold climate and soil full of stones. The first land surveys were a mess. They were badly done, full of mistakes. Some said the surveyors' compasses didn't work right, and there was a good reason for that. Under the forbidding mountains and rocky ground were rich veins of iron ore. So rich that soon mines and forges were scarring the landscape and pouring smoke into the air. Forests were felled for charcoal to fuel the smelters. Plank roads and railways began to snake their way through the rugged terrain.

One of the richest deposits was under Dannemora Mountain, which rises just north of where the village is now. Both mountain and village were named for an iron-working town in Sweden. Some of its people were early immigrants to this corner of New York.

As the iron industry grew, it spawned towns and a canal to carry ingots from Lake Champlain down to the Hudson River. By the time of the Civil War, America's wealth depended on iron. Iron helped to win that war: a war of ironclad ships, iron artillery and locomotives, iron rails and rifles.

In the center of my home town, right next to the gazebo on Malone's New England-style village green, a pair of Civil War cannons point toward the First Congregational Church. (The church, before the war, had been a stop on the Underground Railroad; ironically, respectable townspeople once took big risks to help fugitives find their way to freedom in Canada.) Those heavy artillery pieces were part of that overwhelming weight of iron that won the Civil War. Three decades later, those iron artifacts came back to the North Country, with a plaque that declared, "1861-1865, Presented by the Secretary of War" to our local veterans' post. Amazingly, this small region straddling the Adirondacks, Lake Champlain, and the Canadian border supplied a full quarter of the iron the Union would use to defeat the South.

Long before that could happen, though, the North Country's mines needed labor. And in the 1840s, the state of New York found a ready supply of new workers for this growing industry. Convicts.

Just like today, New York's prison system was shaped by political pressures. Business owners and early unions didn't want competition from prison labor, but they didn't mind letting convicts toil in far-away mines and smelters. The state hired a man named Silas Cook to get this new prison-labor system going.

In the spring of 1845, as soon as the ice broke up, barges brought men from the state's two older prisons, Auburn and Sing Sing, to Lake Champlain's western shore. Guards marched them fifteen miles inland to Dannemora. Waiting on the mountainside was a stockade, which local men had built in the dead of winter, when snowdrifts lay five feet deep on the site.

When those first prisoners arrived in late April, their first task was to build their own housing. Once that was finished, the convicts were put to work in the iron mines nearby.

And ever since, this and many newer prisons have been essential to the region, and to the livelihoods of thousands of people. People like me.

CHAPTER 3
LITTLE SIBERIA

TODAY, THE VILLAGE OF DANNEMORA is one of the biggest of the hundred sleepy towns dotting the Adirondack Park. It's a company town—if the New York State Department of Corrections counts as a "company." Since 1845, what's now called Clinton Correctional Facility has sat on the steep slope above the village's few streets. It's New York's largest maximum-security prison, and it's called "Little Siberia." The name fits for several reasons. First is the severe climate. You won't find harsher winters in America's "lower forty-eight" than in this isolated part of upstate New York. And then there is the remoteness itself. A third similarity to Siberia, and the chain of prisons the Soviets called the Gulag, is Clinton's history of supplying convict labor for mines.

So Dannemora is now, as it's always been, a prison town. That sets it apart from the rest of the Adirondack Park's peace and serenity. It's impossible to drive through on State Route 374 without seeing the rugged old stone buildings on the hillside and the wall that looms along the highway.

It's been more than a century since convicts last went out to mine iron ore. But the prison still puts its inmates to work for the state's benefit. Much of the drama that played out 170 years after the prison opened took place in its modern-day industrial workshops.

Over the decades the Clinton Prison expanded and grew. In

1887, the thirty-foot stone-and-concrete wall was built, a mile around, to surround the prison grounds. Capital punishment by means of an electric chair was introduced in the 1890s and eventually abandoned a couple of decades later. A treatment center was opened for prisoners with tuberculosis. A mental health wing was built for those diagnosed as insane.

In 1929, a riot caused severe damage. In the aftermath, most of the prison's buildings were repaired or rebuilt. The construction work added school space, modern cell blocks, and a free-standing Catholic church on the prison grounds. This unique institution is the Church of St. Dismas, known as "The Good Thief." The name remembers one of the criminals who were crucified alongside Jesus.

Prison architecture in those days consisted of three-story cell blocks to house inmates. Each of a Clinton cell block's three tiers holds one hundred cells, six by eight feet. These are arranged so the back walls of a row of fifty cells share a narrow common passageway with the back walls of the other fifty cells. We call each of these fifty-cell rows a "company." This pattern, with a steel-mesh catwalk running down the middle of each tier, was repeated on all three levels and in all the prison's housing units.

In the catwalk are the plumbing and wiring that serve the cells. Each cell has a sink, a toilet and an electrical outlet. A single overhead light fixture, armored to protect the bulb and keep the wiring out of reach, is controlled by a switch in the cell. The catwalk gives maintenance workers access to each cell's plumbing and electrical service, with no need for any contact with the prisoner.

These eighty-plus-year-old blocks still house most of Clinton's inmates.

As the Clinton prison grew, Dannemora grew with it.

A prison town has its own culture. The prison affects everyone who lives in Dannemora. If you don't work there, your neighbor does, or one of your relatives. Like in any old town a long way from anywhere, generations of interconnected extended families wove a vast web of kinship. If you live there, you definitely know someone who goes inside those ominous thirty-foot walls every day to feed their family. What nobody talks about—not inside the walls, or outside—is the danger. That's just the way of life in Dannemora. For that matter, that way of life extends to many of the other towns within a fifty-mile radius, where thousands of people work in a half-dozen other prisons.

Corrections has its own culture and language, which aren't easily understood unless you're part of it. I made the decision to be part of that culture after I got out of college. I wasn't especially interested in the family business, selling ice. And I noticed that friends of mine were driving shiny new pickups, buying nice toys like all-terrain vehicles, and had plenty of cash in their pockets, all thanks to jobs in the prison system. That made up my mind to choose a Corrections career myself.

I'll never forget the day I entered the Clinton Correctional Facility for the first time. It was 1988 and I was a rookie prison guard. The veteran guards would say I was still "shitting academy food." It's where they sent me to start my on-the-job training. The solid steel door is blank except for a tiny window and a worn handle. It looks like it weighs a ton. That door slamming behind me made a thunderous sound of steel on steel, like nothing I'd ever heard before. The hair bristled on the back of my neck as I realized I was inside until someone let me out. Even for those wearing the state's blue uniform, no amount of training can prepare you for that feeling. I knew I wasn't in Kansas anymore.

The guards, and everyone else on the prison staff, quickly learn to pay attention to their instincts. The secret to survival, the old veterans told me, is trust your gut, keep your guard up, and count on each other. As I put years under my belt, working in other prisons all over the state, I passed those lessons on to the newbies. Unfortunately, as it would turn out, some of the staff at Clinton either failed to learn those lessons or forgot them.

Inside the walls, Clinton Correctional Facility is a small city, parallel to but completely cut off from the village just outside. This self-contained little city features all the conveniences you'd expect. The prison's housing blocks take the place of apartments and houses; its medical department, doctors, and nurses compare to a good-sized town's hospital; and its mess hall stands in for a restaurant. Chapel, outdoor recreation areas, gyms, and training facilities are equivalent to churches, parks, fitness clubs, and schools. And much more so than in most communities, mental health and substance-abuse treatment centers address some of the reasons this small city's residents are here to begin with.

Once inside, I quickly felt something in the air. Prison has energy; I sensed it immediately. Prison also has a smell. Clinton is older than most prisons. It opened 172 years ago. Its aging masonry walls have seen hard labor, one-on-one fights and mass riots, fires, and death. Death from all causes, natural and not. Inmates and guards have been murdered, and of course there were the executions. All of this leaves behind a smell. Its ingredients include blood, smoke, body odor, tear gas, and gunpowder, mixed with the damp, musty stink of stone and concrete. Clinton's unique smell doesn't go away. Everything that happens within the wall's confines stays there. You can't just open a window and air the place out.

Then there's the smell of urine and feces. Let me explain. Imagine yourself as a guard doing your rounds when suddenly you are hit with a potion of excrement thrown by an inmate. In New York State's official terminology, this is delicately called a "throwing incident." What the phrase doesn't explain is that inmates purposely piss and shit into a container, then allow this mess to ferment for a few days. The sole purpose is to throw it onto a member of the prison staff. This is a dramatic way that inmates inform the staff that they are not happy. Thus, another scent is added to the unique cocktail that lingers within and on the walls.

New York's largest prison, Clinton houses some 2,600 of the state's most violent, cold-blooded inmates. Most of them have a long criminal history. In its nearly two-century history, it has been home to an assortment of serial killers, rapists, murderers, and child molesters. It may not be the polite way to say this, but these are two-legged monsters.

Some of Clinton's more infamous inmates have been household names, at least in their own time. Charles "Lucky" Luciano, the Mafia crime boss with the Genovese Family, did time here. Robert Chambers, known in the New York City tabloids as the "Preppy Murderer," was a Clinton inmate. David Berkowitz, the serial murderer the tabloids called "The .44 caliber killer," and who called himself "Son of Sam," got psychiatric and medical evaluations here. And in the 1990s, the rapper Tupac Shakur served time in Clinton after conviction on sexual-assault charges.

For most of the inmate population, violence is a way of life. Simply put, on most days many of them would rather fight than fuck. It's on those days that Dannemora residents hear what's happening inside that looming concrete wall. They can all recall quiet summer nights shattered by the sound of gunshots fired into the recreational yard from one or more of the towers that rise above the wall. But those shots are part of the routine in this particular corner of The Park. Most of the brief interruptions of Dannemora's serenity are quickly forgotten.

Residents know the reason for the gunshots. They know some disturbance in the prison yard has required officers to discharge their weapons. Officially, the shots are a last resort and a life-saving measure to restore order. After more than two hundred years of operating prisons, the State of New York has developed a thick stack of policies, directives, and procedures. These were the result of generations of trial and error, and critical review of policies and procedures that failed, sometimes spectacularly. Some of these methods apply state-wide; others are specific to individual facilities. Like Clinton. All are meant to ensure the safe and secure operation of the state's prisons. And yet, as administrations and politics change, so do policies, directives, and procedures. And then what happens?

Unfortunately, as in Dannemora on one tranquil June night, what happened was catastrophic failure.

CHAPTER 4
AMENITIES AND ACCOMMODATIONS

SHORTLY AFTER CLINTON'S STEEL DOORS SLAMMED SHUT behind them, the convicted murderers David Sweat and Richard Matt found themselves working in the prison's tailor shops. They made decent money. All inmates in New York State prisons get some sort of compensation regardless of whether they work, go to school, or do nothing.

You read me right. "All inmates get" is correct. Every inmate gets paid for going to prison. It's not a lot, but the pay is enough to buy things in the prison commissary or through mail-order companies outside the walls. The commissaries in the New York State Correctional Facilities sell a vast range of items such as cigarettes, canned foods, candy, snacks, soda, and even ice cream. Because of its competitive bidding requirements and volume buying, New York State enjoys purchasing power that lets inmates buy this stuff tax free and for lower prices than what you or I pay at a store.

Inmates are allowed to receive packages from friends, family, and mail-order companies. If a prisoner wants cigars or music, art supplies or a new pair of tighty-whities, he can order them with little or no trouble.

An inmate's life is not all about work or going to school. Let's not forget play time. In the correction system's recreational areas, you'll find basketball courts, handball courts, soccer fields, weight lifting equipment, volleyball nets, and softball diamonds. For those who prefer activities less strenuous, ping-pong, cards, dominos, chess, and checkers are available. Frequently inmates can find a sound-proof music room in which to practice their instrument or prepare for their next gig. Then there's TV. A wide selection of programming is offered for inmates' enjoyment. They can sit back and watch local channels and cable, including sports and HBO. Newly released movies are provided for their viewing pleasure via an in-house system.

Those who like to read or do research will find libraries, including law libraries, second to none. The reading and research materials available to inmates would astound local librarians and make small-town lawyers envious.

New York State also promptly provides for all inmates' medical, dental, and optical needs. Any necessary medication, medical, or surgical procedure and corrective eyewear are provided free of charge.

Housing is guaranteed to be warm and dry. Bedding, clothing, and shoes are always supplied. If newly arriving inmates were welcomed with brochures, they would emphasize the twenty-four hour security and rooms with a view.

The icing on the cake is "Honor Block" housing. Most of New York's correctional facilities have Honor Blocks. These are where the "good" inmates reside. At Clinton, the convicted cop killer David Sweat and the convicted torture-murderer Richard Matt were housed in the Honor Block.

How did that happen?

The Department of Corrections entrusts each facility's superintendent with the authority to manage the Honor Block housing units. A clean slate—behind bars—is one of the factors for deciding who gets to live in the Honor Blocks. The inmate's crime isn't considered, just his behavior once he gets into prison.

Many perks come with living in an Honor Block. The honored inmates are allowed extra time out of their cells to cook or for recreation. They get more liberal hours to use the telephone and have additional shower privileges. Some facilities in New York

State even allow inmates to order food from local restaurants. Delivery only, of course; we do have to draw the line somewhere. No take-out is allowed.

Sadly, a common joke among correctional staff members is that the walls or fencing around the prisons are not to keep the inmates in, but to keep the public out. If they only knew.

CHAPTER 5
RIGHT-SIZING

THE HISTORY OF NEW YORK STATE PRISONS BEGAN in 1797, when a single prison served the whole state. Newgate Prison in New York City was the state's only prison for twenty years. It was eventually replaced by newer prisons—Auburn in the Finger Lakes region and Sing Sing along the Hudson. It was to Sing Sing that convicts were "sent up the river." Both those old prisons are still operating. I worked most of my first year as a guard at Sing Sing.

Because of the iron mines on Dannemora Mountain, the state's third prison would be built in Clinton County, then as now remote from New York's population centers. It's about seventeen miles from Vermont, on the far side of Lake Champlain, and thirty miles from Canada.

By 1973, New York State had eighteen prisons. But that wouldn't be enough. The introduction that year of the so-called Rockefeller drug laws created a huge influx of prisoners who would have to be housed. That created a construction boom as the state drastically expanded its prisons.

In New York, the Department of Corrections handles what are called "state-ready" inmates. They have been convicted or pled guilty to a crime that requires imprisonment for a year or more. Shorter sentences are served in county jails. Those local lock-ups transfer their state-ready prisoners to the DOC—but only when space is available.

To accommodate the influx of inmates, Corrections acquired many vacant state-owned properties, converting some old buildings to prisons. The goal was to reduce overcrowding of state-ready inmates in county jails. Half-way between Dannemora and Malone, in the former iron-mining town of Lyon Mountain, the state turned a vacant elementary school into a minimum-security prison. In other places, the state built "cookie-cutter" facilities. These new medium-security prisons had identical dormitory-style housing. Their layouts, including housing units, mess halls, infirmaries and such, were all exactly the same, all across the state.

Economically struggling regions like the North Country got more than their share of these new prisons. In addition to Dannemora and Lyon Mountain, my home town of Malone now has three state correctional facilities, one after the other along the same road: the Upstate "maxi-max," and two medium-security prisons, Franklin and Bare Hill. After less than two years working far from home and family, I was transferred to the almost brand-new Franklin Correctional Facility.

Just in the three northernmost counties of Clinton, Franklin and Essex, the state also opened prisons in Chateaugay, Altona, Ray Brook, Gabriels, and Moriah. Taking the place of the played-out iron mines and a dying textile industry, the prisons became the region's chief source of jobs.

Even so, the State of New York couldn't build prisons quickly enough to meet the need. That led legislators to explore changing the laws. In the late 1980s, just as I was starting my career in corrections, the Legislature voted twice to reform the 1973 Rockefeller drug laws. Some of these changes allowed early release. The result was that thousands of inmates returned to the streets before serving their full court-ordered sentences.

Even so, massive numbers of inmates kept pouring into the system. In the 1990s, to help cope with the influx, the Corrections bureaucracy in Albany changed its ratio of staff to inmates. The chore of monitoring the custody, care, and control of more inmates with less staff was ordered by people sitting in paneled offices in the state capital, far removed from the realities behind the prison walls. To my eyes, like most of the rank-and-file guards, the state's priority had shifted from public safety to fiscal savings. The unofficial motto seemed to be "Do more with less." That penny-pinching attitude soon became the norm in the department.

New York's prisons began to double-bunk or double-cell inmates. Because of the lower staff-to-inmate ratios, cells or cubicles that had been engineered for one inmate now housed two. Additionally, the gymnasiums were transformed into a housing unit containing hundreds of inmates. No new guards were assigned to these new housing units; the same number of officers was now responsible for more inmates. The loss of the gymnasium for indoor recreation left a void that the state filled by purchasing multi-million dollar seasonal domes. These were air-supported fabric structures used as temporary recreational facilities. In Corrections, they were known as "bubbles."

At its peak in 1999, the state system held more than 71,000 inmates in seventy correctional facilities. Then, however, because of the laws allowing early release to inmates, including sex offenders and the mentally ill, prison populations began to fall.

By then I had passed the exam to be promoted to sergeant. Corrections sergeants are subject to assignment anywhere in the state, and for a few months I was sent to Taconic, a medium-security women's prison just outside New York City. But soon I was back in Malone, at Upstate Correctional Facility, which then was a brand-new "maxi-max" prison. There, security is so extreme that inmates spend twenty-three hours a day in their cells. Their placement into this special housing facility is often due to their violent behavior toward the staff or other inmates. Their daily hour of exercise and fresh air is spent on a fenced-in balcony attached to each cell. After a couple of years at Upstate, I was transferred just a few hundred yards up Bare Hill Road to Franklin, which I still consider my "home jail."

By the late 2000s, the early-release programs and double-bunking allowed the state to start closing prisons, even some that had just opened a few years before. Each year at budget time, the governor's office looked to the Department of Corrections to save

costs by mothballing still more sites. But whenever a prison closing was proposed, towns held rallies to defend important pieces
of their local economies. The arguments always included the
point that the threatened institutions helped keep all New Yorkers
safe. Nevertheless, over the years, sixteen prisons closed, including Camp Gabriels, Lyon Mountain, and Chateaugay right in my
back yard.

Prison closings were just the start of this chronic budget squeez-
ing. Next came a review and audit of all jobs and job descriptions.
Supervisors in each prison were assigned this duty. Their mandate
was to find ways to save money by eliminating both civilian and
uniformed jobs. Like in the corporate world, new weasel words
were used instead of "layoffs" or "downsizing." Trying to "right
size" the number of uniformed prison guards, Corrections combined what had once been separate positions. Surviving staff members found extra duties added to their daily workloads. Guards
were expected to work without breaks or lunch time to complete
all their newly assigned duties. Other jobs were eliminated or
merged after Corrections leadership in Albany deemed them nonessential.

After all the cutbacks, the New York State Department of Corrections and Community Supervision—its full official name since
2011 when the Division of Parole was folded in—now houses
around fifty-four thousand inmates. About twenty thousand corrections officers remain to provide security at fifty-four correctional facilities. More than three thousand of them work in the
seven surviving prisons in my corner of the state. That's almost
two percent of the three counties' total population.

By far the biggest portion of those are the thousand uniformed
corrections officers assigned to Clinton Correctional Facility.
They cover three daily shifts, managing 2,600 of the state's most
incorrigible inmates. The worst of the worst.

PART II
THE INMATES

CHAPTER 6

TWO HARD CASES

IN TWENTY-FIVE YEARS AS A PRISON GUARD, I dealt with and stood face to face with some very scary people. New York State keeps its most dangerous criminals in its maximum-security facilities, which include Clinton. Two of the worst of the hard cases who ended up there were David Sweat and Richard Matt. Both had long criminal histories; both committed especially brutal murders.

David Sweat is a cop-killer. He was convicted of killing Broome County Deputy Sheriff Kevin J. Tarsia before dawn on the Fourth of July, 2002.

Broome County is in New York's Southern Tier. Its biggest city is Binghamton. Tarsia was on night-shift duty early that holiday morning, patrolling in a little place called Kirkwood. In the town park, he happened upon Sweat and his accomplices. They had just burglarized a gun store across the state line in Pennsylvania. Sweat was just twenty-two at the time. After the deputy got out of his patrol car, Sweat ambushed him, a pistol in one hand and an assault rifle in the other. He came out shooting fifteen times, hitting Tarsia a number of times. Then he ran over him with his souped-up gold Honda Accord, dragging him across an asphalt parking lot. The deputy's severe injuries didn't kill him, though. That remained for one of Sweat's companions to do, with the deputy's own .40 caliber Glock pistol. He shot Deputy Tarsia twice in the face.

Sweat was a methodical criminal, with a habit of making written plans. After his arrest for Tarsia's murder, investigators found an outline of the gun shop burglary in a trash can. Fingerprints on the paper were identified as Sweat's. Among his other plans, witnesses said, was one with parallels to his eventual prison break. He used stolen trucks and a stolen camper to hide out in the woods outside Kirkwood.

The court's verdict was guilty of murder in the first degree. The sentence was life without parole. On November 12, 2003, when he was twenty-four years old, Clinton Correctional Facility became home for David Sweat. He remained inside Clinton's walls for nearly twelve years until he finally chiseled and sawed his way out.

All inmates entering the prison system get evaluated by the Department of Corrections. Sweat was motivated by lack of regard for life as well as for the criminal justice system compounded with the lack of emotional control.

Considering the nature of Sweat's crime, the Department of Corrections put him in a special classification. He became a Central Monitoring Case inmate.

That means anyone transporting a CMC inmate outside his assigned prison's secure walls must take special precautions. The prisoner's movements must be tracked. And departmental policy requires that before any CMC inmate is moved, Corrections leadership—in Albany's Central Office Building #2—must grant permission.

Sweat's murder conviction was his second "bid," prison slang for a stint behind bars. He had already done nineteen months in New York's prison system, starting in 1997. The offense was attempted burglary. He was eighteen. The math makes it clear: Sweat has spent nearly half of his life confined to a group youth home or behind bars.

An insight into how he thinks is the shrewd but devious way he always plotted out his crimes on paper. After his first arrest, police discovered a detailed written plan for his attempted heist of the group youth home where he resided.

Broome County jailers searching his cell for contraband then discovered a list of other crimes Sweat was planning to commit. With his history of documenting his criminal plans, I have to wonder if, somewhere, he had written down how he intended to escape from Clinton Correctional Facility. If so, those plans haven't turned up, at least as far as official Corrections records show.

From his childhood on, it was clear to anyone who had any contact with Sweat that the needle of his moral compass was not pointing in the right direction.

I define Richard William "Hacksaw" Matt as a six-foot, two-hundred-ten-pound monster posing as a human.

Matt's arrest history includes twenty different crimes. Murder, kidnapping, robbery, rape, and assault are not an all-inclusive list.

His rap sheet also includes a number of escapes and attempted escapes. It's noteworthy to me that in 1979, when he was still a teenager, Matt escaped from a group home where he had been sent by a juvenile court. He hid in the Allegany State Park—"The Wilderness Playground of Western New York"—while law officers searched for him. While on the run, Matt survived by burglarizing seasonal homes to get food and shelter. This tactic from his first documented escape mirrored how he would behave during his last.

In 1986, under arrest on an assault charge, he escaped from the Erie County Jail in Buffalo by climbing over its perimeter fence. He eluded police for a week before he was captured. This was his second documented escape.

Like his ultimate fellow escapee Sweat, Matt killed without remorse. He was motivated by monetary gain and showed a callous indifference to life.

He earned his prison nickname, "Hacksaw," from the way he dismembered the body of his first murder victim.

In December 1997, he abducted, tortured, and killed his former boss, seventy-six-year-old William Rickerson. The owner of a wholesale food company, Rickerson had hired Matt—and then fired him. Matt had been stealing meat and selling it. Matt and an accomplice kidnapped Rickerson because they believed he had a large cache of money hidden away. They bound him with duct tape and forced him into the trunk of a car, keeping him there in freezing winter weather for nearly thirty hours. His ordeal was punctuated by savage beatings and other tortures as the kidnappers drove from New York through Pennsylvania to Ohio and back.

Finally, enraged at not getting what he wanted, Matt snapped his victim's neck. He then sawed Rickerson's body into pieces. After throwing the dismembered body into the icy Niagara River, Matt fled to Mexico. Empty handed. Of course he never did find any hoard of cash; just $80 and some credit cards from Rickerson's wallet. Within two months, though, his psychotic impulses and his lust for money led to another murder. In February 1998, he stabbed an American engineer several times in the back and the gut, all for the sake of a few hundred dollars.

A Mexican court convicted Matt of murder and sentenced him to twenty-three years. He tried to escape from a Mexican prison by climbing onto a roof, where guards shot him. He recovered from that injury in a prison hospital. If successful, it would have been his third escape.

In 2007, Mexico returned him to United States authorities after he'd served less than half of his sentence. In a Niagara County court, he would then answer to the charges of Rickerson's murder, robbery, and kidnapping. During his trial in 2008, Matt plotted an escape from the county jail. Jailers got wind of this plan and stopped it before he could break out. His score at that point: four attempts, half of them successful.

While the trial went on, authorities took such extra security steps as stationing a sniper on the courthouse roof. Louis Haremski, who prosecuted that case, recalled that Matt swore that if he got away again, he'd never surrender. "Matt told one of the other prisoners that if anybody interfered with him he would 'gut a cop' and not be taken alive."

This undisciplined but cunning career criminal would be convicted of all charges. The sentence was twenty-five years to life.

Matt would enter the Department of Corrections' custody in May 2008 for his third state "bid."

Like Sweat, Matt was classified as a Central Monitoring Case inmate because of his many escapes. He could never be moved outside his prison's walls, regardless of the reason, without an OK from Central Office Building #2 in Albany.

After two months, the state transferred him to Clinton Correctional Facility. It would be his home until he broke out the night of June 5, 2015, his fifth documented attempt. It was his third successful escape—and his last.

Matt was anything but a model inmate. Guards and other prison employees who knew him described him as a "master of manipulation," "psychotic," and "an evil monster." Not surprisingly, it turns out that both Sweat and Matt were on Clinton's so-called "Top 40" list, which actually identifies about seventy-five high-profile or high-risk inmates. The sorts of things that get an inmate on that list include committing a high-profile crime, accepting contraband or manipulating prison staff members. Exactly what both Matt and Sweat were masters of.

CHAPTER 7

BROKEN BOY,
BROKEN TOYS

A CLOSE LOOK AT DAVID SWEAT'S CHILDHOOD provides plenty of clues to how he embarked on his criminal career.

He grew up in New York State's Southern Tier, in Broome County, near the Pennsylvania state line. Born in Binghamton on June 14, 1980, his first home was in Deposit, a small town with small-town values. He and his two sisters were raised by a single mother, Pamela.

It was not a traditional home environment. David's childhood years were filled with assorted house guests and roommates who rotated in and out of the house. Patricia Desmond and her boyfriend lived with the Sweats. She was quoted in a *New York Times* article as saying, "He (Sweat) really wasn't raised into the best society. We drank a lot, we partied a lot. His life was into turmoil." This home environment and irregular schooling fostered David's behavioral problems and violent tendencies.

Several documented instances showed David was already a hellion as a small boy. He displayed extreme personality changes, going from nice to nasty in a flash. This troubled boy often destroyed his own toy cars by smashing them with rocks or burning them. At the early age of nine, his mother and other authority figures became victims of his defiance and other severe behavioral problems. He is known to have thrown a chair and knives at his mom.

Also as a nine-year-old, David hid a butcher knife in his backpack and brought it into his elementary school. The school suspended him.

It was around this time, in the 1990s, that young David became a blip on the radar of law enforcement. Police began to document the boy's toxic environment, filled with empty beer cans and a smoky haze. From his home's constant turmoil and lack of family structure emerged a broken and damaged David Sweat.

His mother eventually admitted she couldn't handle her son. Pamela sent David to her brother's home in Florida. This was her attempt to provide him with a fresh start and some structure in hope of making him a productive member of society. But the plan failed, spectacularly. During David's short stay in the Sunshine State, he stole his aunt's car and wrecked it. That was too much for the uncle and aunt. Their decision was return to sender: back to his mother in New York.

By the time he was a teenager, Sweat had already become the perfect candidate for New York State's "PINS" classification: Person In Need of Supervision. He was placed on PINS at twelve years old on March 5, 1993. The PINS program is designed to change a child whose behavior is dangerous or out of control, or who often disobeys his parents, guardians, or other authorities, diverting him from the criminal justice system.

While he was still in early adolescence, the Department of Social Services intervened and placed David and his sisters in foster care. For a time, he lived in a group youth home on Schiller Street in Binghamton. Things didn't improve there. He was constantly running away; authorities had to return him to the group home. He wasn't willing to stay in school, either. He dropped out of high school in the tenth grade.

What might have looked like a change for the better came in June 1995 when David got his first legitimate job. He worked as a laborer in a summer youth employment program. When that job ended in August, some speculate, he found something part-time that he was good at. He became a dope dealer.

His part-time employment didn't pay very well, though. His

need to supplement his income led him to burglary. At age six-teen, he and another teenage friend planned an elaborate heist, to steal computers and cash from the same Binghamton group youth home where David lived.

It is important to mention that David's plans for this crime were extremely detailed. He drew his own blueprints of the build-ing, showing where the cash and computers were kept. He and his accomplice would conceal their identities by wearing ski masks. He also intended to restrain a female employee, locking her in a storage closet. He wrote down every step of his plan.

The day came when the planning was done and it was time to put the plan into effect. David and his friend donned ski masks. He might not have counted on the disguise making them more conspicuous, not less. The plan went awry when a counselor spot-ted the two masked boys walking across the property and promptly phoned the police.

They quickly arrived and arrested David and his friend. Both were charged with attempted burglary. David's elaborate plan had left out one detail: what to do if you are busted.

David's case was heard in August 1996 by Judge Martin E. Smith of the Broome County Court. When the trial was concluded, David faced a term of five years of probation, which carried many specific terms and conditions. When he passed sentence on David and his friend, the judge would refer to them as "teenaged idiots."

Sweat wasn't really an idiot. Although he never finished high school, he would earn his GED in prison. And later, he was smart enough to manipulate two Department of Corrections employees into helping him break out of a maximum-security prison.

But first, he would have many more brushes with the law. In less than a year, he returned to court with new charges.

This time it was a family affair. David had a cousin, Jeffrey Nabinger Jr., known as Cueball. The two were always seen to-gether; they became partners in crime. Their mothers were sisters and the two boys had many similarities. Like David, Jeffrey came from a broken home and was a high school dropout. Both were well known to law enforcement. With their slim builds, they resembled each other physically. And both lacked the ability to get legitimate employment. The one distinct difference was that David kept his hair cut short, while Jeffrey's was always long, hanging on his shoulders and often covered by a do-rag.

Their partnership culminated in David's arrest on March 13, 1997. The Binghamton Police Department charged him with another attempted burglary and criminal mischief, a catch-all rap for damage done during a break-in. His plan was the same as before: steal cash and valuables, mainly jewelry, from homes. One of the cousins' victims was Jeffrey Nabinger's landlord.

This unsuccessful crime spree sent David to the Broome County Jail to await trial. While incarcerated, his head swarmed with ideas for future capers, which would fill many pages. If he were to be freed on bail or furlough, he wanted to be prepared.

His dream of release never came to fruition. He spent 246 days in the Broome County Jail. During that time, this self-proclaimed rebel became well known for his disruptive and violent behavior toward the staff and other inmates. He sported a "REBEL" tattoo on his left arm. A routine search of cells turned up the detailed list of crimes he intended to commit whenever he got out.

His record—the unsuccessful probation and the new arrest—brought him back into the Broome County Court, where he found himself standing again before Judge Smith. This time the judge gave him two and a third to four and a half years. On November 5, 1997, Smith turned him over to the New York State Department of Corrections. This would be David Sweat's first state "bid." Within days of being received in the prison system, he was sent to Washington Correctional Facility. This medium-security prison is in the Washington County hamlet of Comstock, between Lake George and the Vermont line. It would be Sweat's first introduction to the Adirondack region.

Within less than sixty days after arriving at Washington, Sweat received a misbehavior report for being out of place. Even when he was less than four months away from being released on parole, he would get another misbehavior report, this time for stealing and smuggling. Even in prison, he wasn't capable of obeying the rules or the guards.

While incarcerated at the Washington prison, Sweat did take advantage of its educational and vocational programs. That's where he completed the requirements for his GED, the General Equivalency Diploma.

His vocational training provided him with new skills. He took courses including electrical trades/electrician's helper and industries worker/metal assembler. His new knowledge in these areas ranged from practical skills to specialized training with machines, hand tools, and portable power tools. He also expressed an interest in auto mechanics and a possible future in such work after his release.

In preparation for his release, Sweat was transferred to Buffalo Correctional Facility. He walked out of that prison's gate on June 1, 1999, just days before his nineteenth birthday. He carried with him his GED and new skills in working with electrical systems, as well as knowledge about working with various metals and which tools to use with metals of varying thickness.

After serving just nineteen months, Sweat spent the remainder of his sentence under the supervision of New York State Parole.

The education he acquired in prison gave him abilities he didn't have before. I have to wonder: could this young man have known how valuable these new skills would become to his future?

CHAPTER 8
SWEAT'S ROAD
TO CLINTON

At the time of David Sweat's release from prison, he had spent just over twenty-seven months behind bars, between the Broome County Jail and the state's Washington and Buffalo Correctional Facility. He successfully completed his post-release supervision by the New York State Division of Parole. He reached his sentence's maximum expiration date on August 28, 2000. At the age of twenty, he was a free man.

Free, yes. But also homeless and unemployed. Sweat often stayed with his mother in a house that her new boyfriend rented on Foley Road in Kirkwood. He would couch surf between that place and friends' houses.

Sweat chose not to use the education and skills he'd acquired at the state's expense. Instead, he opted for a set of skills he learned from his fellow inmates. Let's just call them the "tools of the trade."

He became the owner of a gold 1990 Honda Accord. This car gave him the freedom to move around, a luxury he was not allowed in prison. The Accord was equipped with a moon roof and displayed red decals from a company called APC on the windshield and side mirrors. For years these markings have been placed on choppers and hot rods to signify that the ride and its owner are "bad ass" and no one should mess with either one. I find this quite humorous: a bad-ass Honda Accord with a bad-ass driver!

The Accord also sported a yellow "R" on its rear window. We don't know if he put it on, or if it had come with the used car when he bought it. Who knows? Maybe it stood for Rebel. I guess Sweat wasn't interested in keeping a low profile. How many gold Hondas with those identifying stickers could there be?

The exaggerated décor on his car was in keeping with Sweat's interest in guns and tough talk. He boasted about never having enough guns and how he used a portable radio scanner to track police movements. Witnesses would later say he'd often bragged that he'd shoot anyone, including the cops, who got in his way or prevented him from successfully committing a crime.

In March 2002, in rural Delaware County, just east of Binghamton, Sweat stopped in to visit a local business. Marino's Outdoor World is in the little river town of Hancock, New York. It stocks sporting goods, fishing gear—and hundreds of firearms. Sportsmen who patronize the store know its owner as a friendly, knowledgeable professional.

Although Sweat knew his convicted felon status prohibited him from legally buying a firearm, his visit to this well-known landmark served another purpose. He was doing a reconnaissance. What did the gun inventory look like? Was there a security system? What were the fastest ways to get in and out? After taking in that information, he left without attracting any notice.

Not long afterward, on April 25, 2002, local police took a crime report about the store. It seems that two men, both of small to medium build, had thrown a rock through the plate-glass window of Marino's Outdoor World after business hours. A witness said they went directly to a display case holding guns and smashed the glass. Within minutes the two left the store and raced away in a small car.

Seven handguns had been taken. Besides two vintage revolvers, five semi-automatics were missing, including a 9mm Smith & Wesson, a .40 caliber Glock and a 9mm Kahr. Most troubling, an Intratec firearm had also been stolen. This weapon can best be described as a semi-automatic assault rifle in a pistol frame, capable of holding high-capacity magazines for rapid fire. The missing gun, a TAC-9, is one of Intratec's higher-profile products.

Less than thirty days later, a fatal encounter on a Broome County highway would leave an indelible mark on Sweat. He wasn't involved, but the incident was big news for a time. It occurred on May 14, 2002, right in the small town of Kirkwood, where Sweat's mother lived with her boyfriend. On a strip of rural highway between Binghamton and the Pennsylvania line, a routine police traffic stop would end in the driver's death.

Here is what happened. Two New York State Troopers, S. Dean and J. Spero, were parked on the side of U.S. Highway 11 when a 1995 Dodge Spirit drove by. Its New York State inspection sticker was expired. The troopers quickly decided to pursue the car, which had two men in it. The driver was in no hurry to pull over, but eventually yielded to the police siren. As the troopers approached the vehicle, they made note of a U.S.M.C. sticker in the rear window. A quick look through the windows showed the car was clean; a routine traffic stop, the troopers concluded.

But then they started to notice that the car's two occupants weren't acting at all routinely. ID checks showed the men were Michael J. Fisher and Wayne R. Rafferty. The troopers noticed that the men's responses to their questions contradicted each other. Both men showed signs they were extremely nervous. They trembled uncontrollably while smoking cigarettes. Why, the troopers wondered, such extreme anxiety over an outdated safety inspection? They decided to remove the men from the car. Trooper Spero began by asking the passenger, Rafferty, to step out while Trooper Dean stood watch from the front of their troop car.

Trooper Spero had nearly completed a pat-down search when his greatest fear was realized. The driver, Fisher, had gotten out of the car and was pointing a gun directly at him. Spero quickly drew his sidearm and fired two shots at Fisher. Fisher also fired, hitting Spero's fingers and damaging the magazine of his gun. Meanwhile, Dean was also responding, immediately moving toward Fisher, who turned to run, Dean firing at him as he ran. He didn't get far before falling, dead, on a quiet side street. Both troopers' shots had found their mark. A license check showed the Dodge Spirit had been stolen. A more careful search than the troopers' initial look found two ski masks, latex gloves, a Bowie knife, and an empty black holster. The trunk contained stolen weapons: a .38 caliber Smith & Wesson revolver, a Ruger black powder revolver, and a Thompson rifle.

This incident is significant because we know David Sweat was well aware of it. Several weeks later, he was at the nearby home of his mother's boyfriend, Roger Henry. He boasted that if he were ever stopped by the cops after committing a crime, he would do the same as Fisher. To avoid going back to prison, he told Henry and his mother, he'd come out with guns blazing.

Others who later reported him talking this way included a couple of young admirers, "groupies" you might say, named Robert Brown and Jennifer Seely, as well as Sweat's sometime girlfriend Virginia Roberts.

He also talked big about the guns he and his cousin, Jeffrey Nabinger, had been carrying for the past two months. He said he'd bought them. Those guns, of course, would later be traced back to the smash-and-grab theft at Marino's Outdoor World.

The Fisher incident was significant to Sweat for another reason: its location. Kirkwood, the little town where Troopers Dean and Spero had pulled Fisher over, wasn't just where Sweat often crashed on his mother's sofa; it was also the focus of his next criminal plans.

As the summer of 2002 went on, police blotters began to show reports of stolen vehicles from car dealerships in Binghamton and in two nearby small towns: Fenton and Kirkwood. The thieves had a preference for trucks and SUVs. Reported stolen were a 1988 Ford Bronco, 1990 Bronco, 1990 Ford Econoline van and a Ford F-150 pickup that had been modified into a monster truck.

On July 2, in Binghamton, a 1979 Winnebago motor home was reported stolen.

All of these vehicles found their way to Kirkwood, off the grid. Tucked up against the interchange where Interstates 81 and 86 join is a two-lane road called Corporate Drive. It threads its way past a string of light industrial companies before dead-ending at the last one, called Felchar Manufacturing. Behind that plant is a wooded area accessible via a dirt road nestled between Stanley Hollow Creek and the Binghamton Gun Club. Sweat and his buddies referred to it as "One Dirt Road."

It was the perfect spot for partying around a campfire. It was secluded and remote. Paths weaved through the woods and provided a playground for driving their stolen vehicles. Best of all, for Sweat, the stolen Winnebago provided him with something he desperately needed: shelter. He had been living in an apartment in an old house at the dead end of Dickinson Street in Binghamton, but he'd been evicted on June 29. He now had a place to live, party, and plan his crimes.

It's interesting to note that the same day Sweat was kicked out of his apartment, he showed up at the Kirkwood home of Roger Henry, his mother's boyfriend. His cousin Nabinger was with him. Sweat was carrying two semi-automatic pistols; this was one of the times he bragged about having bought them. Henry, who knew damn well that a convicted felon couldn't legally own or carry firearms, asked him to leave and to take his guns with him.

Four days later, on July 3, 2002, Sweat and Nabinger were at "One Dirt Road" with their twenty-three-year-old friend Shawn J. Devaul, from Greene, a town about ten miles outside Binghamton. They were finalizing plans to burglarize another gun store. The target this time was Mess's Fireworks in Great Bend, Pennsylvania, just fifteen minutes from "One Dirt Road." Devaul was an odd choice for a partner in this crime, as he had no criminal record and was gainfully employed.

At approximately 11:15 P.M., the three musketeers piled into Sweat's decorated Honda Accord. They were all carrying weapons with the serial numbers filed off. Sweat had the stolen semi-automatic .40 caliber Glock, Nabinger had the stolen 9mm Kahr, and Devaul had the stolen 9mm Smith & Wesson. Nabinger also had a Chicago Bulls gym bag. Once out of the woods, the car turned south onto the highway and they headed toward Pennsylvania.

CHAPTER 9
DEPUTY TARSIA'S
LAST TOUR

FOR MORE THAN AN HOUR, THE THREE DROVE around Hallstead, Pennsylvania, just two miles past the state line. They were searching for a vehicle to steal. They intended to use a stolen vehicle for their burglary at Mess's Fireworks. They eventually settled on the town's only car dealership, Fuccillo Ford.

According to trial testimony and later confessions, the trio located a green Ford F-150 that had recently been traded in. They took the license plate off the dealership's parts truck and put it on the green pickup. Sweat and Nabinger pounded on the truck's steering column until they broke the ignition, allowing them to hot-wire it. With the truck now started and Nabinger behind the wheel, he would follow Sweat and Devaul in the Honda Accord.

They left the Ford dealership and headed north, back up Route 11. Nabinger enjoyed a cigarette during the ride. He was sporting his signature do-rag, tied tight on his head.

The two-vehicle convoy went past their intended target on the way back into New York State. Just half a mile past the state line, Sweat turned right onto Grange Hall Road, one of the few side streets in that rural area. Only a few hundred yards down the road was the Grange Hall Road Park. It's a flat, open tract with a baseball field, walking track, swings, slides and a pavilion. At the time, its parking lot was bordered by thick brush. Sweat and Devaul parked the Honda in the unlighted parking lot and jumped into the bed of the stolen F-150. They put on ski masks and gloves and lay down for the ride back into Pennsylvania, the village of Great Bend, and Mess's Fireworks.

When they arrived at the store, all three men were armed and wearing ski masks and gloves. Nabinger backed the truck into the metal building's double entrance doors, easily smashing the glass and gaining entry. While the burglar alarm echoed down little Great Bend's deserted business block, they quickly grabbed long guns, handguns, and knives. For easier carrying, they tossed the handguns and knives into Nabinger's Chicago Bulls gym bag. Then they all piled back into the truck and returned north, Nabinger still behind the wheel and Sweat and Devaul riding in the back with the stolen goods.

The three-mile ride from the scene of the crime back to the Honda Accord took just a few minutes. They celebrated their successful heist by lighting up cigarettes in the dark parking lot. While moving the stolen merchandise from the truck into the Accord they noticed a car had just turned onto the Grange Hall Road from Route 11. Devaul thought it; Sweat said it. "Cops."

The configuration of lights on the white Ford confirmed it was a Broome County sheriff's cruiser. As the car's headlights swept into the park, the three thieves scattered like rats. Sweat dove for cover behind the stolen pickup. Nabinger and Devaul took cover in trees and thick brush along the parking lot.

Driving the cruiser was Deputy Sheriff Kevin Tarsia. Turning into the park, he stopped in the middle of the parking lot. His patrol car was pointed north, its headlights and spotlight illuminating the F-150, with visible damage to its back end, and the Honda Accord.

Tarsia stepped out of his car, flashlight in hand, and approached the two apparently abandoned vehicles. As he got closer to the truck, his flashlight beam illuminated an assault rifle, firmly gripped in one of David Sweat's hands. In his other hand, Sweat brandished a stolen .40 caliber Glock semi-automatic pistol.

True to his word, Sweat came out from behind the truck, shooting round after round as quickly as he could squeeze the trigger until the Glock was empty. Some of the rounds missed their mark and Deputy Tarsia's ballistic vest stopped all the other bullets—except one. One round skirted the bottom of his vest and entered his belly, ripping through his intestine and striking a kidney. Tarsia fell to the ground but attempted to return fire from his service pistol, also a .40 caliber Glock.

As Tarsia struggled to get to his feet, Sweat jumped into the Honda and gunned its boosted engine. Slamming it into gear, he aimed it at the deputy. The two thousand-pound car knocked the injured man down, trapping him under the chassis. Sweat kept going across the asphalt parking lot, dragging Tarsia under the car. When the deputy finally became free, he had sustained cuts, scrapes, broken ribs and a fractured femur. He never gave up the struggle to survive.

When Sweat got out of the Honda, he found Deputy Tarsia still alive. Sweat exited the car crying, whimpering, and saying, "I'm sorry, I'm sorry." That was when Nabinger abandoned his cover. Holding the stolen 9mm Kahr semi-automatic pistol, he fired a single shot at Tarsia. After that one shot, the magazine fell from the gun. Nabinger later testified that Sweat had told him to shoot the deputy, something Sweat never admitted. Devaul's statements don't confirm that assertion, either.

What we do know is that Nabinger then took the deputy's .40 caliber Glock pistol and fired two rounds at point-blank range into his face while Tarsia held his hands up in a futile attempt to defend himself. Deputy Sheriff Kevin J. Tarsia had been murdered.

When Devaul emerged from his hiding place, he saw Sweat and Nabinger heading for the Honda. In their haste to get to the car, Nabinger ran into Devaul. Nabinger switched direction and calmly went to the patrol car. He removed the keys and opened the trunk, removing Tarsia's personal duty bag, some arrest forms and road flares. Those items, along with the deputy's service weapon, would solidly tie Nabinger to the murder.

As a light fog began to rise from the nearby Susquehanna River, the three piled into the Honda and raced from the scene. It was 3:45

A.M. on July 4, 2002. They quickly covered the ten miles to "One Dirt Road" and started a campfire. Sitting around that fire, they talked about what had just happened. Sweat and Nabinger would fill in the blanks for Devaul, telling him what had taken place while he was hiding. Devaul crashed first, going to sleep in the Winnebago, while the others stayed up by the fire.

Two hours later, a Kirkwood resident named Michael West was on his way home from his graveyard-shift job. As he passed Grange Hall Road Park, he noticed a Broome County sheriff's car. Behind it was a damaged green Ford F-150. A closer look showed him a body, lying motionless on the pavement, in a deputy sheriff's uniform. West called 911.

First to respond were two troopers from the State Police. Shortly after they had secured the area as a crime scene, they got reinforcements: State Police investigators and Broome County deputies. Sheriff David E. Harder was forced to face the harsh reality that his colleague, a thirteen-year veteran officer, had been brutally murdered. Deputy Tarsia was the first sheriff's deputy to die in the line of duty since Broome County was established in 1806. His colleagues were haunted by the fact that the deputy, who lived on the same road where he died, had left behind a fiancé.

More than a hundred officers from a dozen law enforcement agencies would spend their Independence Day holiday investigating this gruesome crime scene and beginning the search for the perpetrators.

Before noon, Sweat and Nabinger would drop Devaul off at a friend's house in Binghamton. The two cousins went back to Kirkwood for a Fourth of July party at Foley Road, hosted by Roger Henry and Pamela Sweat. While there, they cleaned the two .40 caliber Glocks they had used to kill Tarsia, including the deputy's service pistol. In the garage, with a few invited groupies, they talked about what they had done earlier that day, culminating in their encounter with the deputy. "The cop was in the wrong place at the wrong time," Sweat commented. "Then the cop got shot and run over."

Nabinger chimed in, "He should have been a firefighter."

While Sweat and Nabinger were running their mouths, investigators were processing the murder scene just a few miles away.

For three days, grief-stricken law enforcement officers worked at the crime scene. They gathered physical evidence from the stolen Ford F-150 truck, and collected two rifles, a Chicago Bulls gym bag, cigarette butts, and fifteen spent shell casings. As part of the investigation, Kevin Tarsia's body and car were carefully examined before being removed from the scene. The law enforcement community had lost a brother. No one was going home and no one was going to sleep. The killer or killers were still on the loose, a serious threat to the public.

Broome County's Public Safety Building is in the town of Dickinson, a suburb of Binghamton. It shouldn't be confused with another Dickinson, and the village of Dickinson Center, which are two hundred miles to the north. Those Franklin County communities would figure in this story's conclusion, years later. But now, on the Fourth of July, 2002, Lt. Dale Hamilton of the Broome County Sheriff's Department set up a command post, distributing leads to investigators as they came in. As in any major crime like this, every lead, solid or weak, needed to be pursued. It was an afternoon call the second day, on July 5, that got investigators' full attention. It was a phone call from a sixteen-year-old girl.

The girl named David Sweat as a "likely suspect" in the murder. She talked about how Sweat and his cousin Jeffrey Nabinger always carried guns.

Two investigators went to talk with this young girl face to face. During the interview, she admitted having been with Sweat and Nabinger months earlier when they'd stolen trucks from a used car lot in Fenton. She told the investigators that Sweat had "many guns," semi-automatic pistols, and wanted more. She recounted how Sweat talked about shooting people if they could send him back to prison. She also described Sweat becoming more vocal and even angry following the May incident in which the twenty-one-year-old Michael Fisher had been killed by police. She even told the investigators about "One Dirt Road," the hideout off Corporate Road in Kirkwood, where she said police could find stolen vehicles and guns.

When investigators followed up on this lead, they discovered the stolen vehicles and Sweat's gold Honda Accord, just as the young tipster had described.

Police established round the clock surveillance of "One Dirt Road." They wouldn't have to wait long. By 11 P.M., the night of July 5, David Sweat and his occasional girlfriend appeared, riding bicycles. The watching officers emerged to ask the two for identification and detained them for a short time, then released them.

But when Sweat and his girlfriend, Virginia Roberts, went back to Roger Henry's house, police followed them. And while Sheriff's Department detectives were investigating "One Dirt Road" and their encounter with Sweat, Binghamton police were dealing with Nabinger.

Nabinger and one of his "groupies," Rob Brown, were taken in for questioning after Binghamton police found them standing near a stolen truck at Amsbry and Chenango streets, in an older residential neighborhood right along the Chenango River. Police only questioned the two about the stolen truck and later released them.

Just like Sweat did, Nabinger went to his mother's house. This was on Broome Street in Dickinson.

Despite turning the cousins loose, though, police weren't done with them. Soon after Sweat and Nabinger were first picked up, phone lines were tapped on both Foley Road in Kirkwood and Broome Street in Dickinson. Later that night police recorded a call between the cousins.

While Sweat and Nabinger compared notes, police were gathering evidence from "One Dirt Road." This included samples of human tissue taken from the undercarriage of Sweat's Honda.

Kevin Tarsia's personal duty bag, traffic flares, and a 9mm Kahr semi-automatic pistol were found inside the stolen Winnebago. That was the gun Nabinger used to take the first shot at Tarsia. This evidence placed Sweat and Nabinger at the top of the suspect list; but who was missing? Was anyone else involved?

On Saturday, July 6, investigators wrapped up their work at the crime scene at Grange Hall Road Park. They were moving on. With search warrants in hand, they headed to Foley Road in Kirkwood.

Once the crime-scene tape was removed from Grange Hall Road Park, Kevin Tarsia's brothers began their own search of the crime scene and surrounding area. Steven and Tom Tarsia were armed with a metal detector, but it wasn't the machine's "ping" that led them to a key piece of evidence. Hidden from view, hanging in the brush bordering the parking lot, they found a dark blue "do-rag." With no formal law enforcement training, they had located a critical piece of physical evidence that would turn out to contain DNA. While the Tarsia brothers were notifying authorities of what they had found, Kevin's brothers and sisters of law enforcement were making an arrest for his murder.

At 10:30 that Saturday morning, Sweat stepped out of Roger Henry's Foley Road house into the arms of sheriff's deputies. Within hours of his arrest, he told Broome County Sheriff Sgt. Vasil Yacalis where he had stashed guns near his mom's and her boyfriend's house. But most important, he confessed to shooting and running over Kevin Tarsia. Sweat admitted to being with his cousin, Nabinger, on July 4. This was his explanation for the murder: "I shot the cop first because I thought he was going to shoot at me."

Sweat gave up Devaul. That would give police their third and final suspect.

Officers quickly located the .40 caliber Glock, stolen from Marino's Outdoor World, that Sweat had used to shoot Tarsia, as well as the deputy's own .40 caliber Glock service pistol, the one Nabinger used against him. Both were hidden in the weeds at Foley Road, as Sweat had described.

Nabinger was arrested at 5:30 P.M. as he scurried out the back door of his mom's Broome Street home. As soon as he was in custody, he asked for a lawyer. He was not interrogated and was allowed the courtesy of smoking cigarettes.

Minutes later, at 5:36 P.M., Devaul was arrested by police in Greene, New York, while walking with his girlfriend and their baby.

Devaul confessed to being with Sweat and Nabinger on July 3 and 4. He described in detail their two trips into Pennsylvania, possession of stolen guns, and how they'd stolen the truck, staged Sweat's Honda at the Grange Hall Road Park and burglarized Mess's Fireworks. He told police about their return to New York to unload the stolen weapons at the park, and how his companions ambushed and shot the deputy sheriff. Devaul said the shooting took place out of his sight, while he was hiding in the brush. But he explained that after the three of them returned to "One Dirt Road," he listened to Sweat and Nabinger rehashing in detail what they had done. The police now had everything they needed.

David Sweat and Jeffrey Nabinger, both twenty-two years old, were charged with first-degree murder. Shawn Devaul, twenty-three, was charged with third-degree weapon possession. All were arraigned before Town of Kirkwood Justice Benjamin Weingartner. Each of them requested a court-appointed defense attorney. The judge sent them to the Broome County Jail without bail.

Putting the three suspects behind bars didn't mean any rest for police, though. More than a hundred officers from dozens of agencies had been working the case, processing hundreds of leads. Some Broome County sheriff's deputies had gone more than fifty hours without sleep. Now was the time to secure a conviction.

Sheriff Harder called a news conference Saturday evening to announce the arrests. "We are very sad for the loss of our brother, Kevin Tarsia," he said.

He and others credited solid police work and open communication between agencies for cracking the case. Standing with the sheriff, Major William Foley of State Police Troop C said, "This is another example of what we can do when we join resources like this."

That day and the next, search warrants were served at Sweat's mother's home on Foley Road and at the Nabinger house on Broome Street. Physical evidence was located, catalogued, and seized.

David Sweat and Jeffrey Nabinger were assigned attorneys at taxpayer expense. Because of the possibility of the death penalty, each was also given a second attorney, again at public expense.

On July 10, almost a week after the murder, police visited the apartment from which Sweat had been evicted just twelve days earlier. On the back porch of the Dickinson Street apartment house they found bags of personal property and debris the landlord had removed from Sweat's former home.

Sorting through such trash as urine-filled soda bottles, police found a hand-drawn layout of Mess's Fireworks. The sketch was covered with Sweat's fingerprints. This diagram was one of more than eight hundred pieces of evidence presented in court, which included transcripts of testimony by witnesses, tape recordings of closed-door interrogations, and transcripts of wiretapped phone conversations.

Even though Nabinger wasn't interrogated after his arrest, he had still given damning evidence against himself. Butts from the cigarettes that detectives let him smoke were sent to the state crime lab. They matched DNA with samples from the "do-rag" found at the crime scene.

Before the two shooters went to trial, their accomplice Shawn Devaul was offered a plea bargain in exchange for his testimony and cooperation. On August 9, 2002, he pled guilty to felony weapons possession. Devaul was sentenced to five years in prison and five years of post-prison supervision.

The rest of the case took more than a year to conclude. On July 21, 2003, before Judge Patrick H. Mathews, Sweat pled guilty to one count of first-degree murder. The next day, Nabinger pled guilty to the same charge.

CHAPTER 10
BOY BULLY
TO TEENAGE THUG

IT WAS A SATURDAY, JUNE 25, 1966, when Richard William Matt entered this world, as innocent as any other newborn. He was the second son born to Robert and Judith Matt. His brother, slightly older, was named Robert Jr.

Within five months of his birth, the infant Richard was discovered in a car, alone. This incident resulted in a neglect petition being filed by the Erie County Department of Social Services. Shortly afterward, Richard and Robert Jr. were removed from their home.

Mom had issues. Neglecting her children was at the top of the list. Dad was a low-level criminal who had multiple contacts with the police. These encounters resulted in convictions for assault, burglary, issuing bad checks and possession of stolen property.

The boys were placed in a well-known foster home in Tonawanda, a comfortable suburb of Buffalo. Mr. and Mrs. Vern Edin provided the two little boys with their first safe environment. Unfortunately for Ricky, as he was called in those days, the Edins would be only the first of many foster homes he would shuttle through. While in the Edins' care, the boys attended school and even played Little League baseball. During those early years, Ricky was described as outgoing and brilliant. He was a good-looking child who was beginning to show artistic talents. His first creative outlet was playing the trumpet.

There was another side to Ricky, though. The reporter Jenn Schanz with Buffalo's TV station WIVB delved into his past after he had become notorious. As she reported, an unidentified childhood friend described him as a "funny kid, always funny, always had a big smile on his face, but you know, just couldn't stay out of trouble." The friend elaborated, "He tried to beat me up at the playground; that's the first time I ever met him. That was my first initiation with Rick Matt. He was this bully."

The *Washington Post* quoted a schoolmate, Randy Szokala, who recalled, "He would terrorize kids on the bus . . . Friends of mine knew him. He would just terrorize people. Even in elementary, junior high, he had issues."

Ricky Matt lived in multiple foster homes until he was fourteen and finished the eighth grade. That would be the last grade he completed. Soon playground bullying escalated into trouble with the police, an echo of his father's criminal career. This troubled teenager's misdemeanor and felony arrests furthered his reputation for terrorizing his fellow students. Ricky, who at one time expressed an interest in law enforcement, now found law enforcement was interested in him.

A steadily expanding file included reports of self-inflicted cuts to his arms and major scrapes with local police. His name was routinely found in the Tonawanda Police Department blotter. One of the town's veteran officers, David Bentley, attempted to mentor the boy; his effort was futile. By now, Ricky was a teenage thug, one who became a police informant when ratting on someone would benefit him.

He attempted to steal a houseboat but got caught in the act. This crime resulted in a court judgment that he was ungovernable. In 1980, at the age of 14, he was placed in a secure facility run by New York's State Division of Youth Services. Ricky didn't like being confined and decided to do something about it. He showed a definite flair for escape, getting away from the youth lock-up on horseback. This was the first of what would be a long string of documented escapes from penal institutions.

This teenage desperado, still with peach fuzz on his face, found his way to the Allegany State Park, in a rugged part of western New York State on the Pennsylvania state line. It was eighty miles from where he'd been confined. The Allegany State Park is known as western New York's outdoor playground. Its hundred square miles are filled with nature trails, cabins, lakes, and streams, a popular destination for outdoor enthusiasts.

This detail would later come to sound very familiar. Ricky Matt, the resourceful teenage escapee, burglarized and hid in the park's seasonal camps. The cabins he broke into provided him with food, drink, shelter, and all the supplies he needed while on the run. It took several days for police to track him down, arrest him, and return him to his residential placement.

During the next couple of years, he behaved himself well enough to get out of the juvenile facility. But his freedom was short-lived. His next interaction with the law came in late 1983; he was seventeen. He was arrested and charged with first-degree robbery but pled to a lesser offense, third-degree robbery. Part of a settlement reached in 1984, this got him five years' probation.

A year later, in September 1985, Ricky's criminal side emerged again. At nineteen, under the influence of alcohol and drugs, he was arrested once again. The charges were second-degree criminal possession of a forged instrument and third-degree assault. He was driving a car he'd bought with stolen money, specifically forged checks. Numerous violations of probation would later be added to the charges. It had taken him less than eighteen months to violate the terms of his probation on the earlier robbery conviction. This, his fourth felony arrest, sent him to the Erie County Jail until his case could be resolved in court.

While awaiting trial, he bided his time for months before seeing his chance. That happened on June 15, 1986, when the clever nineteen-year-old Ricky Matt took advantage of a corrections officer's mistake and slipped out of his holding cell. He scaled a nine-foot fence and climbed through the razor wire. Despite multiple cuts to his chest and stomach, the determined, physically-fit teen escaped from the Erie County Jail. This was his second documented escape from a secure facility.

As he'd demonstrated with his earlier horseback escape, Ricky had a knack for colorful ways to get around. This time he caught a ride on a freight train, which took him to within a block of his brother's apartment on William Street in Tonawanda. Big brother Robert Jr. had no problem hiding little Ricky. Robert Jr. had his own issues; he had been arrested on burglary, larceny, and assault charges. Ricky was on the lam for four days until police caught up with him. When he was arrested in his brother's home, he was armed with an ax handle. He was returned to the Erie County Jail, now facing additional charges including second-degree escape.

Ricky's day in court came on July 24, 1986, before Erie County Supreme Court Judge William Flynn. He was sentenced to 1.4 to 4 years for the possession of a forged instrument charge and one year in county jail for the misdemeanor assault charge, the sentences to run consecutively. The escape charge for his four-day walkabout was still pending.

On August 27, 1986, at the age of twenty, Richard W. Matt was received by the New York State Department of Corrections for his first state bid. He was processed at the Elmira Correctional Facility. The routine for new inmates included intake interviews and medical examinations. As with any new inmate, Matt was given a chance to ask any questions. Once an assessment of Inmate Matt's needs was completed, he was transferred to a permanent prison.

While at Elmira, Matt posed for a photograph. A Polaroid image shows him in the light blue uniform shirt of a New York State corrections officer, minus the collar brass and nametag required for officers. He is smoking a cigarette and clutching a corrections baton in his right hand, the leather lanyard wrapped around his wrist. His left hand holds the Elmira Correctional Facility inmate identification placard with his name and department identification number: "Inmate Richard Matt, 86B1754." Written at the bottom of the Polaroid is, "Who said I can't escape this place?" David Bentley, the Tonawanda police officer who had attempted to be a mentor to young Matt, found this photo in his mail.

By this time, Matt had earned a reputation with police as a

manipulator. Any encounter Matt had with law enforcement included him asking for a break or a deal in exchange for information. One of the many officers who knew him was Tonawanda Police Captain Frederic Foels. He described Matt to the *Rochester Democrat and Chronicle* newspaper as the guy you didn't want to hang around with. "We always knew him as Ricky: 'Ricky Matt did this, Ricky Matt did that.' We were very well familiar with him at the time, in the late '80s." He was already known for his violent impulses. Foels recalled, "One time he beat up a girl pretty bad. He got charged for assault second; that's a felony."

CHAPTER 11
CATCH AND RELEASE

THE CHARISMATIC INMATE MATT SPENT TWENTY DAYS at the Elmira Correctional Facility. This is a New York State Department of Corrections maximum-security prison that functions as a reception center. Even though it's close to the state line, this is not to be confused with a New York State Welcome Center.

The staff at Corrections reception centers routinely interviews incoming inmates and evaluates their physical—meaning medical—emotional, and educational needs. The purpose is to place them in the most appropriate facility to meet those needs. Inmate Matt was sent ("drafted") to Coxsackie Correctional Facility, which is on the Hudson River about thirty miles south of Albany.

Coxsackie is a maximum-security prison that houses some 900 male inmates. The majority are in their late teens to early twenties. The prison offers its inmate population many programs for building job skills and the often-needed chance to finish their educations.

Matt took advantage of this opportunity. With his high I.Q., he easily achieved his goal of a high school equivalency diploma by December 1987.

He also kept in touch with Tonawanda Police Officer Bentley with letters and birthday cards.

But that positive direction was a path he could not maintain. Matt received multiple misbehavior reports. In just fifteen months, he was written up for fighting, disorderly conduct, unauthorized exchange of property, harassment, and disobeying direct orders from staff. He wasn't a model inmate in any way, shape, or form.

During that time, Matt was taken back to Buffalo for a number of court appearances and final sentencing for his June 1986 escape from the Erie county jail. That earned him a sentence of 1.4 to 4 years in prison. This was to run concurrently with the identical prison term he was serving for the possession of a forged instrument and assault convictions.

Amazingly, after being convicted of these two felonies, as well as misdemeanor assault, then getting written up by the correctional staff in multiple misbehavior reports for failure to comply with prison rules, Inmate Matt was released to the streets of Erie County early in February 1988. He had served less than a year and a half, just a bit more than his minimum sentence.

The twenty-year-old Matt returned to his previous nomadic lifestyle. He was under the supervision of the New York State Division of Parole.

Back on the streets, Matt was a little smarter, both academically and jail smart. He bobbed and weaved, eluding police, and his illicit activities went undetected for about twenty-four months. During this time, Matt burglarized a home, assaulting and raping the woman who lived there. Matt would not be charged for these crimes until 1991. However, his short-lived freedom ended with other violations of his parole. Matt returned to prison in May 1990.

Once again, he was sent to Elmira Correctional Facility for reception. This time, however, he was assigned to the notorious Attica Correctional Facility to finish his original sentence.

Attica is a maximum-security prison in western New York that houses over two thousand of the state's most dangerous criminals. A majority of those "doing time" at Attica can be considered some of the state's most difficult inmates. Violence and disturbances are normal among Attica's serial killers, hitmen, bank robbers, and mob members. The prison is best known for a deadly uprising in 1971, which led to the deaths of ten Corrections workers and thirty-three inmates.

Matt completed the remainder of his sentence at Attica, getting yet another misbehavior report there. At the end of November 1990 he was released. He was now twenty-four years old. He returned to Tonawanda.

Back on the streets, he was described as charming, brilliant, and brutal. He quickly returned to his lifestyle of terrorizing the people around him and encounters with law enforcement.

He didn't have much interest in working, but when the western New York weather cooperated, he would pick up some work putting in driveways. What he did have interest in was a woman named Vee Marie Harris.

Harris was older than Matt and ignored him at first. But the charming, handsome Matt was difficult to ignore. He was brilliant in the way he impressed girls with his "shy guy" routine, lowering his head and kicking the ground. This masquerade, combined with his well-developed physique, served him well with the ladies. Some who knew him have made mention that he was unusually well-endowed sexually. He was persuasive and captured Harris's heart. Ultimately, he fathered a child with her.

With Matt's new life beginning to take shape, he was taken by surprise when a man by the name of Wayne Schimpf appeared in his life. It seems that Wayne was his half-brother. He had no idea until then that this half-brother even existed.

This might have been the first time Matt had any semblance of a family. He had a girlfriend, a child, and now another brother. Unfortunately, Matt's drinking and other self-destructive behaviors destroyed any possibility of a family relationship with these new-found relations.

The concept "just add alcohol and shake" explains what happened to Matt when he drank. He went from Dr. Jekyll to Mr. Hyde. By 1991, he again developed a pattern of assaulting his baby's mother, as well as the other assorted girlfriends he cavorted with. After what may have been a turning point, an alleged knife-point assault on his girlfriend, his violence toward women consistently rocketed out of control.

Matt's rap sheet quickly filled up, with approximately seventeen arrests on charges including assaults, robbery, escapes, larceny, drunk driving, harassment, attempted unauthorized use of a motor vehicle, attempted possession of stolen property, attempted criminal mischief, disorderly conduct, and multiple vehicle and traffic violations. His records, of course, also outlined his convictions of criminal possession of a forged instrument, escape, and assault. The icing on the cake was two DWI convictions.

In late 1991, at twenty-five, Matt again found himself on his way back to the Erie County Jail. He had been arrested on a long list of charges including burglary, assault, and rape. His willingness to be a police informant when free on the street, and a jailhouse rat when inside, didn't cut him any slack with these new pending charges.

Documents filed at his arraignment outlined an ominous tendency to brutality. Supporting depositions described the brutal beating with a metal object of a woman in the sanctuary of her apartment. Her attacker then raped her while her two children were present. The battered, violated and terrorized victim swore she had never seen Matt prior to the attack.

Matt declared his innocence against these allegations. He told a story of having merely had a bar-room altercation with the victim's boyfriend that night.

Back in the Erie County Jail again, unable to raise $15,000 bail, he waited for his defense attorney to work magic on the pending charges.

As earlier events showed, Matt was both jail smart and physically fit enough to emanate the aura of a tough guy. He experienced no problems in jail while awaiting his day in court.

Before that day came, an opportunity arose for Matt to wiggle out of the latest charges. That came in the form of a prominent, and arrogant, California socialite named David Telstar. This thirty-five-year-old West Coast pretty boy had also found himself in the Erie County Jail.

How did he get there? He had been attempting to enter the United States from Canada, through the Buffalo border crossing, when federal officials ran an identity check. That turned up a warrant from the Santa Barbara County Sheriff's Department, charging him with embezzlement to the tune of $1.6 million. While waiting to confirm the California warrant, U.S. Customs agents detained Telstar. Soon enough, the feds turned Telstar over to local authorities in New York State as a fugitive from justice. After being arraigned, while awaiting extradition to California, he found himself in an Erie County Jail cell.

It didn't take long before he and Matt got acquainted and befriended each other. Weeks passed as both their cases ground their slow way through the court system, giving Matt plenty of time to garner information about his new pal. He was intrigued to learn about Telstar's multiple million-dollar homes, world travels, and comfortable lifestyle. Telstar, for his part, seems to have been intrigued by Matt's violent history. From this mutual fascination would allegedly evolve a murder-for-hire scheme.

The plan was simple. Telstar was to post the $15,000 bail for Matt's release. In exchange, Matt would kill four people for Telstar. Upon completion of the job, Telstar would pay Matt $100,000.

Telstar fulfilled his part of their agreement and arranged for Matt's bail. After Matt's bail was posted, he checked out of the Erie County Jail with his shopping list of people to kill and instructions to burn their bodies. The names on the hit list included Desiree Telstar, David's fifty-year-old socialite ex-wife. Desiree is the granddaughter of movie mogul Harry Warner, the founder of Warner Bros. movie studios, and the heiress to his fortune. Desiree's prominent parents were Los Angeles Police Commission President Stanley Sheinbaum and Betty Warner Sheinbaum, daughter of Harry Warner. Both of their names were on the hit list, along with Walter Valentine, Desiree Telstar's attorney, who had set up the couple's multi-million dollar trust.

CHAPTER 12
MURDER FOR HIRE

DAVID TELSTAR HAD FOUND HIMSELF IN CALIFORNIA after studying at the distinguished Pratt Institute of Architecture in New York City. Pratt Institute is ranked in the top ten of architectural schools in the United States, an impressive addition to any resume. But for some reason he felt the need to embellish his resume in another way: by changing his name. He was originally Mark David Matson. Police speculated that the new name was meant to make him seem more artistic.

Once in California, he settled in at the helm of a small graphic-arts business in Sacramento. Telstar was a talented graphic designer, good looking and charming. He had done what thousands of prospectors before him had done: gone west in search of fame and fortune.

Soon after arriving in Sacramento, Telstar was introduced to Desiree Sperling, an interior designer and art consultant from Los Angeles. Desiree was about fifteen years his senior. She was a California socialite with two daughters to show from her three failed marriages. The thirty-year-old East Coast boy and the forty-five-year-old West Coast girl didn't have much in common except for their taste in fine art and the good life often connected to it.

Sperling had never had much luck with the few men who entered her personal life. She had even been victim of a former business manager who successfully embezzled $2.2 million dollars from her and then later committed suicide. Sperling had plenty to offer any prospective suitors, including the fact she was an heiress to the fortune of Harry Warner, the founder and onetime president of Warner Bros. studio.

In comparison, David Telstar did not have much to offer this movie mogul's granddaughter other than big ideas and a small portfolio. However, at the time in her life when she met Telstar, a little happiness would go a long way.

On February 14, 1986, Valentine's Day, David Telstar and Desiree Sperling were married. The two entered into a comfortable lifestyle in Santa Barbara.

Shortly after their marriage, David told Desiree how he proposed to make them rich. He wanted to combine his ideas and her money to build a future and a fortune. This would be made possible in part with her share of profit from the sale of her family's property in Los Angeles. The property was in the Warner Center Business Park, land that was once Harry Warner's horse ranch. That sale would add another million to Desiree's net worth.

The million from the property sale and a $600,000 settlement from Desiree's earlier embezzlement case were put into a trust fund in 1987. It was established by their attorney, Walter Valentine. The two love birds affectionately named it the Valentine Trust, in honor of their wedding day.

For the next few years the couple used the Valentine Trust to buy and remodel two $1 million dollar homes in Montecito, California. It also secured their lifestyle. But David still wanted more. He wanted a post-nuptial agreement. He wanted half of everything Desiree owned. But three failed marriages had taught Desiree two things: a post-nuptial agreement wasn't going to happen, and the honeymoon was over.

David allegedly became enraged at her resistance to his schemes; the heiress's fourth marriage began to crumble. She felt imprisoned and was fearful of confrontation with him. David threatened Desiree, mentioning his guns, should she try to leave him.

By March 1991, after being married just five years, David began to move the couple's money from the joint $1.6 million Valentine Trust into accounts that only he controlled. According to a six-page divorce affidavit that Desiree would sign, the romantic and charismatic David had become greedy and deceitful.

By now, Desiree's divorce attorney, C. R. Whiston, had been informed of his client's allegations of her husband's cruelty, embezzlement, and threats to kill her. At the lawyer's request, the Santa Barbara County Sheriff's Department launched an investigation of the alleged embezzlement. Detective Greg Nordyk was assigned to the case.

He discovered a money trail that revealed movement of funds from joint accounts in banks in Montecito and Santa Barbara. Banks in San Francisco, Portland, and Palm Springs received deposits to accounts solely controlled by David Telstar.

A supporting deposition from Desiree and the proof that David had taken more than half of the joint Valentine Trust provided Santa Barbara District Attorney Patrick McKinley with enough evidence. He secured a warrant for David's arrest. It got to the Sheriff's Department too late.

In late June 1991, David Telstar withdrew one million dollars in cashier's checks from his new accounts and converted them to traveler's checks. On July 15, he fled to Europe, leaving authorities searching for him.

Detective Nordyk's investigation unearthed a startling discovery in a storage locker Telstar had rented in San Diego. The locker contained financial records, books on money laundering, loaded handguns, and a newspaper article headlined "Without a Trace" about an unsolved murder. It appeared that David Telstar might have had other plans than just making off with his wife's money.

The Santa Barbara County Sheriff's Department, armed with this evidence and the arrest warrant, called for help from the FBI.

Federal agents, with help from informants and from Britain's Scotland Yard, tracked Telstar through England, France, Switzerland, and Singapore. They turned up evidence that Telstar had plans to get plastic surgery and had arranged for a phony death certificate in Brazil.

Amazingly, after Telstar's six-month disappearing act in Europe, he jetted to Canada. It was when he attempted to enter the United States through the Buffalo Port of Entry that Telstar produced his real U.S. passport. In his personal property, he was carrying $13,000 cash, an Air France ticket to Zurich, and a personal computer that quite possibly contained the key to finding the missing $1.6 million. United States Customs agents identified him as a "fugitive from justice," which resulted in his arrest and incarceration with a pending extradition warrant to California. That was how Telstar came to be locked up, without bail, in the Erie County Jail.

He soon learned that the lockup in downtown Buffalo did not feature five-star dining with socialites, background classical music or flowers on linen-covered tabletops. At the jail's mealtimes, he found himself sitting on a stainless-steel stool connected to a stainless-steel table bolted to a concrete floor.

Telstar was totally out of his element, which was obvious to any jail-smart inmate. One like Richard Matt, who quickly identified Telstar for what he was and for what he could provide.

Matt developed a rapport and friendship with this West Coast treasure. As time passed, Matt and Telstar talked with each other about their problems—and possible solutions. Matt was "all in" for helping the California socialite and, not coincidentally, helping himself. Despite working out a murder-for-hire plan, their jailhouse friendship would prove to be one-sided.

Although Matt's part in the deal was to collect $100,000 for killing Telstar's ex-wife, her wealthy parents, and her attorney and burning their bodies, he never intended to provide these services. He did plan to let Telstar pay his $15,000 bail.

Unsuspected by his gullible client, Matt had an even better idea. Once free on bail, detailed instructions in hand for finding his intended victims, Matt was looking for his own deal. He wanted a reduction or dismissal of his pending charges: burglary, assault, and rape. His price would be giving Telstar up to anyone who would listen.

Within days, Matt contacted the authorities in Buffalo, as well as Desiree Telstar and her attorney Walter Valentine. He told them all the same story: he'd been hired to commit murder.

The FBI was soon knocking on Richard Matt's door. The feds were looking for his help. Their talking points included the plot to murder four people and clues to locating the missing embezzled funds.

Matt found himself in the U.S. attorney's office for the Western District of New York, discussing the specifics of the scheme Telstar had hired him for. This bizarre deal amounted to Telstar's $100,000 investment toward a $1.6 million payoff.

Matt went to work as a snitch for the FBI, recording conversations between himself and Telstar. Matt's cooperation helped federal investigators find two separate Swiss safe-deposit boxes under two different aliases.

By the time the Swiss safe-deposit boxes were opened, Telstar had allegedly arranged to have them emptied. It now appeared that with Matt on the street again, Telstar was talking to other inmates who might have the means and the savvy to retrieve the money from the boxes. He offered a substantial reward; five and six figures in cash was Telstar's going rate for this service.

FBI investigators later identified several people who had traveled to Geneva with power of attorney privileges, and emptied Telstar's Swiss safe-deposit boxes.

The FBI investigation had turned up plenty of evidence, including Matt's recorded conversations about the murder plot and the clear path the embezzled $1.6 million had followed. Federal authorities filed charges against Telstar.

Telstar was facing ten years in a federal prison. Matt was lined up to be the star witness against his former jailhouse pal. While this case was pending, Matt, the rat, was well dressed, wearing a bulletproof vest under his clothing in case there was a back-up killer.

The four targets of the alleged plot were all assigned bodyguards.

Before Matt could testify against him, Telstar eventually took a plea to two counts of conspiracy to commit murder against a witness. Telstar went to the medium-security federal prison in McKean County, Pennsylvania, for the next five years, less time off for good behavior. Restitution records revealed he returned to Desiree what he hadn't yet spent of her stolen money.

According to his defense attorney, Matt was offered no deals for his help and cooperation in the federal case. He offered his information out of the kindness of his heart, he and his lawyer would have us believe.

Ridiculous. He gave information hoping that he would get something in return. As the rest of Matt's criminal and prison history proves, nothing is for nothing!

Matt, who was facing charges including burglary, assault, and rape, took a plea to one reduced charge of attempted burglary in full satisfaction of all the others. His sentence included a term of two to four years in state prison. At the age of twenty-seven, Richard Matt was about to start his second state bid.

CHAPTER 13
GLADIATOR SCHOOL

IN SEPTEMBER 1993, BEGINNING HIS SECOND STATE BID, Matt was again sent to Elmira Correctional Facility to be interviewed and evaluated. During his interviews with corrections staff, he expressed no interest in participating in two programs the Department of Corrections offered that might have been helpful to him. One of these was for sex offenders. The other was alternatives to violence. Matt wasn't required to participate in either program, either by the prison system or by the court that sentenced him. He had not been convicted of either rape or assault; those charges had been dropped when he pleaded to attempted burglary. Matt also had a strong reason for not voluntarily attending these programs: fear of being labeled.

Understand that prison has its hierarchy, just like in our free society.

A prison-smart inmate never wants to get labeled as a sex offender. Too many criminals had themselves been sexually victimized as children, and as adults have no tolerance for sex offenders. A tremendous volume of communication flows between inmates; that consistent exchange of personal information means being labeled a sex offender will follow inmates as they move from prison to prison. That label will make for a long and dangerous bid, filled with violence toward anyone with a reputation as a sex offender. Inside the prison walls, the inmate population looks at sex offenders as bottom feeders.

This same prison culture identifies drug kingpins and inmates convicted of organized crimes as the top of the hierarchy. Often these highly respected inmates are family oriented men with wives and children. They especially have a strong distaste for sex offenders and often target them with acts of violence. It's a well-established kind of honor among thieves.

Depending on their crimes, the rest of the prison's population will find themselves somewhere between the top and bottom of the inmates' social structure.

Soon after his intake at Elmira, Matt was drafted—transferred—to Great Meadow Correctional Facility. This is in the town of Comstock, a rural area near the Vermont line, which also has the medium-security Washington Correctional Facility where David Sweat served most of his first sentence. Great Meadow is a much tougher prison. One of New York's maximum-security facilities, it has become so notorious for its inmates' violent ways that it's often referred to as "Gladiator School" by the prison guards who work there.

Among this prison's 1,600 male inmates, violence is an everyday occurrence. Inmates assaulting the staff and each other make Great Meadow Correctional Facility one of New York State's most dangerous prisons, according to Department of Corrections record keepers.

I don't need statistics to know this; I spent two and a half years working at Great Meadow and saw the violence first-hand. That assignment was one of several during the years I worked in maximum-security prisons around the state. As I worked my way up the ranks, I also worked my way back to my home in northern New York. My experience with the most hardened male inmates also included stints at Sing Sing and the Upstate Correctional Facility just outside my home town, Malone. I also worked in Bedford Hills Correctional Facility, New York State's only maximum-security prison for women.

During Matt's time at Great Meadow, he worked in the prison's soap shop and maintained an incident-free disciplinary record. In late 1995, the New York State Parole Board was holding its fall round of interviews and hearings. The twenty-nine-year-old Matt got his turn to meet with the Parole Board.

Board members asked him about his involvement in the high-profile Telstar murder-for-hire plot. This master manipulator was quick to tell the Board that his willingness to agree to the murder plot had always been a ruse. Mustering up all the sincerity he was capable of faking, he assured the board he had planned to save Desiree Telstar's life the entire time. His cooperation with the FBI, becoming their star witness, was the icing on the cake. During his interview, Matt turned on the charisma and spun a wonderful tale about how Telstar had asked him to murder the California four and how he agreed only so he could save the un-suspecting socialites. He had no thoughts of any personal gain, he declared. Matt's story was so heartwarming it should have started with "Once upon a time" and ended with "and they all lived hap-pily ever after."

His story contained enough truth to be plausible. One thing Matt described was how he'd met David Telstar in the Erie County Jail. He told the Parole Board he had noticed a group of black men pushing up on the California pretty boy and stepped in to protect him. By acting as the peacekeeper, he said, he became Telstar's friend.

But doing the right thing, Inmate Matt said sadly, had also put him in danger. His willingness to help law enforcement, he claimed, had gotten him stabbed in Elmira Correctional Facility. This was the result of a hit he said David Telstar had ordered. The point of this story, Matt concluded, was that as long as he remained in prison, he would fear for his life.

On March 14, 1996, Richard Matt was paroled. He promptly returned to the streets of Tonawanda.

But after less than thirty days of enjoying his freedom, Matt was declared delinquent by parole authorities. He returned to prison on August 15, 1996, to serve the rest of his sentence. That concluded on February 21, 1997, when he was again released under parole supervision.

Making up for lost time, Matt was quickly arrested for driving while intoxicated. He quickly pled guilty to this misdemeanor and accepted a sentence of ninety days in county jail, a fine plus a mandatory state surcharge, and three years of probation.

At thirty-one years old and on probation, Matt badly needed a job. He landed one, working for a seventy-six-year-old North Tonawanda businessman, William Rickerson. Rickerson's food-brokerage company bought food items that were nearing their expiration dates and resold them at discounted prices.

Rickerson was kind enough to offer a fresh start to the two-time convicted felon and chronic drunk.

Matt quickly showed his appreciation to the elderly Rickerson by stealing meat and other products the company distributed. Matt took coolers filled with stolen food across the border into Ontario, Canada. He had developed a network of individuals and restaurant owners who would buy the goods at an even steeper discount than they legitimately sold for. Matt was filling his pockets with cash from his lucrative new business. Because he had nothing invested, he was ensured a pure profit.

His new prosperity quickly led him to strip clubs called Mints and Pure Platinum on the Canadian side of the Niagara River. It was in the Pure Platinum jiggle joint in Fort Erie that Matt's attention focused on an exotic dancer from Costa Rica, stage name Karena. Johanna Capretto, AKA Karena, enjoyed Matt's charm, bad-boy humor, and steady supply of money.

Also at Pure Platinum, Matt was introduced to Lee Bates, a part-time employee. Bates was a twenty-one-year-old big boy with dreams of someday becoming a cop—when he wasn't hanging with his stripper girlfriend.

It wasn't long before Bates became infatuated with Matt and willingly became his new mentor's mode of transportation. Matt routinely used Bates and his car to smuggle his stolen food items into Canada. After making their deliveries, the two often went to the strip club to gawk at the girls.

Matt's cash business came to a sudden halt when Rickerson caught him stealing and fired him. Matt was convinced his ex-boss still owed him back wages. He turned to Bates for help in a plan he concocted to recoup this money. With a chilling combination of charisma, coercion, and manipulation, Matt persuaded the young Bates to participate in his plan. Just in case the persuasion wasn't enough, Matt went one step further. He told Bates if he didn't help him, Matt would kill Bates's pole-dancing sweetheart. Bates, with good reason, was scared. He reluctantly agreed.

Looking back, it's not hard to see why Bates took Matt's threats seriously. On their visits to the strip club, Matt had showed Bates just how easily he could get close to his stripper girlfriend. He taunted Bates by summoning the girlfriend to his side, letting him know he wouldn't hesitate to follow through on his threat. He wanted Bates to know that he could get to her anytime he wanted. Matt's physical strength and size only added to the obvious reality: he had not only the desire, but the ability, to harm anyone who crossed him.

On December 3, 1997, Matt and Bates found themselves in an apartment in Buffalo, drinking vodka. It was the home of Matt's half-brother, Wayne Schimpf. Matt talked about money he believed Rickerson owed him, and said he intended to collect it. Matt even called Rickerson from Schimpf's apartment, arguing about the money with his former boss. When Matt and Bates left Schimpf's place, they were armed with a baseball bat, batting gloves, duct tape, and a buck knife.

On this snowy December night, Matt and his accomplice drove to Rickerson's home in North Tonawanda. Matt was convinced that he kept large sums of cash there. Answering a pounding on his door, Rickerson opened it to find Matt and Bates standing there.

The elderly Rickerson, a widower who lived alone, was dressed in his pajamas. As soon as he opened his door, Matt assaulted him, shoving him down a flight of stairs into his family room. Matt demanded cash. When this produced nothing, Matt began savagely beating Rickerson. Matt's search of the house turned up no hoard of cash. What Matt did find was a steel knife-sharpening rod. Matt repeatedly hit Rickerson with this rod and tortured him by ramming it into his ear. The beating and torture continued for about an hour, but produced no mention of any large hidden sum of cash. During his abuse of Rickerson, Matt paused briefly to swig wine and take bites from a stick of pepperoni.

Once he'd had enough wine, Matt poured the remainder of the bottle on Rickerson's head. He pulled off his victim's hairpiece and stuffed it in his pocket. He hadn't gotten the results he wanted. All he'd come up with were a small amount of cash and some credit cards from Rickerson's wallet, and a diamond wedding ring once worn by his deceased wife. Matt decided it was time to hit the road.

Rickerson, still wearing only pajamas, was bound with duct tape and stuffed into the trunk of Bates's car. Wednesday night had become Thursday morning as the kidnappers drove away from Rickerson's house and into the freezing darkness. Where were they taking him?

CHAPTER 14
RICKERSON'S MURDER

WHILE MATT, THE CAREER CRIMINAL, WAS HAVING VISIONS of large sums of cash, Bates's life was flashing before his eyes. He was in way over his head but was committed to this crime and its conclusion.

As this damp, cold December night wore on, Matt kept yelling at Rickerson, "Where's the money? Where's the money?" His victim proved both tough and stubborn. Even while bound with duct tape and stuffed into the trunk of the car, Rickerson refused to answer.

They drove to Matt's place in Tonawanda to regroup. So far, the two criminals had come up with less than one hundred dollars, a few credit cards and Rickerson's deceased wife's diamond wedding ring. They had found it on the elderly widower's hand, where he wore it in her memory.

Having little to show for their efforts thus far and realizing the odds of getting caught were pretty high, they returned to Rickerson's home to do a little cleaning up. After all, robbing and kidnapping someone who knows you and can identify you sure does increase your chances of capture. While Matt and Bates cleaned the house, they left Rickerson locked in the trunk.

When the kidnappers were satisfied that Rickerson's home had been restored to its proper order, they resumed their road trip, this time going south and then west.

As they drove out of New York State into Pennsylvania in the early morning hours of December 4, 1997, Matt continued yelling at Rickerson in the trunk, "Where's the money? Where's the money?"

He wasn't cooperating. He pulled out the wires connected to the car's stereo speakers, kicked at the trunk lid and tried to claw his way out of his cold, dark tomb.

This served only to bring out the worst sadistic streak in Matt. Infuriated, he stopped the car and opened the trunk long enough to beat Rickerson, adding some new tortures to what he'd already done. This began a pattern of stopping periodically on secluded stretches of highway and torturing the man in the trunk. Rickerson suffered numerous painful injuries at Matt's hands. As he repeatedly demanded, "Where's the money?" Matt bent one finger at a time until it broke.

It was early Thursday morning when the two kidnappers made an unscheduled stop in Erie, Pennsylvania, to buy a shovel. By this time, back in North Tonawanda, Rickerson's place of business was opening for the day. His employees wondered why he hadn't showed up at his usual time. It was unusual for Rickerson not to be at work first thing in the morning. His staff tried to call him but got no answer on his home phone.

Meanwhile, the road trip of repeated assaults and torture continued, skirting the Lake Erie shore all the way into northeast Ohio. There, an attempt to dig a hole in the frozen Ohio ground proved as futile as locating Rickerson's imagined stash of cash. The two frustrated kidnappers turned the car around and headed back toward New York State.

Their frustration was about to climax just as their vision of oodles of cash dissolved. The hours of yelling, beating, and torture had produced no information leading them to any money.

By the time they got back into New York State, twenty-seven hours had elapsed. They stopped the car one last time, in a secluded rural area, for one last-ditch effort to force Rickerson to reveal where his money was. By this time, Matt was so enraged he began to take his fury out on Bates. Rickerson shouted, "What are you yelling at him for? He has nothing to do with this. This is between you and me."

Those were Rickerson's last words. Matt reached inside the trunk and, with his bare hands, snapped Rickerson's neck, instantly ending his life. That was too much for Bates, who saw this while standing nearby. He would later admit that he lost control and literally shit himself.

The two jumped back into the car and drove back to Tonawanda. They crossed a short bridge to Tonawanda Island, a small piece of land in the Niagara River, mostly old industrial sites and marinas, deserted in wintertime. There they removed Rickerson's body from the trunk and hid it under a pile of wood along the riverbank. Their road trip ended, Bates and Matt went their separate ways but agreed to stay in touch.

Rickerson's employees reported him missing. The North Tonawanda Police took the report and assigned Detective Gabriel DiBernardo to lead the investigation. A search of Rickerson's home produced no obvious clues to his disappearance—except for a few drops of blood.

While the detective was pursuing the case, Matt was quick to make a confession, but it was to his stripper girlfriend in Canada. He told Johanna Capretto that "He pushed Rickerson and he fell down and died," she later testified. She also said he insisted, "I didn't kill him. I'm not that kind of guy." Matt wanted to assure his sweetheart that he wasn't a bad person. It had been accidental, he told her; things had just gotten out of hand.

Matt was more honest with Bates. Within days, he told him he had returned to Tonawanda Island and gotten rid of the body. Pulling it out from under the woodpile, he'd dismembered Rickerson's body with a hacksaw. He tossed the severed limbs and head into the frigid waters of the Niagara River. He then dragged the torso into the river, which he must have expected would carry it the ten miles downstream to the falls.

During Detective DiBernardo's investigation, he reviewed employment records at Rickerson's food-brokerage company. He wanted to know about the backgrounds of both current and past employees. Interviewing the staff, the seasoned detective quickly learned about Richard Matt's firing for stealing products and re-selling them. But without a body, police had only a suspicious missing-person case, not a clear-cut murder. Working this case would require following other leads.

Soon investigators became aware of Lee Bates and his links to Matt. They connected the dots, from Bates's roles as friend and drinking buddy to delivery driver and strip club pal. In multiple interviews with Bates, police caught him in blatant lies, establishing a pattern of conflicting statements.

When he got wind of this, Matt was quick to warn his friend to keep his mouth shut. If he wanted to stay alive, betrayal was not an option.

DiBernardo began looking at Richard Matt's criminal record, dating back to his early teens. His history of violence and frequent encounters with the criminal justice system troubled the detective.

During this phase of the investigation, Matt checked in with his probation officer, part of his sentence from a DWI conviction he'd gotten while working for Rickerson. Both street-smart and jail-smart, he began to sense he was the focus of official attention. Matt quickly contacted Bates, telling him again to keep his mouth shut. This time, he took the warnings one step further. He told his former partner that if he crossed him, he would kill him and his entire family.

Bates had stood and watched while Matt tortured, then killed, William Rickerson. He knew for a fact that Matt was capable of executing his threat.

About three weeks after Rickerson's disappearance, detectives from the North Tonawanda Police Department again questioned Bates. This time, he began to tell a piece of the truth. He admitted to police that he had sometimes helped Matt peddle the meat stolen from the food broker. He wasn't ready to tell the whole truth, however. For many reasons, Bates continued his deception with the detectives.

He was fearful of being arrested for the kidnapping and murder of Rickerson. He was even more fearful for his own and his family's safety from the psychotic Matt.

In early January 1998, a man and boy walking the banks of the Niagara River made a gruesome discovery. The two found a human torso floating in the ice-cold water off Fisherman Park in North Tonawanda. This was less than 500 yards downstream from Tonawanda Island. It seems the river's currents weren't as reliable a disposal system as Matt must have thought. Within weeks of this finding, police divers located two legs in about twenty feet of water, also downstream from Tonawanda Island. DNA testing confirmed the torso and legs belonged to the missing Rickerson.

These finds made front-page headlines in all the local newspapers. Now police had no doubt: they had a murder on their hands.

With the pressure mounting, Matt felt compelled to have another conversation with his girlfriend about Rickerson's death. They were sitting in Johanna Capretto's motel room in Fort Erie, Ontario, when he made a slightly more truthful confession to her. While he smoked a cigarette, he dropped his earlier story about an accidental fall. In fact, he told her, he had snapped Rickerson's neck. But he assured her that had been an accident, too.

As he was getting this half-truth off his chest, Matt knew it was time to run. He offered Johanna the diamond ring he had stolen from Rickerson. She allegedly took the ring but soon panicked and flushed it down the toilet. As Matt left her motel room, he helped himself to her hard-earned tips. What she may not have realized was just how lucky she was: he'd stolen her money but left her alive.

Matt's next stop was his half-brother's apartment in Buffalo. He confessed to Wayne Schimpf that he was in a lot of trouble, showing him a newspaper article about Rickerson's murder. He told Wayne he had done it—but by accident.

Reading the newspaper clipping, Schimpf was unnerved when he got to the part about the dismembered body being discarded in the Niagara River. "How did you do it? How did you hack him up, with a chainsaw or something?"

Matt turned toward his half-brother, looked him in the eye, smiled, and answered, "With a hacksaw." He then told Wayne, "I can do another seven years, but I can't do life."

Matt told Schimpf he needed a car to get out of town. He wanted to use Schimpf's van. Schimpf refused to let him take it. Then Matt made a highly persuasive argument. "You're my brother, you're my blood," he told him. "I love you. But I'll kill you."

As Matt drove away from the Buffalo apartment with Wayne's van—and his identity—police were already beginning to close in.

CHAPTER 15
MATT TAKES A RIDE

ON JANUARY 5, 1998, LEE BATES WALKED into the North Tonawanda Police station. He had something important to say to the cops he'd been lying to for weeks. "Your job is to protect and serve. He is coming to kill me." Police didn't have to ask who he was talking about.

Bates was clearly uncomfortable explaining why he had lied to detectives during the earlier interviews. He told them he was afraid of Matt. He said he'd feared being killed on the spot if he hadn't helped Matt with the crimes against Rickerson. Bates broke down crying. He spilled his guts to the police. He described how Matt had tortured, killed, and dismembered his former boss. Bates made especially certain to tell police that Matt had threatened to kill him and his family if he talked.

Unknown to Bates at the time, Matt had fled western New York, driving Schimpf's van, Capretto's cash in his pocket. So as not to risk having its license number checked when crossing the border, he ditched the van in Brownville, Texas. He crossed the Rio Grande River on foot; his final destination was Matamoros, Mexico.

North Tonawanda is on the north side of the Erie Canal, the boundary between Erie and Niagara counties. So when Lee Bates appeared before a grand jury in February 1998, it was in Niagara County. He testified about his role, as well as Richard Matt's, in the death of William Rickerson. His testimony was part of a plea deal that Bates and his lawyer made with the Niagara County District Attorney's Office. Bates cooperated, hoping for both leniency and protection.

While Bates sat in the Niagara County Jail, awaiting his next court date, Richard Matt sat on a barstool in Mexico, stalking his next victim.

According to authorities in Matamoros, an American going by the name of Wayne Schimpf had noticed an American businessman at the bar holding a wad of cash. The gringo calling himself Schimpf followed the man into the restroom. Not content to rob Charles Perrault of hundreds of dollars, Matt fatally stabbed him.

Running from the bar, the attacker was caught by police within minutes. When arrested, Matt told the Mexican police his name was Wayne Schimpf.

By the time his case was heard, of course, the Mexicans knew he was Richard Matt. Without ever seeing the inside of a courtroom, Matt was convicted and sentenced to twenty-three years in a Mexican prison. In a jail interview years later, the Buffalo TV news reporter Rich Newbert asked Matt how many times he'd stabbed Perrault. Matt's answer was chilling. "I don't know. Till he stopped moving."

Shortly after being imprisoned in Mexico, Matt reached out to his one-time mentor, Tonawanda Detective David Bentley. His letter was mostly complaints about his treatment at the hands of the Mexican justice system. He wrote about never seeing a judge and having a defense attorney who spoke only Spanish. He wrote about receiving his twenty-three-year prison sentence via a letter from the judge, written in Spanish. At the time, Matt didn't speak or read Spanish. He claimed his jailers beat and abused him and extorted money before he could get a cell with a bed and toilet.

Interestingly, when he wrote to Bentley, Matt also shared previously undisclosed details of the assault, kidnapping, and twenty-seven-hour horror story that ended with William Rickerson's barbaric death.

Matt had served just four months of his twenty-three-year sentence in Mexico when Lee Bates began serving his prison sentence of fifteen years to life for his role—and guilty plea—in Rickerson's murder. This young man who had once wanted to become a cop had shifted from one side of the law to the other. It was Bates's first bid with the New York State Department of Corrections.

Not long after Bates went to prison, his family received a letter sent from the Matamoros prison. Written by Richard Matt, the letter had been postmarked in Texas. In the letter, Matt offered the Bates family a deal. He said he was willing to assume full responsibility for Rickerson's murder, clearing Bates of his involvement, in exchange for a hefty price of $10,000. Considerately, he even outlined how he wanted that paid: $5,000 in fifty-dollar bills and the rest in hundreds. Matt admitted that he'd been present during the murder but said Bates was just as guilty as he was.

The Bates family didn't bite on this ridiculous proposition. Matt was nothing but a pain in the ass for them. He was also a pain in the ass for his Mexican jailers. He was anything but a model prisoner. He attempted to escape, getting as far as a rooftop when an alert jailer spotted him and shot him. This was Richard Matt's third documented escape attempt, and only the first that was unsuccessful.

By January 2007, Matt had served about nine years of his twenty-three year sentence in the Mexican prison for the murder of Charles Perrault. That month he found himself in an airplane flying north to the United States. This private flight from Mexico to Houston was a one-way trip for its fifteen passengers, all fugitives from justice in the United States. It wasn't just their seat belts that kept these high-profile, well-known individuals secure in their seats. And it's highly unlikely that they were offered complimentary food and beverages, either.

On arriving in Houston, the fifteen fugitives were greeted by heavily armed U.S. Marshals. Taking control of the clandestine mission, the marshals moved their charges from the airport to the Federal Court House in Houston, supported by an assortment of firepower that included snipers on rooftops on and around the building. This extraordinary security was aimed at potential violence from Mexican drug cartels.

Among the fifteen fugitives were four Mexican drug lords with various cartel affiliations. The eleven Americans in the group were wanted for serious crimes including murder, drug trafficking, kidnapping and sex offenses.

This shipment was part of a prisoner exchange negotiated between the U.S. State Department and its Mexican counterpart. In several exchanges like this during 2007, some 108 fugitives from justice were returned to the United States from Mexico. In return, Mexico received eighty-seven fugitives from the United States the same year.

The U.S. Marshals are this nation's primary fugitive-hunting organization. The Marshals Service has a field office in Mexico, with the sole mission of tracking down fugitives. The marshals pursue anyone who flees the United States into Mexico, as well as people from Mexico who flee into the United States. Those they capture are processed under the authority of both the United States and Mexican constitutions and both countries' laws.

All fifteen of the fugitives in the January 2007 shipment were arraigned before a federal magistrate in Houston. The marshals then arranged to transport them to the appropriate jurisdictions for further proceedings.

North Tonawanda police were notified that Richard Matt had been extradited and was returning to Niagara County under escort of the U.S. Marshals. They delivered him at the Buffalo-Niagara International Airport. When Matt emerged from a commercial flight from Houston, he was handcuffed and in leg irons. When local police escorted him from the airport, he refused to answer questions from a reporter.

Almost ten years after the crime, the forty-one-year-old Matt was sitting in the Niagara County Jail, waiting for his day in court to answer charges for the assault, kidnapping, and murder of William Rickerson. For more than a year, he was held without bail while prosecutors and defense attorneys jousted over a variety of motions. The sensational nature of the crime made Matt something of a celebrity in the small Niagara County seat, the old canal town of Lockport. This also put unusual burdens on local authorities.

As the case dragged on, Niagara County Sheriff Tom Beilein and his deputies were tasked with keeping Matt in custody. They were well aware of his history of escapes. In February 2008, a month before the case was scheduled for trial, Beilein got reports that Matt was plotting to escape. This high-profile and high-security defendant was reported to have said he would kill anyone who stood in his way. A fellow inmate said Matt told him he would "gut a cop" if he met any resistance during his escape. He also vowed he would never be taken alive.

Sheriff Beilein received information that Matt was attempting to get a diamond glass cutter to use in escaping. The intel also said Matt intended to return to Mexico if he succeeded in breaking out. After his nine years behind bars in Mexico, Matt had established a number of contacts with drug lords who were willing to help him, sources said. If his escape was unsuccessful, the sheriff's contacts reported, Matt intended to kill himself.

Jailers responded by moving Matt to the jail's special housing area. Taking an inmate out of the general population is a standard precaution. Greater security and less mobility equals no escape. The Niagara County Jail's special-housing inmates are locked down with little to no movement allowed. With meals and other services delivered to his cell, Matt would have spent a quiet thirty days awaiting his time in the courtroom.

Although jail authorities were able to foil this escape plot before it materialized, it was documented as Matt's fourth try to break out.

After more than two days of jury selection, on March 13, 2008, Judge Sara Sheldon Sperrazza oversaw opening statements on one of the most gruesome murders in Niagara County's history. It wasn't just the trial that had a high profile. So did the security arrangements that surrounded it.

Sheriff Beilein and his staff were in charge of the extraordinary effort to protect the court officers, jury, and public while in Matt's presence. Escorting Matt to and from the Niagara County Court House was the duty of the Sheriff's Department Corrections Emergency Response Team. Much like the state-level CERT, part of the Department of Corrections, members of the county's CERT are specially trained with semi-automatic weapons and the sort of gear used by most police department SWAT officers. CERT members are also trained to deal with defendants requiring high security, those considered disruptive, or physically strong inmates. Given his prior escape history, and the accusation that he snapped a man's spine with his bare hands, Matt fit into all these categories.

The officers who escorted Matt to court were armed with semi-automatic pistols and assault rifles. Once in court, the escort officers supplemented the deputies already assigned to courthouse security. Because of what they had learned about Matt's background and drug-cartel connections, twice the usual number of Niagara County deputies were on duty in the courtroom. Meanwhile, deputies armed with sniper rifles were posted around the outside of the courthouse.

Inside the courtroom, other security precautions were taken. Protective glass was removed from the wooden tables used by counsel. Court officials feared that if the glass was shattered, Matt could use it as a weapon. Off hours, when court wasn't in session, deputies frisked the entire area around the courtroom to ensure no dangerous contraband was stashed there.

The most powerful tool Beilein used was an electrical belt that Matt wore under his clothing. This remote-controlled device could deliver a 50,000-volt shock to the defendant in the event of a disturbance or escape attempt. During the entire trial, a deputy whose identity Matt didn't know held the remote control for the belt.

When not in court, Matt was housed in what the Niagara County Jail called administrative segregation. Inmates are placed in this special housing arrangement for several reasons. One reason to separate an inmate from the jail's general population is security concerns. With Matt's documented escape history and information about another possible escape plot, Beilein was taking no chances.

Two other developments reinforced the jailers' fears and led to additional security precautions. First, Matt bought a pair of Adidas sneakers with hard soles, which were less apt to get cut while climbing over a fence topped with razor wire. Then there were the weekly deliveries of cash to Matt by a woman who lived in Niagara Falls. During one visit, she gave him two fifty-dollar bills.

The jury and the courtroom spectators saw none of this. The jurors—nine women and three men, with four alternates—occasionally glanced at Matt, who came to court dressed in fashionable suits and with his hair slicked down. Handsome and physically fit, he made a good impression during testimony and the lawyers' arguments. He listened intently, occasionally jotting notes on a yellow legal pad as he sat with Public Defenders Matthew Pynn and Christopher Privateer.

Special Prosecutors Lou Haremski and Joe Mordino provided the jury with a clear picture of the defendant. Testimony from those who knew him—acquaintances, an old girlfriend, the police officer who had attempted to mentor him, even his own half-brother—described Matt as charming, but also brutal and deadly.

Pynn didn't have a strong reply to what these witnesses said. "I can't explain it. I can see him as a guy who would have a lot of friends," he said.

Matt's other lawyer, Privateer, told the jury, "William Rickerson died in December 1997. The question is, who did it? We know Lee Bates admitted to it."

When it was Bates's turn on the stand, he testified about his need for money and gave a blow-by-blow account of the assault, kidnapping, and murder. Over two days of testimony, he described in detail the horror William Rickerson endured at Matt's hands.

Johanna Capretto told how Matt had confessed to killing Rickerson, offered her the victim's diamond wedding ring, and then stole her tips when he was on his way out the door.

Called as a witness for the defense was Detective David Bentley, who had attempted to mentor the teenaged Matt. He described the letters Matt had sent him from the Mexican prison, which included details of the crimes against Rickerson. That information, which investigators had never disclosed publicly, could only have been known to someone who was present during the crimes.

Before the trial ended, Matt sent a threatening letter to Bentley. Even though called by Matt's own lawyers, Bentley had not helped his case. To his former mentor, Matt wrote, "You lied in court to fuck me over for the D.A. You also make it very clear that we are not friends. I'll remember both . . ."

Matt's own half-brother, Wayne Schimpf, told the court how he was freaked out when Matt showed up at his apartment, first confessing to the murder and then demanding his van. He elaborated on Matt's description of cutting up Rickerson's body with a hacksaw.

The icing on the prosecution's case was the so-called "Matamoros Letter," mailed to the Bates family, asking for $10,000 to clear Lee Bates. The envelope contained Matt's DNA and handwriting samples tied him both to the letter and to the crimes.

After four weeks and testimony from thirty witnesses, the trial ended with closing arguments that took more than two hours.

New York State law defines second-degree murder as a killing committed under several specific conditions. Those include intent to kill; reckless conduct showing "a depraved indifference to human life"; and killing while committing another serious crime, including kidnapping and robbery. All three of these were applied to Richard Matt. The laws concerning kidnapping and robbery have similar provisions. That means a defendant, like Matt, can be charged more than once with murder, kidnapping, and robbery for the same crime.

The jury deliberated only four hours before returning with a guilty verdict. Richard Matt was found guilty of three charges of second-degree murder, two charges of first-degree robbery and three charges of first-degree kidnapping.

When the court reconvened for the sentencing, Judge Sperrazza sentenced Matt to twenty-five years to life in prison for the crimes against William Rickerson. It was 9 A.M. on Friday, May 30, 2008.

Sheriff Beilein wasted no time in getting rid of this hot potato. As the ink dried on the court's commitment order, Niagara County transferred Matt to the custody of the New York State Department of Corrections. As he began his third and final bid, this charming, clever criminal would keep an eye out for new people he could manipulate.

PART III
THE PLANS, THE SCHEMES

CHAPTER 16
THE COMPLACENT GUARD

ONE OF THE TWO PRISON EMPLOYEES HELD LEGALLY RESPONSIBLE for Matt's and Sweat's escape is a former uniformed guard named Gene Palmer. He began his career in 1987 as one of New York State's more than twenty thousand corrections officers. His career ended in 2015 at Clinton Correctional Facility, with a guilty plea and a transfer into a cell in the county jail. Early in his career, Palmer had honed the valuable skill of getting information from inmates. The information he obtained often helped guards find contraband, drugs and weapons—all taken from inmates other than the informants. The payoff? The inmates who provided the information would get rewards.

At Clinton, Palmer was assigned as an escort officer. This meant he would walk with inmates moving from one part of the prison to another. That duty gave him access to just about every corner of Clinton's many buildings and its sprawling grounds.

As the years went by, Palmer became relaxed, even complacent, in his duties. He forgot that he was surrounded by criminals. By his own admission, he didn't properly frisk inmates he escorted within the prison walls. He neglected to require his "rats" to walk through metal detectors.

And as Palmer relaxed his standards, something else started to slip: the quality of the information he got from the inmates. Sure, he could find out who had contraband—if that inmate had an enemy who wanted to do him dirty or just wanted some of his stuff for himself. But the sort of intelligence that helps head off trouble and keep prisons safer? Not so much.

Palmer considered himself a "go-to guy" at Clinton, someone who could get things done, both for fellow guards and for inmates. He wouldn't hesitate to tell you so, either. "Everybody looked up to me," he later told investigators. But not everybody shared his high opinion of himself. After all his bad decisions blew up in his face, Palmer would claim that he'd gotten valuable information from Richard Matt about trouble brewing in the prison. He said he reported this to his superiors.

They weren't impressed. The prison does have an intelligence-gathering team, called the Crisis Intervention Unit. Palmer wasn't part of it. Maybe that was because his intel never seemed to pan out. Donald Quinn, the first deputy superintendent at Clinton, said Palmer was "real dramatic" but seldom had anything valuable to report. Once, Palmer warned, "You're going to lose your prison . . . It's a powder keg and it's about to explode. My informant tells me that when it goes, they're going to show no mercy." When Quinn heard this, he asked Palmer for his evidence. He didn't have any.

Palmer might not have been so high on himself if he'd known what Quinn called his stream of worthless tips: the "disinformation highway."

Quinn's boss, Steven Racette, was Clinton's superintendent. He said his leadership team called Palmer "Chicken Little." As in, "The sky is falling." Racette and his deputies "quickly figured out that his information wasn't reliable," he said later.

But it wasn't his Chicken Little act that cost Palmer his career. It was another series of bad decisions that unwittingly helped a couple of vicious felons pull off an audacious prison break. After a quarter century in the Department of Corrections uniform, he knew all the policies and procedures that clearly define acceptable staff conduct. He chose to blatantly disregard them. Even if you credit his pleas that he meant well, the fact was that he directly undermined the prison's security.

Sweat and Matt, who proved more clever than their guard, manipulated Gene Palmer's ego and his thirst for information. Then, once he had compromised himself, they exploited his weakness.

As escort officer, Palmer's chief duty was accompanying inmates between their Honor Block cells and the tailor shops in the Industry Building. He held this position for the final eight years of his nearly unblemished twenty-seven-year career with Corrections. Palmer also had the opportunity to work overtime shifts on weekends due to staff shortages. He often served those shifts in the Honor Block.

Both of these duties put Palmer close to Richard Matt. Over the years, the guard came to trust the convicted killer. Matt built on this relationship, assuring Palmer that he would kill any inmate who dared to assault his good friend in the blue uniform. Matt also fed Palmer information that let him to find and seize contraband, including drugs and such home-made weapons as shanks or shivs. The grateful Palmer would reward Matt by giving him property that had been confiscated from the targeted inmates. Those perks ranged from food to a television. Palmer would go one step further, giving Matt the permit required to own such a prized possession as a TV set. Throughout his career, as investigators later determined, Palmer had acted as the prison's Robin Hood, taking illicit property from some inmates and giving it to others as payment for information.

Palmer's duties gave him freedom to move around the prison without being deemed "out of place" by his supervisor. He used that flexibility to visit counselors, Program Committee members, the medical staff, and the package room's personnel. With all of these, he would be an advocate for Matt, and eventually Sweat, too.

Matt was astute enough to recognize Palmer's thirst for information as a vulnerability. Once their relationship was well-established, Matt found it easy to manipulate Palmer and exploit his soft spots. Both Matt and Sweat recognized that they could only benefit from cultivating the gullible guard.

Both of these inmates considered themselves artists. But only Matt could justify that claim. He was an accomplished draftsman. His drawings and paintings became valuable commodities inside the prison—and out. But to properly profit from his talent, to market his artwork, he needed someone with ready access to all corners of the facility. Palmer was happy to oblige, for a price. He served as a conduit for Matt to trade his artwork for things he needed—or for favors. Palmer's commission for these services consisted of paintings and drawings for which he paid little or nothing. He also served as an intermediary for staff members he trusted, helping them to get artwork from the prison's self-taught Rembrandt.

All this was entirely illicit. Prison regulations explicitly ban these sorts of black-market barter transactions.

Defying the rules and apparently oblivious to the consequences for soliciting and receiving inmate artwork, Palmer would seal his fate by extending his commerce beyond the prison walls. He began smuggling Matt's artwork out of the prison and smuggling in paints and brushes. Another service he provided to Matt was bringing him photographs that the inmate artist would recreate as paintings. Some of these were for himself, but he carried photos from other buyers, too. Ultimately Palmer would get more than a dozen pieces of art from Matt.

So why the big deal over paints and brushes? These aren't considered contraband in prison. Inmates Matt and Sweat could have ordered their art supplies from an outside vendor. It's how they came into Clinton that was the problem. But this was very useful to the inmates. By manipulating Palmer into smuggling supplies into the prison, they confirmed that he could be bought. Once they knew this guard was willing to violate Department of Corrections policies, they had a perfect candidate for extortion.

Matt also persuaded Palmer to violate a cardinal principle for the prison staff: to be even-handed in enforcing rules and offering privileges. Instead, he began playing favorites, becoming an advocate for certain inmates while strictly policing others. Palmer was the catalyst who let Matt gain power among his fellow prisoners. He would tell Palmer that some workers in the tailor shop were possible trouble makers. Palmer would see to it that those inmates got reassigned. The message was clear. If you didn't kiss Matt's ass, your days in the tailor shop were numbered.

When escorting Matt from the tailor shop to his cell, Palmer often let him bypass the walk-through metal detectors. Department directives require that all inmates go through a metal detector between work place and cell. Every time, every day. Matt's manipulation of Palmer paid off every time he was able to evade this security measure.

Palmer would warn Matt and Sweat when to expect cell searches. He gave them access to the catwalks behind their cells so they could hide the paint Palmer had smuggled in for them. Most amazing of all, Palmer let Sweat venture unescorted onto the catwalks behind the Honor Block cells with instructions to modify the electrical wiring! This was a forbidden favor for specific inmates. Sometimes inmates get ahold of electrical appliances that exceed the capacity of their cell's single outlet. That trips the breaker, killing all power to the cell. A staff member then has to manually reset the breaker switch. But to reduce the possibility of breakers tripping, a circuit can be rigged to allow a greater power draw. Inmates who wanted more juice would submit a request to Matt. He would pass this black-market work order to Palmer. Palmer, happily letting Matt pull his strings, would give Sweat the assignment and the tools needed, and let him onto the catwalk.

However smoothly this little system worked, though, this is prison. And in prison, nothing is free. Not information, not electrical upgrades, not artwork. For everything, there is a price to be paid. Sometimes the price is high and means losing your job. Gene Palmer didn't recognize that he was no longer the one in control. In his daily interactions with inmates, he disregarded his training and the employee manual. By violating the department's policies and procedures, he became a resource for prisoners dealing in contraband.

Far more seriously, Palmer became a broker for misconduct by other prison staff members, misconduct that would come to a disastrous end.

CHAPTER 17
LONELY, UNDISCIPLINED, CORRUPTIBLE

ALLOW ME TO INTRODUCE JOYCE MITCHELL, the second of the compromised prison insiders who took a fall after the escape. This full-figured wife and mother, fifty-one years old at the time, actively helped Sweat and Matt make their escape. She started her Corrections career in March 2008, with the job title of industrial training supervisor. She was employed by the prison system's revenue-producing arm, called Corcraft. Her assignment was a tailor shop at Clinton Correctional Facility. This job paid Mitchell $57,600 plus benefits. For a North Country native with a community college degree, this was a great opportunity.

She already knew a good deal about the job. Mitchell's husband, Lyle, had been a civilian supervisor for Corcraft in one of Clinton's other tailor shops since September 2005. Now that both were working in the prison, they could car-pool to work together from their home in Dickinson Center, a fifty-five-mile drive to Dannemora.

Joyce went through the training required for all new civilian employees. Mandatory courses included departmental policies, directives, and procedures; security procedures; tool control, key control, and emergency control procedures; and a unique class called "Understanding Games Inmates Play." The state's corrections training courses explicitly describe how to maintain a professional working relationship with inmates. New staff members are taught how to keep a safe and professional distance and avoid befriending the inmates. One very specific directive: never reveal personal details about themselves.

Although Joyce had no experience working in a prison, her training, instincts, and common sense should have prepared her for this position. As a parent, she should have already known a great deal about how to cope with manipulative behavior, poor impulse control, and other character flaws that criminals share with children. Staff members, both uniformed and civilian, could have been great mentors and resources for Joyce. She would also have the advantage of her husband, Lyle, and his three years of experience in the tailor shop.

She also should have known something about working in a position of public trust. She had managed to get elected three times to the post of tax collector for the town of Dickinson. And yet that little town, with just a few hundred residents, doesn't enjoy a good reputation for sound financial management. In 2014, a state audit said the local governing board "did not effectively oversee the town's financial operations." Local leaders failed to audit the financial records of several town offices, including the tax collector, a state report said. The state audit doesn't specify whether those failings went back to Mitchell's time in office. What her history as a small-time elected official does show is that she had some political pull. To me, that's a more likely explanation than her skill with a sewing machine for how she got her lucrative job in the prison system.

Digging a little deeper into Joyce and Lyle Mitchell's history unearths a more complex story. On the one hand, they both had experience in the textile industry. They had met while working at a company called Tru-Stitch, which once operated several huge mills in Malone and nearby towns. Those mills employed hundreds of local residents, making slippers for name-brand clothing retailers. But just like the iron mines before it, the textile industry abandoned the North Country. Tru-Stitch closed its Franklin County operations in the 1990s, a major kick in the teeth for the local economy. Joyce Mitchell found work with another company, Gildan, which made T-shirts, but its plant eventually closed in 2007. Those jobs meant that, just like her husband, she could claim experience in garment production when she applied to work for Corcraft.

But while she would oversee inmates working at sewing machines, Mitchell herself hadn't been very skillful when she was a stitcher. A former co-worker told *People* magazine that she wasn't good at the precision work her job required; Tru-Stitch kept moving her from workstation to workstation to try to find something she could do.

Something else Mitchell's fellow employees knew about her: "She would talk about men," the co-worker recalled. "That's all she would talk about."

That gets us to the other side of Joyce and Lyle's history at Tru-Stitch: a history of dishonesty and betrayal. Not only did they meet while working there; not only did they have sexual trysts on the plant grounds while on the clock; they were each married to other people when their affair began.

Joyce Mitchell brought one other thing to Dannemora that she'd picked up at Tru-Stitch: her nickname. Around Clinton prison, both staff and inmates called her "Tillie." It seems that when she first went to work at the slipper factory, her mother, also named Joyce, was already employed there. And so rather than have to keep two "Joyces" straight, her co-workers assigned her the name Tillie.

Whether she was more a "Tillie the toiler" or a "Tillie the tramp," events in the Corcraft tailor shops would soon make clear.

CHAPTER 18
CORCRAFT'S TAILOR SHOPS

THE STATE OPERATES A NUMBER OF INDUSTRIES within its prison walls, all under the name Corcraft. It isn't just license plates, though they're still part of Corcraft's product line. It also manufactures highway signs, office furniture, clothing for inmates and uniforms for guards.

At last count, Corcraft employs more than 275 civilians and 2,100 inmates in fourteen prisons. Corcraft's revenue is in the neighborhood of $50 million per year, the state has reported. This income helps offset the cost of operating the prisons. And working for Corcraft helps inmates learn job skills that might help them make an honest living once they get out. Many of those workers, though, are lifers. They'll never get out.

Clinton has eight Corcraft tailor shops, each employing around fifty inmate workers. The shops are in the Industry Building, which is on the prison's south side, closest to the streets of Dannemora. Its workshop windows offer a view of the perimeter wall, the foothills of the Adirondacks and, from the upper stories, the village of Dannemora itself.

A tour through one of the tailor shops at Clinton brings you into a large room lit by fluorescent lights hanging from the ceiling and natural light pouring in from south-facing windows. Through these, the Adirondack Mountains rising just a dozen miles away are a tantalizing vision of freedom for the imprisoned workers. Filling the room are rows of tables, each holding an industrial-grade sewing machine. Each has its own task light. For obvious reasons, the machines are bolted to the tables. The simple metal work tables measure about two by four feet and contain a single drawer each. The whirring sound from dozens of sewing machines pervades the room. You can feel the vibration from dozens of needles moving in and out of fabric. The floor is lined with remnants of thread and scraps of cloth the inmate workers discard as they sew.

A typical day in the tailor shop begins when the inmates, clad in green prison attire, are escorted in by a corrections officer. Someone like Gene Palmer. Each inmate is expected to sit at his assigned sewing machine as soon as he arrives. Inmates typically bring earphones and a portable radio/cassette player for music while they work. More up-to-date devices like iPods aren't allowed. When he arrives, each one is issued a seam ripper and blunt-tipped safety scissors. These tools are collected and accounted for before inmates are allowed to leave their work area.

The industrial training supervisor—Joyce Mitchell, for example—assigns the workers' duties, offers instruction as needed and inspects the final products. The tailor shop's security is monitored by a corrections officer who sits at a desk raised two steps above the shop floor. This guard's post, in each shop, is right next to the civilian supervisor's desk, on the same platform. I know how this works; I've been that guard in tailor shops in other prisons.

For an inmate at Clinton, working in a tailor shop is a plum assignment. The hourly wage, which can range from twenty-six to sixty-five cents, is excellent by prison standards, and workers stand to earn bonuses, too. The criteria that determine work assignments are designed to encourage good behavior and ultimately make managing the prison easier.

A Program Committee is in charge of assigning inmates to jobs, school—formal education—or vocational training. The committee usually includes security supervisors, senior counselors, and educational supervisors. In making assignments, they consider factors like the inmates' educational needs, criminal history, and disciplinary record. They will also listen to opinions from corrections officers who know the inmates better than they do. Of course, in some cases as it would turn out, those guards only think they know the inmates.

Qualifying for a tailor shop job requires meeting a high standard: a good work ethic and good behavior. Those who get those coveted positions are paid according to their performance and production. Their wages are placed directly into personal accounts, from which the inmates can later draw as they wish.

One important reason for the good pay is that it helps guarantee a steady stream of revenue for the prison. The tailor shop is a business that provides income for the State of New York. The eight tailor shops at the Clinton Correctional Facility get about $10 million in orders each year.

In December 2003, just weeks after Sweat arrived at Clinton, he was assigned to one of those shops. It seemed like a good fit. His work ethic and job performance earned him promotions and transfers to other shops where the work was more demanding and the pay better. By the time Joyce Mitchell was hired in March 2008, Sweat had four and a half years of experience sitting at a sewing machine.

Joyce's job with Corcraft meant she would work in the same building as her husband, Lyle, but in different shops.

A condition of employment was that Joyce would go through forty hours of training. This included orientation both to Clinton Correctional Facility as a whole and the Corcraft Industry building. Within a week, she was supervising some of New York State's most violent inmates as they worked at their sewing machines. At the beginning, she was a relief supervisor, filling in as needed for fellow staff members who were out sick, in training, or on vacation.

Five months after Joyce started her job, a new inmate was assigned to the tailor shops. It was Richard Matt. His assignment came in August 2008, just a few weeks after he arrived at Clinton.

Like everyone who starts work in the state's prisons, Joyce Mitchell attended the training session titled "Games Inmates

Play." Presented as a video, it's also part of the refresher training required for all staff members. It shows scenarios in which inmates try to manipulate the prison staff. The video cautions employees against two cardinal sins: becoming too friendly with inmates and sharing personal information with them. Two of the tailor shop workers, Matt and Sweat, could easily have played the roles of the inmates in the training video. Both Joyce and Lyle Mitchell watched the training video many times. They also ignored it.

The state's comprehensive training program has been developed over decades of experience. It's been used successfully to educate thousands of Corrections employees. With Joyce and Lyle Mitchell, though, it would prove utterly ineffective.

Joyce's orientation and initial training exposed her to a new world. It introduced her to the ever-present potential for violence, manipulation, extortion, riots, escape and hostage-taking: dangers that all Corrections employees confront every day.

But she was sure she knew better, as events would prove. Instead of taking her training seriously, Joyce Mitchell actively cultivated personal relationships with both Sweat and Matt. She shared personal information about her unhappy marriage to Lyle. She confided in these inmates about her dissatisfaction and loneliness. And she also let them know that she held a life insurance policy on her husband. A policy that made him worth half a million dollars—when he was dead.

It didn't take long for Joyce's first few bad decisions to begin compromising her. This self-proclaimed devoted wife and mother, a regular church-goer, the coach of a girls' softball team, let her emotions get the better of her judgment and willingly opened herself up to blackmail. Before it all ended, she would become New York State's poster child for prison breaks and pocket pool.

CHAPTER 19
TAILOR SHOP TROUBLES

SWEAT AND MATT EACH BEGAN WORK IN ONE OF CORCRAFT'S industrial tailor shops soon after arriving at Clinton.

The two inmates worked in many of the eight shops, directed by several civilian supervisors, producing a variety of garments. On separate occasions, security investigations led to both Sweat and Matt being removed from the tailor shops. But both were eventually allowed to return.

Many tailor shop workers are assigned to cells in A-Block Housing Unit, which is Clinton Correctional Facility's Honor Block. Sweat entered Honor Block in November 2010 after seven years at Clinton. Matt had been there since June 2009. They shared common interests in drawing and painting and soon became friends and cell neighbors. Sweat worked in the tailor shops without incident from November 2003 until September 2014. In performance evaluations during those eleven years, his supervisors described him as a highly skilled worker. In January 2012, he was assigned to Tailor Shop #1. Because he was so good with a sewing machine, he was given the additional duty of "instructor."

Between August 2008 and September 2011, Matt's employment with Corcraft was also uneventful. His civilian supervisors often rated him as an average or above average worker. But two separate incidents triggered security investigations that got him removed from the tailor shops.

The first was in September 2011. On a day that he didn't have Palmer to wave him around the metal detector, Matt had to submit to a mandatory search on his way back from work. He was carrying twelve needles he had smuggled out of the tailor shops in a portable radio battery compartment. This triggered an investigation that started with a frisk—a thorough search of Matt's cell. This turned up other contraband items meant to be parts of a homemade tattoo machine. The next steps were a misbehavior report and a disciplinary hearing. Matt was found guilty of promoting prison contraband. He was sentenced to thirty days confined to his new cell. This is called "keeplock." The infraction cost him his Honor Block housing; he was reassigned to D Block, three buildings away.

But immediately after serving his thirty days of what amounted to house arrest, he went right back to the tailor shops. Within two weeks, he got a promotion and a pay raise.

It was less than a year later when Matt was pulled out of the tailor shop again. In August 2012, the female civilian supervisor in his shop discovered an unsigned typewritten note. It alleged that she had carried on an inappropriate relationship with one of the inmates she supervised. Addressed to her, the note attempted to extort $500 from her.

The extortion attempt didn't work. Its intended target immediately turned the note over to Pat Smith, Corcraft's senior industrial superintendent. Smith reported the matter to Stephen Brown, the deputy superintendent for security, who ordered an investigation. That probe exonerated the shop supervisor of any misconduct. But for security reasons, seven inmates, including Matt, were removed from the tailor shop.

Six months later, Matt asked the Program Committee to let him return to the tailor shops. Advocating for Matt was Corrections Officer Palmer. This was not a normal duty for someone in his position. As an escort officer, Palmer would not have been expected to speak, pro or con, about inmates' proposed job assignments. In spite of Matt's recent removal from that assignment, the

Program Committee agreed to send him back. And a few months after that, Matt returned to his previous home in Honor Block.

While this was going on, troubles were brewing in one of the other tailor shops. Starting in 2012, prison staff members and inmates began noticing Joyce Mitchell interacting inappropriately with the inmate workers in her workplace. Vicki-Lynn Safford was the industry quality-control supervisor. She said later that Mitchell "treated them more as an employee or a friend . . . she didn't keep the distance."

Bradley Streeter, who would become Mitchell's supervisor in 2013, called her an "inmate lover" who "tried to sweet-talk them into getting things done her way." Mitchell herself said she found it difficult to maintain a proper separation from inmates. "I will visit with the guys," she would admit. "It's like you get a rapport with them because you're in that same room with them every day of the week."

Safford had a slightly different take on that rapport. "She always flirted around the shop and laughed and stood close to all inmates," she remembered. "But it was more so with Sweat and Matt."

Other witnesses included Corcraft supervisors and uniformed guards. They reported that Mitchell had behaved contrary to Department of Corrections policies and directives. Like Safford and Streeter, these employees also observed her treating inmates like close friends instead of maintaining the required professional distance. Joyce's supervisors at Corcraft addressed these issues and tried counseling to modify her behavior. She resisted and pushed back. Her supervisors saw that her behavior didn't get better; it got worse. Now openly defiant, she started to bring contraband food items for the inmates. These included home-baked treats like brownies or cookies, packaged candy, and the occasional new recipe. Once she brought Sweat a Big Mac, one of the other inmate workers said. Why he would want a cold hamburger—the nearest McDonald's is in Malone, forty-five minutes away—is a mystery, but every time Joyce smuggled something into the prison, she gave Sweat more and more power over her.

All this eventually led to what the DOC calls a counseling memorandum, which her supervisor Pat Smith issued in 2012. Under departmental procedures, only after repeated informal counseling does a supervisor put something on paper. The paper trail continued with a performance evaluation that Smith wrote the next year. This addressed Mitchell's inappropriate behavior and was critical of her job performance. Joyce responded to this by filing a grievance, claiming Smith was harassing her. She took her complaint over her bosses' heads, directly to Thomas LaValley, the prison's superintendent at the time.

That tactic paid off. While DOC and Corcraft managers tried to resolve the grievance, Joyce and Lyle Mitchell carried an air of empowerment. Smith, who had tried to pull Joyce back into line, saw the two on their way back from a meeting with LaValley. The Mitchells "were walking by my office whistling and smiling," she said, "because they had been to the superintendent and the superintendent was telling us to back off." Others used the word "smug" to describe Joyce's attitude.

Her inappropriate behaviors continued into the next year. Joyce blatantly ignored her supervisors. Allan Trombley, the guard assigned to her shop, later testified that she had said, "I'm going to do what I want to do, whether they like it or not."

During this time, in July 2013, Matt was assigned to cell A-6-22 in the Honor Block. A month later, Sweat was moved into cell A-6-23, right next door. Both worked in Tailor Shop #1 during the day and lived next door to each other at night. Soon this sinister partnership would gain its third member, without whom they wouldn't have been able to carry out their schemes. That happened in November when Smith reluctantly assigned Joyce Mitchell to supervise Tailor Shop #1. That decision put this problem employee in contact with two inmates who knew how to benefit from her undisciplined ways.

Corcraft was under pressure to fulfill vendor orders but a hiring freeze ordered from Albany made it impossible to hire anyone new. That put Pat Smith in a bind. As Clinton's Corcraft superintendent, she had to ignore Joyce's performance problems because the risk of losing orders would mean losing revenue. In this case, it seems that a bad employee was better than no employee.

In the aftermath of Joyce's complaints of harassment, her formal grievance, and her new assignment to Tailor Shop #1, Smith decided she had had enough. She had tried to do her duty, documenting Joyce's inappropriate behavior, to no avail. Washing her hands of the whole business, she retired. Her replacement, Scott Scholl, had been assistant industrial superintendent for five years. He knew all about both of the Mitchells and the controversy that surrounded them. But he chose to ignore the questionable activities occurring in the Mitchell tailor shop.

Later, state investigators would have harsh words for Scholl, calling him a much less effective manager than his predecessor. Even though Mitchell's behavior showed no improvement, Scholl never considered it a serious matter of concern. Asked directly about this afterward, he rambled all around the point: "I don't know that it ever came to me to the point where, in my opinion, I thought it needed to be put on paper or to pull her out."

And so, by his passivity, Scholl made it possible for Mitchell's behavior to escalate from unprofessional to criminal.

CHAPTER 20
ROMANCING AND CONTRABAND

AFTER OUTMANEUVERING HER MANAGERS, JOYCE MITCHELL took on her new duties in Tailor Shop #1 in late 2013. Like before, though, she was supervising some of the state's most violent inmates. While different skill levels might get them assigned to different shops, all the inmate workers were cut from the same cloth. All had violent histories. All posed potential risks to the staff. None of this seemed to bother Joyce. In fact, she seemed to revel in the danger. Under her attentive eyes, these inmates would work at their sewing machines, turning green fabric into prison uniforms. In her growing infatuation with dangerous men wearing those same state-issue uniforms, was she seeing "fifty shades of green"?

When she took over Tailor Shop #1, Mitchell had accumulated just shy of five and a half years of experience in the prison. Although Matt and Sweat were just two of the fifty inmates she supervised, the staff and inmates almost immediately noticed signs of a developing personal connection. It appeared as if Joyce Mitchell was craving attention from Sweat. Witnesses reported that anytime Sweat walked past Joyce's desk, she would engage him in a conversation, often about nothing. An inmate who saw many of these conversations said "lots of laughing, giggling" made him certain the two had some sort of relationship. With time, Mitchell began to share details about her personal life. She told Sweat she was lonely, and confided in him about her un-happy marriage to Lyle. It wasn't long before intimate conversations turned to physical contact. Many times, both the staff and other inmates saw her arm draped over Sweat's shoulder.

Matt and Sweat quickly identified Joyce Mitchell's vulnerability. They saw her unwillingness to follow protocol or obey the DOC's policies and procedures. Sensing that her loyalty was skewed, they watched for a chance to benefit from her blatant disregard for prison rules. Sweat later gave Matt full credit as the master manipulator. When asked how he figured out that Mitchell might be able to help them escape, Sweat answered, "Matt did."

In July 2014, the administration at Clinton Correctional Facility received an anonymous letter through the in-house mail system. It alleged improper conduct in Tailor Shop #1. It also accused Joyce Mitchell and Allan Trombley, the shop's guard, of racial bias against black and Latino inmates. The letter described a romantic relationship between Joyce and Sweat. The two of them would regularly go together to Tailor Shop #9, an unstaffed parts room next to their own shop, the letter said. When they returned, they never brought any parts. The accuser implied they were inspecting each other's parts while behind closed doors. Administrators told Joyce about the allegations and gave her a copy of the letter so she could respond. Joyce chose to fight back. She showed the anonymous letter to Sweat and Matt, hoping they could tell who had written it.

Meanwhile, her official response was to submit a statement denying any wrongdoing. Prison security conducted an internal investigation. The investigation confirmed that other prison employees had observed Joyce with her arm around Sweat, part of what appeared to be a personal relationship. During the time that Joyce's relationship with Sweat was under scrutiny, Matt seized the opportunity to bond with her. He turned on the charm, feigning interest in her, to endear himself to her.

In August 2014, Mitchell made a deal with Matt for a painting. His price was to ask her to get him two pairs of lighted reading glasses, handy—as it would turn out—for working in dark spaces. Joyce bought the glasses on eBay for less than $10, smuggled the contraband into the prison and gave them to Matt.

The lighted glasses paid for a portrait of Joyce's son, which Matt painted from a photograph she'd given him. Each piece of this transaction—soliciting the painting, giving an inmate a personal photograph, and smuggling contraband—directly violated Department of Corrections policies and directives.

Corrections Officer Gene Palmer re-entered the story at this point. He served as the courier for the finished painting, getting it though the maximum-security prison's gate and delivering it to Joyce and Lyle Mitchell's car for them to take it home.

Within a few weeks Mitchell commissioned another painting. This time, Matt's price was a pair of exercise gloves. Even if never used to grip bar-bells, the gloves would be useful when handling cutting tools. Mitchell dutifully bought the gloves and smuggled them into the prison. Palmer again served as intermediary, delivering the gloves to Matt's cell. The second painting was of Joyce's two dogs, also made from a photograph. When that painting was ready, Palmer once again was the courier, bringing the art to Joyce and Lyle's vehicle.

In early September 2014, Matt asked Joyce to place a phone call to his daughter, another clear violation of department rules. Mitchell not only made the call from her cell phone at home, she acknowledged to Matt's daughter that what she was doing "was wrong" and could cost her job.

Significantly, Lyle Mitchell was fully aware of the contraband glasses and gloves his wife had smuggled into the prison. He knew they had been traded for the two paintings that hung in their home. He knew these were firing offenses. Afterward, he would claim that he'd warned his wife about what she was doing: "I told her . . . 'Never, ever again. It ain't worth losing your job over.'" But his attitude softened when he found out one of the inmate paintings was supposed to be a gift for him.

Lyle Mitchell never reported his wife's actions to any Clinton Correctional Facility official. He also never reported that Palmer had helped get the paintings out of the prison. When he was asked about this later, Lyle had what for him might have been a blinding insight: "I guess I should have." But somehow he never managed to accept his own responsibility. It was the fault of the prison guards assigned to the front gate, not his, Lyle would insist, that Joyce was able to sneak so much contraband behind the wall. His excuse for his silence was to say, "There's nothing worse than being a snitch in jail." That's true—for inmates. Not so for prison staff members responsible for doing their jobs honestly.

It was also in September 2014 that Sweat got a written misbehavior report. The stated offenses were interference and staff harassment. Scott Scholl, the recently appointed industrial supervisor, said that in a conversation in the shop, Sweat had insulted a Corcraft employee he blamed for an ordering snafu. "So, did you take care of that dumb bitch that fucked up . . . the order for the zippers?" Instead of acting on his own, Scholl reported the matter to a higher ranking official, Capt. David Lucia. He told Scholl to write up the misbehavior report. It was the only one Scholl would write in ten years of supervising inmate shop workers. This was also the first misbehavior report Sweat had gotten since arriving at Clinton. At his hearing, he was found guilty. His punishment included removal from Joyce Mitchell's tailor shop and eviction from his cell next to Matt's.

Several people, including the hearing officer and at least one inmate, believed the charge against Sweat was a pretext. They thought Lucia's real motive was to break up the unhealthy familiarity between Sweat and Mitchell. The inmate said, "She really had a crush on Sweat. There's no question about that. A serious crush." Sweat suspected he had taken the fall because management didn't want to face up to Mitchell's misbehavior. He was right.

When she learned about Sweat's reassignment, Joyce was overcome with emotion. She broke down and cried. By now there was no doubt she had developed what she later referred to as "kind of" romantic feelings for Sweat. Those feelings were clearly visible to the other inmate workers. They later said she appeared angry through her tears and announced to the tailor shop workers that she wanted a drink when she got home.

Every week after Sweat's disciplinary reassignment, Mitchell approached her supervisors to urge his return to her tailor shop. Despite her obvious inappropriate interactions with Sweat when he was under her supervision, Mitchell's superiors took no disciplinary action. Her demonstrated readiness to allege workplace harassment made them reluctant to challenge or reprimand her.

What they did do is to make suggestions about how she should deal with her inmate workers according to departmental policy. For a short time, she complied. But soon she was back to her old habits—which would not just be noticed, but thoroughly exploited by Matt.

CHAPTER 21
LAYING THE FOUNDATION

SWEAT'S SENTENCE AFTER PLEADING GUILTY TO HIS MISBEHAVIOR REPORT was thirty days of "keeplock," confinement to his cell. In addition to losing his place in the tailor shop, he would be removed from the top-floor Honor Block cell next to Matt's. But after imposing Sweat's sentence, the hearing officer suspended it. That meant that while Sweat still lost his tailor shop job, he could stay in the Honor Block. Just two levels down.

Sweat's new cell was on the first floor. Called "the flats," this is where the Honor Block's indoor recreation takes place. Right in front of Sweat's new cell, all the housing unit's inmates gather to watch sports on TV, play board games, and socialize. On the flats, each cell is constantly in view and subject to almost constant noise. Although these six-by-eight cells contain the same necessities found in every cell at Clinton—a bed, sink, toilet, and electrical outlet—the constant inmate and staff traffic means they offer no privacy or quiet.

Sweat had also lost his daily interactions with Joyce Mitchell. With him gone from Tailor Shop #1, Matt became Joyce's new attendant. He also gained the privilege of escorting her to the unoccupied Tailor Shop #9—the parts room. Investigators learned later that she had openly confessed her sexual hunger to this inmate. He was never one to let an admission of weakness go unexploited. What, exactly, was going on in that room?

Matt took full advantage of this new situation. He systematically tested Joyce's loyalty to the Department of Corrections. Even though he was allowed telephone privileges, he continued to ask Joyce to phone his daughter. Not only did she make these calls, she also communicated with Matt's daughter by text messages. Matt then asked her to call the wife of another Clinton inmate. She seems not to have realized that with each violation of departmental policy, she surrendered more power to Matt.

As time passed, Joyce remained undeterred. She became bolder and more brazen. By October 2014, she had become an accomplished smuggler of contraband. She would place smuggled items in the single drawer at Matt's workstation, either before the inmates and security staff arrived in the morning or when they were in the mess hall for lunch.

Some of that contraband had culinary value, but that wasn't why Matt asked for it. From October 2014 until June 2015, Joyce Mitchell smuggled in more than seventy containers of black and cayenne pepper. Matt was thinking ahead; he wouldn't be needing these illicit products until he was outside the walls. He didn't need the original packaging, either. As sold, these packages included an anti-tampering foil seal, which might have set off a prison metal detector. So working in her kitchen in full view of her husband, she would empty the pepper into plastic bags, ready to deliver the next morning.

I have to wonder if Lyle Mitchell was aware that his wife was routinely violating the department's rules. Their shared hour-long daily commute provided plenty of opportunity for them to talk about the smuggled paintings they had carried home and put on display in their house. It's highly unlikely that Lyle failed to notice the baked goods, bags of pepper, and other repackaged items Joyce frequently took to work.

Another witness to Joyce's inappropriate contacts with the inmates finally decided he'd had enough. Allan Trombley, the guard assigned to her shop, had become increasingly unhappy with Mitchell's behavior. By January 2015, he wanted out. He followed Corrections protocol for securing a different position within the walls. As openings occur, the positions are posted and guards have an opportunity to bid for them. Normally these jobs are awarded to guards who have the most seniority. It may take multiple attempts, bidding for different positions, to secure a new job. Trombley said it was impossible for him to effectively perform his duties in Tailor Shop #1. He was well aware of the grievance and harassment charges Mitchell had filed. He was also aware that Mitchell's previous supervisor had retired; he didn't want his own career to go off the rails because of her.

Trombley complained to Streeter, the shop boss, that Mitchell was letting her shop get completely out of control. "You see why I'm bidding out," he told Streeter. "It's all the time." But it would be another five months before Trombley received his bid award.

While he waited, he took a passive, look-the-other-way approach to his job. He was biding his time in a position that had become frustrating for him. He had butted heads with Joyce too many times, to no avail, and didn't want to suffer the repercussions experienced by others who had challenged the Mitchells. Regardless of his motives, this earned him plenty of blame.

After the escape, the inspector general's report would show no tolerance for his position. "Mitchell's numerous acts of misconduct in the tailor shop occurred in the presence of a negligent correction officer, Allan Trombley," the report said. "According to staff and inmates alike, Trombley routinely failed to perform his duties, instead spending much of the day reading at his desk."

Meanwhile, though, as the rumors about Mitchell and Sweat became the talk of the tailor shops, Mitchell decided to fight back. She complained to Racette, the prison's new superintendent, about gossip among the inmates. She blamed Vicki-Lynn Safford, the quality-control supervisor, for spreading the rumors. She also brought Gene Palmer into it, saying he had "informed me that inmates had come to him with the same insinuations." Mitchell insisted the gossip "was putting my life and job in jeopardy." Racette kicked the matter upstairs to the department's Office of Special Investigations in Albany. The OSI looked into the matter—but not very deeply. It concluded that the stories were baseless. But exactly how they came to this conclusion is a mystery.

The OSI investigators interviewed Sweat, Mitchell, Safford, and several other civilian supervisors in the tailor shops. Sweat put the blame for the rumors on Safford. Not true, Safford replied. She said she'd never told anybody anything about a relationship between Mitchell and Sweat. And that, as far as the investigator was concerned, was the end of it. But nobody interviewed Trombley, the guard who had been a daily witness to the shenanigans in Tailor Shop #1, or Bradley Streeter, Mitchell's direct supervisor, to whom Trombley had reported what he'd seen. Trombley would have been the key to exposing Mitchell, but fearing retaliation, he didn't take the initiative to speak to the investigators. Nobody talked to David Lucia, the captain who had yanked Sweat out of the shop to get him away from Mitchell. And for some reason, the investigation didn't include a search of Sweat's cell. That might have found some very incriminating evidence.

That evidence concerned a plan Matt and Sweat had come up with at the beginning of 2015. Their first idea about how to escape was to dismantle the locking mechanisms on their cell doors. Once out of their cells, they would slip out of the Honor Block, cross the Industry yard, and climb over the thirty-foot perimeter wall with a makeshift rope.

Their first challenge would be the cell door locks. For obvious reasons, they couldn't be taken apart with ordinary tools. Security screws that could be opened only with special star-shaped screwdrivers held the locks together.

So Sweat, using Matt as his middleman with Joyce, asked her to bring them some of those security screwdriver bits. To be sure she got the right size, Sweat pressed a lump of artist's clay into one of the security screw heads in his cell's door lock. The impression this made was allowed to dry; then he painted it and pressed the wet paint onto a piece of paper. This created an exact image of the security screw. Matt gave this paper to Joyce so she could determine the correct size bit.

Mitchell bought a boxed set of security screwdriver bits at a

WANTED
CONVICT ESCAPED FROM N.Y. PRISON

RICHARD MATT
AGE: 48

6', 210 POUNDS

- WHITE MALE, BLACK HAIR, HAZEL EYES
- TATTOOS ON BACK, CHEST AND SHOULDERS

CALL **1-800-GIVE-TIP** IF YOU HAVE INFORMATION

WANTED
CONVICT ESCAPED FROM N.Y. PRISON

DAVID SWEAT
AGE: 34

5'11, 165 POUNDS

- WHITE MALE, BROWN HAIR, GREEN EYES
- TATTOOS ON LEFT BICEP, RIGHT FINGERS

CALL **1-800-GIVE-TIP** IF YOU HAVE INFORMATION

(Photos courtesy NYSDEC)

The main gate of Clinton Correctional Facility in Dannemora, New York. Once the center of a mining community, the town became the epicenter of a massive manhunt. *(Photo by Charles A. Gardner)*

The Clinton Correctional Facility perimeter wall dominates the streetscape. The tailor shop building where the convicts worked can be seen above the perimeter wall. *(Photo by Charles A. Gardner)*

Inside Tailor Shop #1, supervisor
Joyce Mitchell became involved
with convicted murderers
David Sweat and Richard Matt.
*(Photo by Darren McGee/
New York State Governor's Office)*

Joyce Mitchell leaves Plattsburgh
City Court on June 15, 2015.
*(Photo by Rob Fountain,
courtesy Press-Republican)*

David Sweat's cell was located in Honor Block, where inmates enjoyed privileges earned by good behavior. *(Photo by Darren McGee/ New York State Governor's Office)*

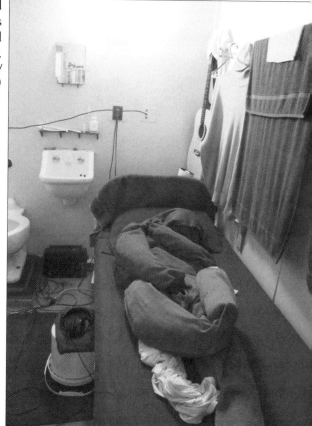

Sweat and Matt used hacksaw blades to etch holes in the cell walls behind their beds. Sweat's cell is shown in this photo. *(Photo by Darren McGee/ New York State Governor's Office)*

The bracket that supported this heat pipe passing through the brick wall between B and C Blocks in the subterranean tunnel was the first of many underground obstructions faced by the inmates. *(Photo by Darren McGee/ New York State Governor's Office)*

During many nights working on their escape route, the inmates cut this hole in the steam pipe at the base of the perimeter wall. This was one of the final tasks they completed in the tunnel that allowed them to escape. *(Photo by Darren McGee/ New York State Governor's Office)*

Governor Andrew Cuomo
flew to the prison within hours
to examine the cells and
escape route.
(Photo by Darren McGee/
New York State Governor's Office)

Governor Cuomo descends
a ladder that was part of
the escape route.
(Photo by Darren McGee/
New York State Governor's Office)

Governor Cuomo stands on
the catwalk behind Matt's
and Sweat's breached cells.
*(Photo by Darren McGee/
New York State Governor's Office)*

Governor Cuomo views
the manhole from which
the inmates escaped.
*(Photo by Darren McGee/
New York State Governor's Office)*

Residents of the local area saw law enforcement searchers everywhere. *(Photo courtesy NYSDEC)*

New York State Department of Corrections CERT searchers played a key role in the manhunt. *(Photo courtesy NYSDEC)*

Four-wheel-drive vehicles were necessary to transport searchers through rugged terrain. *(Photo courtesy NYSDEC)*

Much of the manhunt took place in the beautiful but challenging landscape of the Adirondack Park. *(Photo courtesy NYSDEC)*

The first search perimeter was just outside the Village of Dannemora,
but it quickly expanded to more desolate areas as the manhunt grew in scope.
(Photo courtesy NYSDEC)

National media with mobile satellite trucks reported the ongoing story
from Owls Head, New York. *(Photo by Charles A. Gardner)*

Correction officer John Stockwell and his dog, Dolly, went to check his family's hunting camp—and nearly came face-to-face with a killer. *(Photos by Charles A. Gardner)*

Belly's Mountain View Inn accommodated the hordes of police and media that streamed into rustic Mountain View, New York. *(Photo by Charles A. Gardner)*

Matt and Sweat broke into Charlie Champagne's camp to steal food, liquor, and gear. *(Photo by Charles A. Gardner)*

When correction officer Bob Willett, Jr., opened the door to his family's hunting camp, he found evidence of unwanted visitors. *(Photos by Paul Marlow)*

Roadblocks were set up by law enforcement officers who carefully checked vehicular traffic. *(Photo courtesy NYSDEC)*

U.S. Border Patrol Agents on ATVs took part in the search. *(Photo courtesy NYSDEC)*

Emergency medical services from the town of Constable tended to Sweat after his capture.

Prison guard Tim Brown and his family were heading to a campground when their camper was shot by Matt on State Route 30, approximately 25 miles from the Canadian border. *(Photo by Charles A. Gardner)*

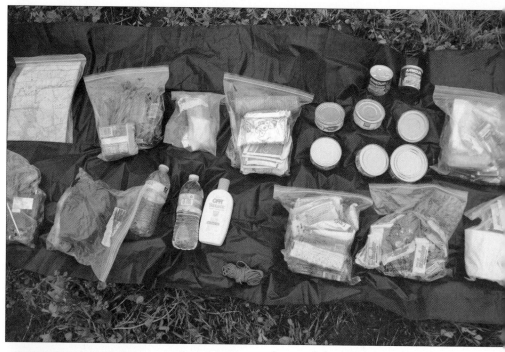

Some of the contents of Sweat's backpack found when he was captured.

Sweat spent his last night of freedom in this hunting tree stand.
(Photo by Charles A. Gardner)

store in Malone. Following directions from the two inmates, she smuggled in three of the bits. That included the one that looked closest to the image they had given her and, just to be sure, the next smaller and larger sizes. Matt successfully got the three contraband security bits out of the tailor shop and back to the Honor Block. For whatever reason, they didn't get flagged by the metal detector. Sweat promptly went to work, trying to dismantle the lock. But he quickly found the tools were too small to turn by hand.

So they went back to Joyce and asked her to get them some Allen-wrench-style star tools. These have an "L" shape that makes them easier to grip and turn. She complied without hesitation. Within a few days she had smuggled in the latest escape tools.

Despite Joyce's help, the two inmates eventually abandoned their first escape plan. Matt, who was overweight and had other health issues, realized he was physically unable to climb the prison's thirty-foot wall. So they hatched a new plan. Now the pair planned to get into the tunnels that run under the housing units, crawl into the unknown until they found the sewer system, and then escape to freedom. If this sounds like the plot from the 1994 prison escape movie *The Shawshank Redemption*, it's not completely coincidental. As their plan evolved, Matt and Sweat would joke about parallels to that movie.

First, though, for the new escape plan to work, Sweat and Matt would have to again occupy adjacent cells in the Honor Block. The problem was that only tailor shop workers, like Matt, were housed on the Honor Block's top floor. Somehow, Sweat would have to get back into one of the tailor shops.

The answer came in the form of Corrections Officer Gene Palmer. In mid-January, 2015, thanks to Palmer's advocacy, Scholl agreed to return Sweat to work in the tailor shops. It seems that financial benefit to Corcraft trumped the prison's security concerns.

The assignment didn't totally ignore the problem between Sweat and Mitchell. To keep him away from her, he was assigned to Tailor Shop #8, the one farthest away from #1. As a further precaution, Corcraft's civilian supervisor there was instructed to contact Scholl or Safford if Mitchell was seen anywhere near Tailor Shop #8.

Within two weeks after Sweat came back to the tailor shops, Matt asked for him to be returned to his former cell, A-6-23. Although Palmer used his influence to make this happen, one snag remained. The inmate who already occupied that cell next door to Matt's wasn't interested in moving. He had a price, though. He eventually agreed to move after Matt got him some $100 worth of cigarettes and two huge homemade pornography books—called "short-eyes" in New York's prisons. It's prison; nothing is free. And a big stash of cigarettes and porn was a small price to pay for freedom!

With Matt and Sweat again next-door neighbors, they began to carry out their new plan. For the next 133 days, they spent their days in the tailor shops and their nights working on their escape route.

PART IV
THE BREAKOUT

CHAPTER 22
BREACHING THEIR CELLS

GIVING UP ON THE IDEA OF SCALING THE PERIMETER WALL forced Sweat and Matt to refocus their attention downward, on the tunnels underneath the prison. They were confident that access to the catwalk behind their cells would lead them to the tunnels and ultimately a way out. The catwalk area is familiar to the inmate population. It contains the electrical and plumbing arteries for individual cells. Some inmates are assigned jobs as assistants to civilian plumbers and electricians. Those inmate workers frequently accompany those contractors onto the catwalks to make repairs.

First order of business was to breach their cells' metal rear walls. These were steel plate, 3/16ths of an inch thick. For this, they needed cutting tools. Matt's next order was for a tool he was entirely too familiar with, and that his fellow inmates associated with him: hacksaw blades. Joyce Mitchell, who no doubt had heard other inmates calling Matt by his nickname "Hacksaw," saw no reason not to oblige. On February 16, 2015, at the Walmart in Malone, she spent less than six dollars for half a dozen hacksaw blades. Ineptly trying to conceal her transaction for the tools, Mitchell first used her debit card to buy a number of household items. Immediately after those were rung up, she paid cash for the six blades at the same checkout.

First thing the next morning, when Matt came to work, he

found the blades already in his work station. He smuggled the hacksaw blades back to his cell by taping them to his torso, but still had to avoid the metal detector. Palmer, who had become lax and complacent over his long prison career, solved that problem by allowing him to bypass it.

The post-escape investigation concluded that Matt got the blades to his cell either directly from the shop or by faking an attack of sciatica, which would let him go to the prison infirmary. Palmer was "almost certainly" the guard escorting him, the inspector general's report said. One of the other tailor shop inmates said Matt never claimed to have back pain unless Palmer was on escort duty, to be sure that cooperative officer would let him go around the metal detector.

Palmer later admitted that he had routinely escorted Matt from the shop to his cell without frisking him or putting him through the metal detector.

Back in his cell, Matt passed three of the blades to Sweat. Each inmate snapped his three blades in half, then wrapped the shortened pieces in cloth, secured by rubber bands. Those improvised handles gave them a better grip and protected their hands from the sharp steel as they worked.

Another precaution taken was to pad the legs of their steel bed frames with cloth. This muffled the noise when they slid the beds away from the wall. Fully prepared now, they began working on their cell walls. First, they used a blade to score the steel surface. Over many hours, the repeated scratching eventually produced a small hole. With this monumental task accomplished, they were able to fit their miniature saws into the holes and begin sawing in earnest. There's no way to disguise or muffle the noise of a hacksaw blade cutting steel. That meant Matt and Sweat had to work while their fellow inmates were gone every evening, two floors down on the flats, the Honor Block's first floor. The guards didn't find this unusual; both men had been in the habit of cooking or painting in their cells during the 6:30 to 10:00 P.M. recreation period.

On the flats, most of the inmates watched sports on wall-mounted televisions or played cards or dominoes. The routine noise from hundreds of men and several TVs was loud enough to conceal the sound of steel blades sawing steel. Still, to be safe, Sweat and Matt took turns keeping watch during evening recreation. Prison slang for a lookout is "crow." One would saw while the other kept an eye out for guards. They alternated twenty-minute shifts. The one not sawing used a mirror to watch for guards on security rounds. When a guard was coming, or if the cutting got too loud, the "crow" would knock on the wall. The inmate cutting would stop and pretend to be painting, watching TV, or sleeping.

One evening, the inmate in cell A-6-21, on the other side of Matt, didn't go to recreation. When he overheard the sawing noise from Matt's cell, the inmate called out, "What the hell you doing over there?" Matt replied that he was cutting a piece of canvas for a painting. The next-door neighbor may have concluded that it was best not to question Matt's explanation. He knew, like everyone else on the block did, why Matt was called "Hacksaw."

The two inmates' habit of remaining locked in their cells when most others had gone to recreation didn't attract any official attention. If inmates are quiet and behaving in their cells, officers aren't going to make an issue of it. It's quite common for inmates to remain in their cells, where they can feel safe. And so nobody questioned Matt and Sweat's choice to stay put, apparently to paint or eat dinner, every evening for months.

Of course, cutting through steel walls is slow. Two inches was considered a good night's work. Cleaning up afterward involved a magnet, a contraband item that inmates can get by dismantling a cassette player. The magnet picked up the metal filings, which were flushed down the cell's sink or toilet.

About three weeks into the project, Sweat was first to finish the hole through the back of his cell. It was the size of a doggie door. Matt lagged behind; his hole took an additional week. At this stage, the two inmates had used only a single hacksaw blade each. By mid-March, after thirty nights of work, both inmates had breached their cells and gotten into the catwalk. Every day, they informed Joyce Mitchell of the progress they had made the night before.

They were now faced with the task of camouflaging the cutouts. They taped over the freshly cut edges and painted the tape in the color used for cell maintenance. This was no problem; inmates were encouraged to keep up appearances in their cells, and conveniently supplied with prison-issue paint. This blended the repair with the surrounding area so it wouldn't be obvious to the guards passing by on their rounds. Their beds also blocked a direct line of sight. Add to that a little clutter, throw a shirt here and a towel there, and a hole is effectively camouflaged.

A month after embarking on their mission, Sweat and Matt had overcome their first major obstacle. "We just kept going," Sweat said, "because you can't stop." They had reached the point of no return.

CHAPTER 23
A SUBTERRANEAN MAZE

IT WAS SWEAT WHO FIRST BLAZED THE TRAIL TOWARD FREEDOM while Matt was still busily sawing. Even though still surrounded by the prison's thirty-foot walls, Sweat said later, he felt free as he squeezed through his just-finished hole and stepped onto the catwalk. Heightening that sense of freedom, he broke a cardinal prison rule by leaving his state-issued identification card behind in the cell. Failure to have his I.D. card in his possession at all times earns an inmate a misbehavior report. Whenever he ventured into the forbidden catwalk space and beyond, Sweat placed a mannequin in his bed. This mock-up of his sleeping self was made from sweatshirts and sweatpants stuffed with clothing and sheets. The dimly lit prison block assisted in the illusion that he was sleeping peacefully under his covers.

On the other side of the wall, the catwalk area is always lit. But during the time Sweat and Matt were using that space, the Honor Block guards rarely ventured in during the night shift.

Now Sweat used a tactic he might have borrowed from the movies, but with a twist. Instead of a poster of Rita Hayworth or Raquel Welch for camouflage, as in *The Shawshank Redemption*, Sweat used some of his own artwork. To guard against his doggie-door-size exit hole being detected while he was at work in the tunnels, he covered it with a painting. He rigged cardboard handles and attached magnets to secure the art to the wall. With a painting covering the hole, his bed in place, and a dummy in the bed, it was unlikely his absence would be noticed.

Sweat quickly worked out a routine for getting into the tunnels. From his exit hole, he walked to the end of the catwalk and lowered himself three stories through a space between the catwalks and the backs of the cells. Plumbing and electrical conduits in this narrow space served as rungs and hand-holds for descending and climbing.

When he reached the bottom of the catwalk space, he found decades of discarded cigarette butts, trash and other debris in standing water that had been thrown from the three tiers above. The tunnels that branched off from here were just as filthy. As he began to explore, he discovered a labyrinth, filled with a maze of pipes and wires, twisting and turning left and right and extending under much of the prison.

On his first night of reconnaissance, Sweat found his way through the tunnels under A-Block (the Honor Block), the laundry and the B-Block housing unit without encountering an obstacle. However, his explorations literally hit a brick wall. He came to a sudden halt at a masonry barricade between B-Block and C-Block. That wall was penetrated by a round opening connecting the two housing units, just big enough for electrical conduits and plumbing to pass through. These were held by a single pipe support. This hanger blocked Sweat's passage through the opening. He returned to his cell, shared his adventure with Matt, and described the obstacle they faced.

The next two nights, dressed in dark clothing—like a ninja, he later bragged—and armed with hacksaw blades and lighted glasses that Mitchell had given Matt, Sweat worked to cut the pipe hanger. He was able to move it enough to squeeze through the opening. He wondered whether Matt's size would prevent him from getting through.

When Joyce Mitchell got her next progress update, she learned they needed a measuring tape. Every good seamstress has a measuring tape. She had one in her desk drawer in Tailor Shop #1, with the words "National Guard" proudly imprinted on the case.

She supplied it to Matt, who smuggled it back to his cell and used it to measure his girth. Sweat then took it to measure the opening between B-Block and C-Block, satisfying himself that it was big enough for Matt.

Once Matt had finished sawing his way into the catwalk, it was time for both inmates to create a system for their nightly tunnel forays. First on their agenda would be guidelines for dealing with the guards. Both inmates knew the routines and what to expect when the Honor Block's regular staff members were on duty. They had observed those officers for over a year. They could anticipate security rounds and be sure they were in their cells and visible. But if relief officers were working, the inmates took the precaution of not leaving their cells. Not knowing the relief staff's habits, they didn't risk the chance of being taken by surprise.

It's worth noting that Sweat would claim later that he'd done nearly all the work. He promoted the idea that Matt was too fat and out of shape to be climbing down to the tunnels and back every night, much less doing the heavy work of bashing or sawing through masonry and steel. I don't believe that. True, Matt was not in prime physical condition. But he was also not the sort of person to sit back passively while someone else found a way out of prison. After all, he had attempted four jailbreaks already in his criminal career and succeeded twice.

So while Sweat's after-the-fact interviews with police always feature him as the solo escape artist, only at the end bringing his fat friend along, I believe the two inmates were both active participants from the start. Whenever Sweat claimed he worked on a task alone, I'm confident that Matt was in on the work, too.

On nights when the regular staff was on duty, this was their routine. They waited for the midnight shift to finish the 11 P.M. count. Then, under cover of darkness, either Matt or Sweat or both would slide through the holes in their cell walls and crawl into the unknown. The next hundred or so nights were spent with one or both of them establishing an escape route through the prison's tunnel system.

CHAPTER 24
MITCHELL GOES DEEP

EVERY DAY IN THE MONTHS BEFORE THE ESCAPE, Joyce Mitchell placed herself in compromising positions with Matt and Sweat. As she walked through Clinton Correctional Facility's gates, she always passed the Office of Facility Administration. On any of those days, she could have stopped in, admitted her culpability, and prevented the escape.

The inmates' continuing manipulation drew her deeper and deeper into their scheme. She had already given them tools essential to their escape and other contraband to help guarantee its success. Now far beyond violations of departmental rules, she had entered felony territory when she smuggled in the first piece of contraband. It wasn't long before she agreed to become an active participant in the escape by serving as get-away driver.

Almost daily, Mitchell exchanged love notes with Sweat, who was out of her direct reach in the most distant of the tailor shops. Matt was the courier for these hand-written notes, which expressed her romantic and sexual feelings. She confessed to Matt that she yearned for an intimate relationship with his friend. One of the shop's other inmates later reported overhearing Mitchell tell Matt, "Hurry up and get Dave back here. I'm horny as fuck." Sweat's notes to Mitchell mirrored those sentiments, although insincerely. He sprinkled his messages with requests for items needed for the escape plan. Soon after her confession to Matt, both staff and inmates in Tailor Shop #1 noticed that Mitchell was spending a ridiculous amount of time sitting side by side with him. She even moved an inmate out of the work station next to Matt's so she could use the now-vacant chair. It didn't take long for Mitchell's sexual hunger to shift from Sweat to the readily available Matt. This new relationship was consummated in the romantic setting of Tailor Shop #9, the parts room. Other inmates were enlisted to watch for guards so that the trysts wouldn't be interrupted.

Matt and Mitchell never went into the parts room without Matt placing a fellow inmate as a lookout. Matt rewarded his "crows" with favors, sometimes as simple as allowing them a sniff of his fingers after his rendezvous with Mitchell. Remember, it's prison. Nothing is free.

Mitchell allowed Matt to store his personal property in her staff locker. He became a hero to the other inmates who were able to watch him grope and fondle their supervisor. All this should have been visible from his elevated guard post, but Trombley never saw a thing. Sick of the conflict with Mitchell, he was making time and looking the other way for his own sanity.

Some members of the prison staff did notice things, though. Obvious to many of them was a change in Joyce's appearance. She was coming to work sporting revealing tops and had begun dieting. Safford said, "I noticed that she was wearing make-up and lower-cut shirts and she had lost weight." By late May, Gene Palmer had spotted "cleavage," he reported later. But like so many things Palmer was privy to, he admitted, "I didn't bring it to anyone's attention." Another guard, Mary Lamar, did make Mitchell's clothing an issue, Palmer said, reporting her concerns to a shop sergeant, who passed the issue up the chain of command.

But Scholl blew it off. "I didn't find that she was inappropriately dressed," he said. And Joyce, herself, would insist to the bitter end that she was slimming down and wearing sexy clothing for Lyle's benefit.

It may have been around this time that Joyce, like a love-sick teenager, started to dabble in verse. Investigators would find a ruled notebook, the kind a school child would use, in which she had written this love poem in red ink. She titled it "Dreams."

Dreams are good
Dreams are bad
Dreams of trees
Dreams of grass
I Dream of you
But now I know dreams don't always true

That's not my typo in the last line. The missing word is exactly how she wrote it. It's not clear just who she was dreaming of, but she predicted one thing right. Her dream of a serious relationship with a maximum-security inmate didn't have a prayer of coming true.

Even when they couldn't slip off to the parts room for sex, Joyce and Matt found an alternative. Several times, he would stand next to her desk so she could reach into his pocket. He had cut a hole in the pocket so she could massage his penis. Even though it was played right next to Trombley's desk, their friendly game of "pocket pool" went undetected by the security staff and other inmates.

Mitchell went so far as to take photographs of her naked body, make prints, and bring copies to Matt. Besides betraying her employer, it seems that Joyce had no loyalty to her husband, either. But she might have rationalized her behavior; after all, back in their Tru-Stitch days, adultery had been the basis for Joyce and Lyle's original relationship.

Her contraband smuggling now included liquor. Not bottom-shelf rotgut, either. Favored brands included Bacardi 151 rum and Wild Turkey bourbon. She poured the liquor into plastic water or soda bottles that she gave to Matt. To help ensure the loyalty, and the silence, of the shop's other inmates, he shared the alcohol with them. Mitchell later said Matt told her he sometimes shared the booze with Palmer, the easy-going escort officer. At least once a week, Mitchell brought Matt some contraband food. More than once she brought him envelopes supposedly containing paints and brushes.

This started to bother Sweat. He worried that Matt's excessive and unnecessary requests were increasing their chances of getting caught. Sweat asked his co-conspirator to stop asking for contraband they wouldn't directly need for their escape.

The contraband pipeline did become more focused. In early April 2015, Mitchell started to assemble items that Sweat and Matt would need for life on the run. At their request, she gathered a compass, tent, sleeping bags, fishing poles, hatchet, rifle, shotgun, ammunition, and more hacksaw blades. The blades would be used to cut down the shotgun's barrel. Much of this gear belonged to Joyce's husband. Most of these bulky items would remain in Joyce's custody, to be brought along in her Jeep when she rendezvoused with the inmates outside the prison's walls.

In mid-April, Mitchell smuggled a Rand McNally Road Atlas into the prison. More than a hundred large-format pages included detailed maps of the United States, Canada, and Mexico. The edition she chose had a metal spiral binding. Matt worried that the wire binding increased the chances it would be detected. Mitchell told Matt she didn't think the atlas was necessary, because her car had a GPS system. Nevertheless, she made him copies of the book's New York state pages, using a copier in the tailor shop.

As the escape gear accumulated, Matt asked Joyce to help make plans for after the escape. This included telephone inquiries about vacation cabins in the neighboring state of Vermont. The idea was that the two would check in as husband and wife, along with their "nephew," Sweat, then hide out until the coast was clear. Joyce obediently made these calls from her home phone, but reported that the properties she'd researched were too expensive. Just like the Department of Corrections, their little conspiracy had to operate within a tight budget.

During May, Mitchell agreed to help Matt with a scheme to earn cash by bringing contraband into Clinton for another inmate. The plan was that this other inmate's wife would deliver a package to her in the Alice Hyde Medical Center's parking lot in Malone.

Mitchell exchanged several telephone calls with the inmate's wife. The conversations, which included coded messages, resulted in a time and date to hand over the package. The contraband would be hidden in a "Lean Cuisine" frozen meal box. Mitchell would smuggle it into the prison and Matt would then deliver it to the other inmate. For this service, the conspirators demanded a delivery fee of $500. Three hundred was for Mitchell and the rest for Matt. That seemed easy to Joyce. After all, she was dieting— "I eat Lean Cuisines"—so this latest contraband package would look normal.

After a flurry of phone calls, at first to a "Diane" or "Diana," and then to someone going by the name "Bree," Joyce got cold feet. The last of these calls would come just a day before the escape. Afterward, investigators tracing the call through Mitchell's phone records found that "Bree" was, in fact, married to a Clinton inmate. But, of course, she swore she didn't know a thing about any plot to smuggle drugs into the prison. In any case, whether either Joyce or "Bree" was telling the truth, this is one scheme that didn't pan out.

Joyce would claim later that even she had misgivings about some of Matt's requests. She said she wouldn't bring him a handgun, knife, or cell phone that he'd asked for. Sweat, though, said Joyce "was all for" smuggling the gun, and that he had to talk her out of it. Same thing with the cell phone, he said: it would be too easy for guards to detect.

Sweat wasn't the only one worried about the volume of Joyce's smuggling. In May, her husband, Lyle, cautioned her again, questioning the amount of contraband she was sneaking into the prison. But despite admonishing his wife—or so he claimed— Lyle never did anything to stop her or report her illegal behavior. Weirdly enough, what he did do was to confide in Sweat! He told the inmate that he was aware of his wife's smuggling and worried that somebody might be trying to extort her.

To head off the danger that Lyle's bumbling curiosity might wreck their escape plan, Sweat and Matt came up with a cover story. It was much like one Lyle had fallen for earlier. The idea was that Matt was working on a painting to be a surprise gift for Lyle. Sweat explained later, "I told Lyle, I said, 'Listen, I talked to Matt, and you didn't hear this from me, because you're not supposed to know, but the reason she's bringing stuff in, I guess you've got a birthday or an anniversary or something coming up? And I guess he's making something for you. She's got him making something for you. . . . ' I said, 'You didn't hear that from me.' I said, 'That's where the stuff is going.'" Lyle's curiosity, or at least his vanity, was satisfied. "He was fine with that," Sweat said.

Lyle's failure to report his wife's criminal misconduct made him just as guilty as Joyce. But now he had a much bigger—and deadlier—problem.

Joyce and Matt were now talking about her husband as "the Glitch." They considered that glitch an impediment to their plans and began calculating ways to get rid of Lyle. That added a deadly new twist to their plot. The other inmate workers in Tailor Shop #1 had heard Joyce openly discussing her rocky relationship with her husband. She also mentioned, within earshot, that Lyle was worth more dead than alive: $500,000 more. With the help of a life insurance policy on her clueless husband, Joyce concluded, she could cash out of one relationship and finance a new one.

She and Matt discussed several plans before deciding to kill Lyle at their home. Those they considered and discarded included driving a semi-conscious Lyle off a cliff near their house at Dickinson; murdering him inside the prison walls; or sedating him the night of the escape and letting Matt and Sweat kill him. By this time it was clear that the success of both the escape and the murder plot depended on Joyce's participation.

Of course, this scheme had one important problem. Much later, State Police interrogators would ask Sweat about it. How, they wondered, did Joyce think she could collect on a half-million-dollar insurance policy if she ran away with two escaped convicts? "Sweat's response," an interviewer dryly noted, "was that she was an idiot."

CHAPTER 25
SUBTERRANEAN STRUGGLES

SWEAT'S REMOVAL OF THE PIPE HANGER between B-Block and C-Block opened the way to the tunnel under C-Block housing unit. There the two inmates found a concrete cover bolted to the floor. They immediately thought this was their ticket to freedom and sawed through the bolts that secured it. But removing the slab exposed only rotten wood and solid concrete. This would not be their way out.

For days they explored the maze of tunnels. Their self-guided tour took them under the C-Block, D-Block, and E-Block housing units and the prison hospital. Their tunnel travels were a treasure hunt. They scavenged a discarded bolt, covered in rust; construction rebar; an empty water jug; a misplaced extension cord with a work light; a wooden mop handle; and an unused pipe hanger. All these items would later prove useful.

One night the tunnels bore a gift in the form of a construction job box. What were the chances, the inmates wondered, that the box was filled with tools? Using tweezers and a paper clip, Sweat quickly picked the lock and opened the lid. They were disappointed to find it held nothing usable. As a precaution, though, they re-locked it.

In a tunnel under C-Block, they discovered a large-diameter insulated pipe lettered "LPS," which meant low-pressure steam. The prison's utilities including power, heat, telephone, and sewer all penetrate under the perimeter wall. Nothing goes over. Matt and Sweat knew that following those services to their source would translate to a way out. The insulated pipe led the inmates to a solid brick wall between C-Block housing unit and the Industry Building. With a hacksaw blade, they cut the end of the rusty bolt they had found earlier, creating a crude chisel. The discarded pipe hanger served as a pry bar. With those makeshift tools, they began to slowly chip away at three layers of bricks.

The bricks, reinforced with concrete, proved a formidable obstacle. The inmates' arduous labor let them remove only a few bricks each night. At the end of each night's work, they carefully returned the bricks to their original position. The structure had to look intact if the tunnels should be inspected.

Unknown to them, though, they had nothing to worry about. Years earlier, Clinton's guards had abandoned tunnel inspections. This happened in the mid-1990s when the prison guards' job descriptions were restructured under cost-saving orders from Albany. New job descriptions meant nobody was specifically assigned to inspect the tunnels—a duty that had formerly been a routine part of a designated officer's job.

In one of many ironies surrounding the escape, Clinton Correctional Facility administrators had recognized the problem and recently established a new tunnel inspection policy. But it didn't take effect in time to discover evidence of the escape attempt in progress. After the fact, of course, Corrections leaders in Albany concluded that tunnel inspections were a good idea after all. They are once again a part of the prison's security routine.

After two weeks of undetected but futile labor, Matt and Sweat had not come close to breaching the solidly built foundation wall. More exploration, in hopes of finding a way around, was also futile. One night, while passing beneath one of the housing blocks, Sweat said, a guard on a catwalk high above tossed down a lit cigarette butt. It narrowly missed Sweat before sizzling out in the muck at his feet.

Their luck changed when they discovered an eight-pound sledge hammer, lying outside the job box they had found earlier.

They gained momentum using the sledge hammer and their modified bolt/chisel to level solid hits against the bricks and mortar. To mask the noise, they timed their hammer blows to coincide with rhythmic banging from the heat pipes. The forgotten sledge hammer became their key to penetrate the wall; by late April they had opened a hole large enough to get to the other side.

They were now under the Industrial Building that housed the Corcraft tailor shops. After a brief tour of the tunnels, the low-pressure steam pipe led them to the base of the prison's century-old perimeter wall. This is where the pipe enters the prison after a three-block run from the heating plant, which is well outside the wall. The heat pipes are encased in steel sleeves that pass through the perimeter wall. Through a void between the pipe and its sleeve, the inmates were able to see into a tunnel that went under the streets of Dannemora. They deduced that the tunnel led to the power house, easily visible to them every day through the tailor shop's windows. Seeing their way out, they next had to contend with the perimeter wall's foundation. Adding to that task's difficulty was the sauna conditions the steam pipes created.

The two worked in blistering heat, chipping away at the perimeter wall's concrete base. To help make this bearable, they moved air with a small fan brought from one of their cells. They plugged the fan into an extension cord bought from the prison commissary. With a pair of tweezers standing in for a screwdriver and skills Sweat had learned during his first prison "bid," the cord was wired into a nearby light fixture. The other extension cord, the one they had found with the work light, let them see what they were doing.

As they chipped away at the concrete, Sweat and Matt shared a few laughs about *The Shawshank Redemption*. The movie's protagonist, Andy Dufresne, took twenty years to chisel his way through Shawshank Prison's walls. The two Clinton inmates joked with each other that they would need only ten years to breach their prison's perimeter.

If they were to get out sooner, they needed real tools. Revisiting the job box proved beneficial. Apparently a contractor who had been working in the tunnels had stashed a trove of useful tools in the box since they first investigated it. They found power tools including an angle grinder and drills, an LED headband light, disposable breathing masks, a steel punch, and a two-pound sledge hammer. They pilfered the hammer, punch, headband light, and dust masks, all of which proved helpful in their nightly attacks on the wall. Only the two-pound sledge hammer was returned to the job box before dawn every morning. They never did return the eight-pound sledge, punch, headband light, or dust masks. Within days, they broke the steel punch. The contractor noticed it was gone and replaced it with a new one. Irresponsibly, he never reported to security that he was missing all the other valuable escape gear.

Even so, the inmates needed more tools. The next love note to Joyce asked her to get them heavy-duty work gloves, special hardened drill bits for concrete, two chisels, and a steel punch. Joyce had a busy evening, starting with her shopping. First, she bought the tools, then picked up two pounds of fresh hamburger. When she got home, she carefully embedded the tools in the ground beef before putting it in her freezer. The next morning, the meat was frozen solid. She carried the tool-laden hamburger package past security without hesitation and without detection. Then she arranged for a clueless Corrections Officer Palmer to deliver the meat.

Accustomed as he was to taking contraband to inmates as payment for paintings, Palmer didn't question the delivery of frozen hamburger. He had no idea the contraband meat also contained contraband escape tools. Within hours after retrieving the tools from their edible packaging, the inmates were back at their exhausting task, chipping away at the perimeter wall. With two concrete bits in hand, they returned to the contractor's job box to retrieve a power drill. Much to their chagrin, the power tools were gone. A few days later, the entire job box had vanished.

With that handy source of tools gone, they resumed their work on the perimeter wall one hammer blow at a time. Progress was slow and exhausting. Then, during the second week of May, the inmates noticed that their work was less uncomfortable than they had been accustomed to. The air in their cramped work space was beginning to cool. Sweat touched the pipe, he recalled later: "I realized it's cold." On May 4, with spring far advanced, the steam heat had been shut off and the pipes drained.

A gentle tap with the eight-pound sledge confirmed two things: first, that the pipe was empty; second, that banging on the pipe with a sledge hammer and chisel would be a big mistake. The metallic clang echoed loudly down the tunnel. "Man, you could hear that fucking thing go all the way down to the power house, all the way the other way, and come all the way back," Sweat said. "It was really loud; it echoed the whole way." He came to a simple conclusion. He decided they would cut into the empty pipe with their hacksaw blades, use its eighteen-inch width as their way through the perimeter wall, then cut their way out of the pipe to freedom.

In his cell, Sweat made a notation on a calendar, documenting the date he started to cut into the steam pipe. Old habits die hard—he liked to write down his plans. First task was to strip off the layer of insulation around the pipe. The work of cutting into the dormant heat pipe's three-eighths-inch thick wall began. The hacksaw blades Joyce had so graciously delivered in February made quick work. The two were able to cut approximately ten inches each day.

The blades eventually wore out. Sweat wrote another love note to Joyce asking for two more hacksaw blades. Of course, she delivered. She used a proven technique: hide the tools in frozen hamburger. Again, Palmer would deliver the contraband meat. His claim that he was totally unaware of what was hidden inside rings a little false, though. He would tell investigators that when he saw the frozen beef, he told Mitchell, "Tillie, don't be doing this." And he confessed that "I knew we were in a gray area with the meat." He admitted later that it seemed odd that the hamburger didn't have a supermarket label or bar code on it.

Whatever reservations Palmer might have had, he still took the meat to Matt. "Here, I don't want nothing to do with this," he claimed to have said as he delivered it. And any scruples he might have had didn't cover the goulash Matt cooked from it after Sweat extracted the hacksaw blades. "I may have eaten some," Palmer admitted to the inspector general's staff.

About this time, Matt gave Joyce two pills. Investigators later concluded they were narcotic painkillers that had been prescribed by the prison's medical staff. Joyce assumed the same thing and that she could sedate her husband with them. The plan was for her to give the pills to Lyle on the night of the escape, knocking him out. She took the pills home and hid them in her purse.

Once a man-sized hole had been cut into the steam pipe, the next challenge was figuring out where to cut out of the pipe on the wall's far side. If they cut too close, they risked being trapped and needing to cut another hole. They used the wooden mop handle they had found to probe the perimeter wall's thickness, sliding it through the steel sleeve between the steam pipe and the concrete.

From mid-May until June 4, the inmates worked diligently to cut their way out of the steam pipe. The LED headband light they'd stolen from the job box provided illumination. For ventilation, they taped plastic trash bags together. A fan they'd bought from the commissary blew fresh air through this improvised ductwork to keep them cool. These career criminals, who had proved unable to function honestly in the outside world, showed considerable ingenuity in getting out of prison.

Sawing their way out of the pipe required working on their sides. They used a rolled-up blanket for a pillow, a recycled Mountain Dew bottle with a spray top to cool the cutting area, and socks for elbow pads. To stay hydrated, they refilled the discarded water jug they'd found from a spigot in one of the tunnels. For energy, they brought a fistful of granola bars they'd bought in the commissary.

As Matt and Sweat worked efficiently toward their ultimate breakout, their co-conspirator Joyce Mitchell got an unpleasant shock. On June 4, a Thursday, she learned that Trombley had finally been reassigned, and that a new corrections officer would be on duty in Joyce's shop the next day. She was in a room filled with her co-workers when she read the written announcement from a clipboard. Joyce was furious. She created a scene, throwing the clipboard to the floor. She knew the new guard, who had worked in her shop as a relief officer. She knew he was a straight arrow, a stickler for prison rules and state directives. This news left her both resentful and worried. Mitchell confessed to Gene Palmer that she feared "He's going to come here . . . and he's going to lock up Matt."

As it happened, that was the night the final cut was made through the steam pipe. In the after-midnight hours of June 5, the inmates slid the cut-out piece of steel between the remaining pipe and the layer of insulation wrapped around it. From inside the pipe, they kicked their way through the fiberglass. They had successfully hatched their scheme. Like baby birds finding their way into the world, the inmates emerged from the steam pipe and into another tunnel. This tunnel, they knew, was outside the prison's wall and would take them to the power house three blocks to the south.

They scurried through the tunnel all the way to the power house, finding the end secured only by a single steel gate. It was wide open. But they feared that someone working in the plant might see them. So they retreated to one of the many ladders and manholes they had passed between the wall and the plant. These would be better, less visible places to get out.

The manhole they selected had a cover chained to the ladder with a simple padlock. With one of their precious hacksaw blades, they severed the chain within minutes. They pushed the manhole cover up and looked around. They were at the intersection of Barker and Bouck streets, exactly a block from the prison's south wall. It was a welcome and familiar sight! This street corner was clearly visible from the windows of Tailor Shop #1. More important, it was easily accessible for their getaway car.

Any concern they had about being seen from the wall towers was unwarranted. Neither of the two towers in view of this intersection was manned on midnight shifts. In fact, they had been unstaffed for almost two decades, yet another of the cost-saving measures ordered by Corrections officials in Albany. Measures that in retrospect looked tailor-made to help inmates escape.

CHAPTER 26
"TIME TO GO, KID!"

AFTER RETURNING TO THEIR CELLS, THEY SMOKED A SHARED CIGARETTE to celebrate their first brief moment of freedom in years. It was still early morning on Friday, June 5, 2015, when they put the final touches on their escape plan. Both agreed that zero hour would come immediately after the last inmate count at 11 that night. As soon as the Honor Block was quiet and dark, they would slip out of their cells onto the catwalk and be on their way.

Sweat wrote his last love note to Joyce Mitchell. He told her, "Tonight's the night" and gave their willing accomplice her final marching orders. First, he wrote, she should give the two pills to "The Glitch," ensuring that Lyle didn't interfere with the plan. Then she should pack all the outdoor gear, including Lyle's rifle and shotgun, into her Jeep and drive back to Dannemora. Sweat instructed her to be at the corner of Barker and Bouck Streets at midnight, with the engine running. Well aware that he was dealing with someone less resourceful than himself, he offered detailed advice on how she should act. "Have the headlights off on the running SUV and be outside the vehicle pretending to be talking on your cell phone to avoid drawing attention to yourself."

As the prison's final work day of the week dawned and the cell doors opened, the inmates of the Honor Block's company A-6 filed out for breakfast. As he had promised two weeks earlier, Matt gave his prized possession, his television, to the inmate next

door in A-6-21. What was he paying for? Was the TV a pay-off
for the inmate's loyalty or merely his silence? Had the neighbor
heard the cutting noises, night-time movement on the catwalks, or
talk about a breakout? If so, odds were good that he'd soon be
suffering a spell of forgetfulness.

After breakfast, the inmates were escorted to the tailor shops.
Matt delivered Sweat's final love note to Joyce. Then she spent
the first half of the day sitting next to Matt's workstation, chatting
with him.

But her old, bad habits were out of synch with Tailor Shop #1's
new reality. There was a new sheriff in town. The newly assigned
corrections officer was not going to tolerate any unauthorized activity under his watch. In the first hours at his new assignment, he
observed idle inmates and Joyce Mitchell's unprofessional conduct with Matt. He quickly challenged Mitchell about her behavior, and ordered the inmates to get to work. Mitchell exploded.
She yelled at him from across the room, "Leave my fucking inmates alone. If they don't have any fucking work, they can't do
no work now, can they?"

The officer's response was calm and professional, but blunt.
"We can't be having this in the shop."

Mitchell tried to outflank the officer, calling the easy-going
Scott Scholl to ask that a sergeant be sent to her shop. Instead, it
was Bradley Streeter, Mitchell's direct supervisor, who showed
up. He reprimanded Mitchell and told her, "You can't yell at your
officer."

Mitchell chose to remain defiant. "Fuck I can't."

It was clear to the newly assigned officer, after just a few hours
of watching Mitchell's interactions with the inmates, that she was
a security risk.

Unfortunately, because of the time that any systematic follow-
up would have taken, the new guard's conclusion came days too
late.

The work day ended without any other incident. But on this Friday, instead of his usual "See you Monday" farewell to Mitchell,

Matt walked out of her tailor shop for the last time with his fist raised in the air.

Back in their cells, Sweat and Matt had an urgent discussion about Mitchell's loyalty. Sweat questioned her commitment to showing up for their midnight rendezvous. Matt tried to reassure him. "He told her, he said, 'Listen, you have to be there at twelve,'" Sweat recalled. "She's like, 'I'll be there, I'll be there' . . . And he told her, 'If you're not there, we're dead. They're going to kill us.' He says, 'You understand, if you don't show up, they're going to kill us. We're dead.' 'No, no, I'm going to be there. I'm going to be there.'"

As they prepared for their big night, Sweat packed carefully. He had a soft guitar case that he loaded with supplies including clean T-shirts, underwear, socks, a sweater, and new boots. He had traded a painting with another inmate to get the boots. He also packed twenty packages of peanuts, forty Sunset Bakery chocolate chip chewy granola bars and twelve sticks of pepperoni, all bought from the commissary the day before.

Matt stuffed a similar assortment of supplies into a makeshift backpack he'd pieced together in the tailor shop. He made it from the green state-issue fabric used for prison uniforms. Like his partner, Matt had a new pair of boots, which he had bought by mail order. But he didn't pack them, maybe he was planning to wear them during the escape. He would come to regret that decision.

The food, however, was well chosen. Everything would keep well without refrigeration, and was loaded with nutrition in comparison to its weight. Excellent trail food, as any experienced hiker would tell you.

At about 9:45 P.M., as the other inmates returned to the housing unit from evening recreation, Matt and Sweat ate their dinner of salad and chicken. This would be their final meal behind bars. Matt passed bowls of extra food to the inmate next door and told him to enjoy. He told him not to worry about returning the bowls. It had been quite a day for this inmate. A television set in the morning and then lots of food in the evening. Chances were excellent that he wouldn't see or hear anything the rest of the night.

When the officer assigned to Tour 1, the midnight shift, conducted the 11 P.M. count, Sweat confirmed that it was Ronald Blair, one of the regular guards. Sweat disliked Blair because he was one of those "balls-on, by the book" officers. That meant, among other things, that he always confirmed that each inmate was present when conducting the count. He used his flashlight and demanded that each inmate move to confirm that the cell contained a living, breathing human. This was all according to Department of Corrections directive. It was also the result of an embarrassing mistake early in Blair's career. He had once missed a dummy filling in for an inmate who later turned up in another cell. While probably a matter of illicit sex instead of an escape attempt, it still made a strong and healthy impact on the young guard's career. So now, fourteen years later, Blair remained a stickler. He was always the one making the night's first count, and always made sure he saw every inmate.

Sweat considered this by-the-book behavior unnecessarily disruptive to his night's repose. Other inmates might have tossed a container of fermented piss and shit on the officer to show their displeasure. But Sweat had an even better idea. He was tickled pink that he would thoroughly humiliate Blair and destroy his career by escaping on his tour.

Once the count was done, it was safe to place the stuffed mannequins in the beds and cover them with sheets and blankets. Matt left behind a note that said, "You left me no choice but to grow old & die in here. I had to do something! 6-5-15." He inscribed a second message on one of his paintings. It depicted the actor James Gandolfini in character as Tony Soprano from the HBO series *The Sopranos*. With a black Sharpie marker, right next to "Tony's" face, he wrote, "Time to go Kid 6/5/15!"

As he slipped through the hole in his cell wall, Matt committed an oversight that would have major consequences in the days to come. He unintentionally left behind his newly purchased boots, overlooking them in the shadows of his cell, illuminated only by the housing block's night lights. Unlike his obsessively organized co-conspirator, Matt wasn't the sort of guy who made written plans or relied on checklists.

As the inmates descended to the tunnels, they left taunting notes in two places that had challenged them. The first depicted a space alien with crossed arms and the words "Are you trying me Punk!" They left this stuck to a pipe between B-Block and C-Block housing units, where they had spent two nights laboring.

At the perimeter wall, they had spent nearly thirty nights sawing on the steam pipe. There they left a note depicting a smiling Asian caricature with the words, "Have a nice day!" One other thing they left behind was a tote bag. Like Matt's backpack, it had been crafted in the tailor shop. It would be found the next day in the tunnel next to the steam pipe. It held all their tools and the copies Joyce had made of the road atlas' New York State map.

Sweat was first to slither through the steam pipe, going in feet first. As Matt followed, head first, Sweat had to haul him along using a bedsheet as a rope. The tight squeeze pulled Matt's pants down. When he emerged from the pipe with his pants half off, Sweat joked, "Matt, I didn't know you cared."

Out of the pipe's confines, they had no trouble moving through the power house tunnel, getting to the manhole around a quarter to midnight, ahead of schedule. For the next ten or fifteen minutes, they caught their breaths and waited for Joyce to arrive. Every so often they would peek out from under the manhole cover, checking the time, watching for her Jeep.

CHAPTER 27
CHANGE IN PLANS

EIGHT AND A HALF HOURS EARLIER, WHEN HER WORK DAY ENDED at 3:30 P.M., a still-defiant Joyce Mitchell walked past the Clinton Correctional Facility's administrative office on her way to the gate. It would be her last opportunity to do the right thing, but of course she didn't stop. She had nothing to say about the impending escape or anything else that had happened in the previous 133 days. Mitchell never looked back.

With her husband Lyle driving west on State Route 374, Joyce rode by his side. As the highway angled north toward the border, they turned left onto Brainardsville Road. In less than an hour, they were in Malone, the only sizeable town on their way home to tiny Dickinson Center. They stopped for dinner at the King's Wok Buffet, a Chinese restaurant in a strip mall on the edge of town. During her dinner with her husband, Joyce didn't reveal the escape plot. She didn't mention the inmates' plan to murder him, or her intention to collect the insurance money.

Directly across U.S. 11, visible from the King's Wok's windows, is a New York State Police substation. Even at this late hour, Joyce could have driven across the highway and, with just a few words, foiled the escape plan. Instead, she ordered dessert.

Soon after the Mitchells got home, Joyce diagnosed herself as having a panic attack. Her symptoms included chest pains and a flushed face. She lay down for a nap. When she woke up before

9 P.M., the symptoms hadn't gone away. Lyle drove her back to Malone and the Alice Hyde Medical Center. Shortly after midnight, in the early hours of Saturday, June 6, the hospital admitted her for observation. At about that time, of course, her partners in crime were skulking in the shadows of Dannemora's back streets, wondering where the hell she was. After ensuring that his wife was resting comfortably, Lyle returned home to tend to their dogs and go to bed. At the hospital, Joyce had drifted off to sleep before she was able to tell her husband something very important: don't go home, because two convicted murderers are on their way to kill you!

When midnight arrived, Matt and Sweat had no idea that their getaway driver was almost forty miles away, waiting in the emergency room. They pushed the iron cover aside and clambered up the manhole's iron rungs. Dressed in T-shirts and prison-issue green pants, carrying a soft guitar case and a homemade backpack, they stood in the intersection of Barker and Bouck streets, a block from the prison. They were surprised to find this part of Dannemora had so many homes. Even so, they tried to blend into the neighborhood and not attract attention.

A streetlight high over the corner cast a bright glare on both streets. Too bright.

Within minutes, a local resident would confront them. Leslie Lewis III, the young stepson of a prison employee, lived right on the corner. At a quarter after midnight, he was riding home from a date. When he got out of his girlfriend's car, he spotted somebody in the shadows behind his house. He yelled, "What are you scumbags doing in my backyard?"

The man he'd seen apologized and said he was on the wrong street. As the stranger stepped back onto the sidewalk, Lewis noticed that he was carrying a guitar case on his back. A couple of doors down Barker Street, Lewis saw a second man "crunched down in a yard," he told police later. "It looked like he was going through a dark colored backpack." Lewis reported, "The guy I chased out of the yard ran toward the other guy. They both started walking at a fast pace south, towards Smith Street" in the direction of the prison's power house. Nothing about these two men's explanation or appearance aroused his suspicion—at least not enough to alert the authorities.

Sweat, as it turned out, would tell the story differently. Lewis' description of the guitar case made it clear it was Sweat he had ordered off his property. But a month later, when his former partner couldn't contradict him, Sweat claimed it was Matt who had blundered into Lewis' backyard. "I'm yelling at him, 'What the fuck are you doing, man? Where are you going?' And the guy sees him." This would be typical of what Sweat told interrogators. If he could make himself look good—smart or brave or resourceful—at Matt's expense, that's how he would tell it. It might be a self-serving retelling. But, for what it's worth, most of Sweat's accounts line up pretty close to what other evidence shows.

The encounter told Matt and Sweat that lurking in the shadows, waiting for Joyce Mitchell, wasn't working. It was time to move on. Now.

They hurried away from Lewis, going another block down the hill, away from the prison walls, to Smith Street. They turned west, walking between scattered houses on their right and mostly empty, wooded land sloping down to the prison power house on their left. After a few blocks, they turned right again, climbing steep, narrow Manley Street to get to Highway 374. They were far enough from the prison that they wouldn't be noticed by the guard in the corner tower. Hoping Mitchell had just been delayed, they thought they might flag her down as she drove down Dannemora Mountain and into town.

Waiting by the roadside, though, was starting to spook them. They were still too conspicuous. So they retraced their steps, back to the corner of Barker and Bouck Streets, hoping to find Joyce Mitchell's Jeep idling there.

But a few more minutes of waiting convinced the two, Sweat said later, that their elaborate scheme was a bust. Joyce was a no-show. Their master plan had depended on her and on them all being a couple of hundred miles away before the morning head count. They had no Plan B. "Well, I guess we're gonna have to go on foot now," Sweat remembered saying.

Now, suddenly, it began to matter that Matt had forgotten his new boots.

Once again, they returned to Route 374, which they knew from studying their *Rand McNally Road Atlas* was the only way out of town to the west. Their now-abandoned plan had called for driving that way, eventually to pick up Interstate 81. Once on the Interstate, three hours and you're out of New York State. And so, lacking a better idea, they headed west anyway. But even in the after-midnight darkness, they felt dangerously exposed. Several times, when they saw headlights or heard a car approaching, they jumped off the road and into the woods. This wasn't going to work. Even in the early morning hours, there was just too much traffic.

Fortunately for the fugitives, right where Route 374 takes a sharp swerve to the north to climb over Dannemora Mountain, they found an alternative. A quiet back way, Hugh Herron Road, turns off to the left. They seized this first chance to get away from the highway. As the night wore on, they walked steadily down the Hugh Herron Road, southbound for the time being.

By the time the first glimmers of light appeared in the sky to their left, they had walked about five miles down the little-traveled side road. They hadn't seen anybody. And—as far as they knew—nobody had seen them.

PART V
THE SEARCH

CHAPTER 28
DISCOVERY

SATURDAY AT CLINTON CORRECTIONAL FACILITY BEGAN AT 5 A.M., ten minutes before sunrise. The public-address system squawked with an order for all 288 inmates in the Honor Block: stand or sit up in bed for the morning's master count. As inmates began to stir, one by one their cells came alive with light.

Corrections Officer Ronald Blair was finishing his night's shift as he'd begun it, with a count of Company A-6. To begin the morning count, he walked up the back staircase to the block's top floor. As he passed each cell, he made sure he saw its occupant before moving down the line. As he reached the middle of row A-6, he noticed two cells were still dark.

It was about 5:17 A.M. when Blair reached cell A-6-23, which belonged to David Sweat. He ordered the inmate to get up but saw no movement. He reached through the bars, grabbed the bed and shook it. Still nothing. He grabbed the sheet and pulled it off. "I almost threw up," he admitted later. In the bed, what he saw was a mannequin made from clothing. And no inmate.

SHIT! Stumbling back from the bars in shock and disbelief, Blair went to the next cell, also still dark. Number A-6-22, inmate Richard Matt. Here again he uncovered a dummy. The guard, by now thoroughly flummoxed, had an audience. The inmate in A-6-21 was watching silently through the bars. He never said a word, but glanced at his new TV, which he hadn't yet turned on. Right now, the show in progress right outside his cell was far better than anything he could find on the tube.

Blair sprinted to the stairway and tumbled down. His heart was beating out of his chest, and a huge lump hung in his throat. *Where the fuck are those inmates?*

Prison life offers no opportunities to toughen the feet for hiking. By the end of the night, Sweat was better off than Matt, who had neglected to bring his new boots. But both were starting to suffer. "We can barely walk," Sweat would tell interrogators nearly a month later. "I mean, we got huge blisters on our feet." And as traces of dawn began to appear, they realized they couldn't keep going south.

"We just have to wing it," Sweat recalled telling Matt at that point. "We'll walk north, northwest, stay out of the Adirondacks area; because if you go too far to the south, it's just, it's really bad, it's all swamps and lakes and stuff and you could get lost in there for days."

He was right. In those mountains, even people who *want* to be found sometimes stay lost for days.

It wasn't yet 6 A.M. when the corrections officers in the Honor Block made a panicked call to the watch commander's office. Two inmates were missing. Supervisors, bolstered by extra guards, immediately raced up to the third tier. They unlocked the two vacant cells, confirmed they were missing two inmates, and quickly discovered the holes in the back walls.

Within minutes, the midnight shift's watch commander ordered that the entire prison be locked down. Inmates who were already on their job sites were hustled back to their housing blocks. All inmates were locked into their cells. Once every member of the civilian and security staffs was accounted for, a top-to-bottom search of the entire prison began.

The Department of Corrections dictates detailed procedures to be followed in these situations. And even though it had been more than a hundred years since anybody had broken out of the state's largest maximum-security prison, the staff knew exactly what to do. The administration and key personnel were told about the two missing inmates. While department leaders in Albany were being notified, outside police agencies were also alerted.

Supervisors began working through the protocol. Guards were assigned to secure the two cells, preserving all the potential evidence. Others were assigned to make phone calls, start writing incident logs and begin the pursuit: to track down the escaped inmates. Still others had to be sure the facility kept running, and that the thousands of other inmates were under control, escape or no escape. All this activity began before additional guards arrived, summoned to keep the prison in its locked-down status.

The objective was to safeguard the physical evidence and avoid contaminating any of the areas the escapees had breached. Each space—cells, catwalk, tunnels, manhole—was considered a crime scene. Protecting the evidence was a priority, with guards assigned to watch everything that was being found. The staff was ordered to allow only necessary personnel into the crime scenes. Any contamination might compromise evidence.

Village, county, and state police were called in to help pursue the fugitives. The prison system activated and deployed its Corrections Emergency Response Teams, which are skilled and trained for emergency situations such as this.

Inside the walls, guards simultaneously searched the roof above and the tunnels below the Honor Block. First Deputy Superintendent Donald Quinn, who arrived at the prison within minutes after the alarm was sounded, personally conducted the underground search. Accompanied by a sergeant, he found the passage the inmates used between B-Block and C-Block and the note they left there. Soon they also discovered the breached brick wall in the tunnel between C-Block and the tailor shop. Finally, they reached the perimeter wall's foundation, saw the hole cut in the dormant steam heating pipe—and found the last of the escapees' taunting notes.

It was only after Quinn had explored the tunnel between the power house and the prison, seen the cut chain under the manhole cover, and discovered the holes in the steam pipe, that he was certain the missing inmates had gotten all the way out.

A lot of work had to be done. The prison staff had to take over jobs normally done by inmates. No inmates were allowed to go to the mess hall or medical department. All 2,600 of them had to be fed and cared for in their cells. During a lockdown, all meals and any medical treatment have to be delivered.

Guards searched every inch of the prison. All gates and bars were inspected. All tools were counted. All cells searched for contraband. All this is standard operating procedure during any lockdown. Most of the contraband that turned up was handmade weapons. But guards would report that news of the escape had affected inmates' attitudes, and not for the better. One insider reported that during a cell frisk two days after the escape, inmates attacked three guards. "We lost a lot of credibility because of this escape," the anonymous source told the Plattsburgh *Press-Republican*. The inmates were "going wild," he said. "They are dissing us, and we are going to have to fight like hell" to get that credibility back.

Meanwhile, outside the walls, the State Police were mobilizing to catch the escapees and to discover how they'd gotten out. One of their first missions was to find Joyce Mitchell. The newly assigned guard in Tailor Shop #1, who had clashed with Joyce more than once, immediately blew the whistle on her as soon as he learned Matt and Sweat were gone. Already, by seven in the morning, Mitchell's name was being thrown around in connection with the escape.

One important detail the new guard mentioned immediately was how Matt had given Mitchell the raised-fist salute when he left work Friday afternoon. Once again, the prison was full of talk about her chummy-chummy relationships with inmates, going back at least three years.

As it happened, Joyce quickly figured out that police were looking for her. They didn't have to track her down; she came to them. When Mitchell was discharged from the hospital just after 11 A.M. Saturday, she turned on her cell phone to discover a long list of missed calls, most of them from the State Police. Perhaps figuring she'd be safer with the police than with two vengeful es-capees, she immediately went to the Troop B barracks in Malone.

Within a few hours after the two Honor Block cells had turned up empty, State Police investigators were questioning Mitchell about her possible involvement. At first, she played coy and de-nied knowing anything. The next day, Sunday, June 7, the State Police showed up at the Mitchells' house to resume their ques-tioning. About an hour into the interrogation, Mitchell made a partial confession. She admitted she had smuggled escape tools into the Clinton prison. A day later, police declared Mitchell to be a "person of interest." This was announced to the media. As the public learned her name, she would quickly become the most hated person in the North Country.

CHAPTER 29
LOCKDOWN, OVERTIME, AND A MEDIA BLITZ

THE LOCKDOWN THAT BEGAN THE MORNING THE ESCAPE WAS DISCOVERED came just a week after Corrections leadership in Albany had said "no" to a preventive lockdown at Clinton. State policy says prison superintendents can't decide on such measures themselves, but have to ask permission. A lockdown requires overtime. And overtime, of course, costs money, which nobody in Albany was willing to spend. The Clinton prison's administration had asked for the lockdown after seeing clues that something big was stirring inside the walls.

The prison's superintendent Steven Racette directed his deputy Donald Quinn to ask Albany for its OK in response to a violent disturbance on May 31. Thirty-five or forty inmates had gotten into a brawl in the recreation yard. According to the state inspector general's report, guards fired several canisters of "CS" tear gas to quell the disturbance and restore order.

Experienced prison guards know this sort of thing can signal something more serious is coming. It's extremely common for inmates to create a ruckus when they know a major incident is about to occur. They don't want to lose their privileges. Prison brawls are often a way to alert security that something is brewing. If some inmates attempt to escape, the others know they stand to pay a high price. There are no secrets in prison. Among prison guards, we sometimes state this truth as a riddle: "Q. What are the three fastest ways to communicate?" "A. Telephone, telegraph, or tell-an-inmate."

The bond among Joyce Mitchell, Matt, and Sweat was well known. This relationship afforded Matt and Sweat bragging rights, vitally important in a place where status is everything. It's also likely that inmates heard suspicious noises during the many nights of clandestine work in the tunnels. But to report something like this to the guards is not good for an inmate's health. It's a cardinal prison rule: snitches get stitches. But saying something directly isn't the only option. It's not unheard-of for a few inmates to sacrifice their freedom for the greater good of the entire inmate population. That's a plausible explanation for the May 31 fight. The participants may well have gambled that their disturbance would trigger a lockdown and a search for contraband, which could have discovered and stopped the escape plan. But in a strange alignment of motivations, when both inmates and prison officials wanted a lockdown, Corrections officials in Albany said "No."

Well-informed observers think a facility-wide lockdown and frisk between May 31 and June 5 might well have changed the outcome.

But speculation and second-guessing would come later. Now, in the immediate aftermath, Governor Andrew Cuomo and his Acting Department of Corrections and Community Supervision commissioner, Anthony Annucci, abandoned their Saturday morning plans. For the governor, those had included going to Long Island to watch a high-profile horse race, the Belmont Stakes. He missed seeing the thoroughbred American Pharaoh winning the Triple Crown that day. But as it turned out, this change of plans may have been the political equivalent of a triple crown for Cuomo. Until that day, the governor hadn't been having a very good year.

Cuomo and the acting commissioner, trailed by staff entourages, arrived at Clinton later on Saturday for a tour and news conference.

The visiting officials from Albany paraded through the prison with cameras and cell phones documenting the escape route and crime scenes. In one of many ironies surrounding the case, this was a violation of several departmental policies, including strict rules against cell phones and cameras inside prisons. In other words, top state officials were breaking some of the same rules about which they would later beat up on Corrections officials. The governor's entourage gave their photos and video to the news media and posted them on social media. Soon the public was seeing images of the pipe chase behind Sweat's and Matt's cells A-6-23 and A-6-22. They saw the governor on the steel ladder that descends to the levels beneath the prison's tailor shops where the escapees had worked.

As the tour progressed, the world saw the hole cut into the dormant steam pipe that just weeks earlier had heated the prison. Images went across the airwaves of the taunting note with the Asian caricature and the words "Have a nice day." Finally, TV viewers got a good look at the manhole where Bouck Street crosses Barker Street, the spot where the escaped murderers emerged from the steam tunnel. But before this could happen, the governor's staff had to tidy up the scene for their boss's photo opportunity. They ordered a police tracking dog and its handler out of the area.

Apparently indifferent to investigative protocols, the governor, acting commissioner, and their staffs crossed crime-scene tape and handled physical evidence while touring the escape route. Investigators watched silently as this parade of people contaminated active crime scenes. Why Albany big-wigs allowed photos and video from the crime scene to be publicized, the investigators couldn't understand. But they kept their mouths shut.

This didn't go unnoticed. One law enforcement insider complained to the *New York Post* that Cuomo had meddled in the investigation and in fact had hampered it with his high-handed approach. That source told the *Post* that the governor had refused to enter the State Police command post until his aides kicked out everyone who wasn't a state employee.

Other media also noticed how eager the governor was to get in front of the cameras. The escape was a welcome distraction from what had been an unsuccessful year for him politically.

Political reporter Alexander Burns wrote in *The New York Times* that for Cuomo, the escape was "an unexpected break from the deepest political doldrums of his time in office." Less than two days after his "whirlwind" tour of the Clinton Prison, the governor "was ready for a full-fledged media blitz," the *Times* said. Burns pointed out that the drama in Dannemora began near the end of a state Legislature session "that has been deeply frustrating for Mr. Cuomo." The governor's agenda was going nowhere. And the only place his poll numbers were going was straight down.

So when network anchors asked him to tell them all about the escape story, Cuomo "energetically obliged," as Burns put it. The Monday after the break, the governor would make five different TV appearances, without any inconvenient questions about anything besides the escape. Burns reported that the governor hadn't held a regular news conference in Albany since February. With the horse race at Belmont forgotten, racing up to Dannemora and talking gravely with national TV anchors was a perfect chance to get favorable air time. And, while he was at it, to get away from those pesky state-capitol reporters in Albany.

"Seeking visibility in a crisis has long been central to Mr. Cuomo's method of governing," Burns wrote. Just in the few months before the escape, the governor had made sure to get in front of the cameras covering a train wreck, a nuclear-plant fire, and even reporting on fallout from the African ebola epidemic. It's a technique Cuomo learned early, when he was an aide to his father, Mario Cuomo. In 1983, the first Governor Cuomo went to Sing Sing prison to help negotiate an end to an inmate uprising there. That visit boosted his reputation nationwide as a leader, a lesson his son never forgot.

Andrew Cuomo didn't rely just on network TV to promote his involvement in this new prison story. His staff also posted pictures on Flickr.com, showcasing his visit to Dannemora. His Twitter feed was also busy, reminding followers about his appearances in the national media.

On this media blitz's first day, the governor and his acting department head gave a news conference in Dannemora. It was staged so parts of the prison's wall and a gate formed a backdrop for the cameras. This "media opportunity" gave the public its first of many looks at the escapees' mugshots. The speeches Governor Cuomo and Acting Commissioner Annucci gave were short and critical of the prison's administration. It was obvious that someone was going to be held accountable in addition to Matt and Sweat.

It may have been unavoidable, but that first day's announcements spread one major error, which took weeks to correct. The governor and others kept saying the inmates had cut their way out using "power tools." For days afterward, news reports were full of speculation about how much noise those non-existent power tools must have made, and how it could have been that nobody noticed. It must have seemed impossible that two desperate men could have accomplished so much just with hammers, chisels, and a handful of broken hacksaw blades.

When Cuomo and Annucci first spoke to the media, visible in the background were two columns made of stone and concrete. They flanked one of the prison's entrances. During the escape emergency's first hour, a staff member accidentally ran his vehicle into one of those rock-solid pillars, knocking it from its foundation.

Within weeks, other seemingly rock-solid pillars of Clinton Correctional Facility would also topple.

CHAPTER 30
SHELTER IN PLACE

AS SOON AS THE ESCAPE WAS DISCOVERED, prison officials called on the State Police for help. Corrections officers immediately set up roadblocks and sent out patrols near the prison, while troopers did the same farther afield. The roving patrols formed a perimeter and dragnet around Dannemora. One thing prison officials didn't do was to sound the siren mounted on top of the power house. While it was meant to alert the village if an inmate escaped, it hadn't been tested in years, and had never been used for real. Nobody had escaped from Clinton since 1912. In fact, Clinton Superintendent Steven Racette said later, he decided not to use the siren because nobody would know what it meant.

Within an hour, law enforcement assets including tracking dogs and air support were on their way. The village of Dannemora became "Ground Zero" for the local, county, state, and federal agencies that responded.

Major Charles Guess of State Police Troop B was put in command. Troop B covers the largest and most sparsely populated of the state's nine police districts. That includes Clinton and Franklin Counties and most of the Adirondack Park. Guess's troopers are familiar with the wilds of northern New York State. He was no stranger to prison issues, either. His headquarters, in a little place called Ray Brook just outside Saranac Lake, is just a few hundred yards from the state's Adirondack Correctional Facility, and just a little farther away from the Federal Correctional Institution, Ray Brook.

His mission was two-fold: investigate the crime, to determine how the two inmates had gotten out; and of course to capture them. Before joining the State Police, the fifty-four-year-old Guess had served in the Army Rangers, first as an infantryman, then as a helicopter pilot, and in more specialized duties. Other valuable experience came from assignments with State Police Aviation, SWAT and Emergency Management. Major Guess would lead and coordinate officers from many different agencies through what became New York State Police's biggest and most elaborate manhunt ever.

In pursuing the first part of Guess's mandate, his troopers had quickly found a prime suspect in Joyce Mitchell. By the second day, she had already begun to talk, spilling increasingly useful information.

Meanwhile, outside the walls, the search quickly picked up steam. That first day, about 200 searchers were deployed. Guess wouldn't discuss their specific tactics with the media, but they included house-to-house searches in the village and roadblocks outside it. Forest rangers were put to work leading Corrections Emergency Response Teams searching woods and the vast countryside. By Sunday, with 250 officers on the case, checkpoints had been put up on all major roads. Besides those I'd encountered near the border and my home in Malone on day one, the press reported that checkpoints had been set up on state highways on both sides of Dannemora and one to the south on Pickett's Corners Road. This was just outside a tiny community called Saranac. Nobody knew it at the time, but at that last location, the roadblock was in exactly the right place; just hours too late.

Local agencies that answered the call included police departments from Plattsburgh and Malone and the sheriff's departments and district attorney's officers from Clinton and Franklin Counties. Broome County's sheriff's office, remembering that David Sweat had murdered one of their own, sent help. The New York State Police dispatched their Aviation Unit, Special Operations

Response Team, Bureau of Criminal Investigation, Forensics Identification Unit, Uniformed Police, and canine and specialized bloodhound units. Other state agencies included Forest Rangers, Department of Environmental Conservation officers, and the Department of Corrections Emergency Response Team, and Crisis Intervention Unit. Vermont sent its Special Weapons Tactical Unit. The federal government was represented by Immigration and Customs Enforcement, the Border Patrol, U.S. Marshals, FBI, and the Department of Homeland Security.

State police began the search, but were quickly joined by the local agencies and what would soon be a vast horde of prison guards. As I'd discovered that first morning, federal agencies joined in immediately. Help came even from the Coast Guard and the Vermont State Police Marine Task Force on Lake Champlain. Other jurisdictions were on the alert, too: north of the border, the Royal Canadian Mounted Police were watching for the escapees.

In my years as a corrections officer I'd gotten familiar with the department's standard operating procedures for every sort of incident, from riots in prison yards to escapes. The goal is always to get reinforcements into position in five minutes or less.

Every prison has equipment ready to set up roadblocks in the event an inmate goes missing. It's pre-planned, pre-packaged, and pre-boxed, ready to grab and go with only minutes' notice. Guards are assigned by name to collect a specific numbered box and go to a designated roadblock location. In the box are everything from signs warning motorists "Stop ahead: roadblock" to bug spray for the officers.

For a major event like the Clinton break-out, right behind the local corrections officers come CERT teams from around the state. During my time on the CERT team at Upstate Correctional Facility, we would train every month for a variety of scenarios. Each of us had to be ready to move on short notice. When the phone rings, when you get that dreaded call, you grab your "go" bag. This contains necessary clothing and a supply of cash, because there's no telling where you might end up or how long you're going to be there. That personal bag gets stashed inside a second "go" bag, full of tactical equipment, that's kept at the officer's assigned prison.

Once "go" bags are in hand, the CERT officers are put on a bus. During the bus ride, they get a briefing from a supervisor, explaining the nature of the emergency and where they're going. As in this case, to Clinton County.

For those of us living nearby, those first couple of days our daily tasks were clouded with anxiety and trepidation. We were surrounded by a gut-wrenching feeling of dread. Knowing what kind of men had broken out of prison, we waited for what seemed like an inevitable piece of bad news come Monday morning. News that somebody hadn't shown up for work. That one of our friends or relatives wasn't answering their phone. That a car normally parked in a neighbor's driveway was unaccountably missing. I know I breathed a huge sigh of relief when Monday came and went, and that awful news never came.

Still, the authorities had every reason to fear that Matt and Sweat might have stolen or hijacked vehicles. So the State Police's first reaction was to throw up roadblocks. But the escapees were just as likely to have holed up somewhere near the prison, either in empty buildings or by taking homeowners hostage. Every day, teams were assigned to systematically search homes, garages, and other structures.

Then, of course, there was the good chance that the inmates were on the run somewhere in the vast Adirondack countryside. Roving patrols, in a variety of motorized vehicles and on foot, combed the area's rural roads and backwoods trails. Police aircraft had joined in the search on day one.

Along with the influx of searchers, all the major national and state news media flocked to Dannemora before the first weekend ended. A new fixture on the landscape was the TV remote truck, with its telescoping antenna tower. Daily—and sometimes hourly—updates began appearing in print and on the air. Within days of the escape, the news reporters' chatter was surmising that Sweat and

Matt were in Canada or Mexico. The world was watching and wondering: where were the escapees?

Meanwhile, in a search for clues about where the escapees might be headed, and how they had gotten out, investigators began interviewing the prison's staff.

The dragnet included high-tech methods. Warrants were issued to authorize wiretaps of the escapees' known associates. Cyber-crime investigators monitored bank activity and money transfers by the people under suspicion. They also watched emails, text messages, and social-media contacts.

Within a day, New York State had offered a $100,000 reward: a $50,000 payment for the capture of either of the two escapees.

But in the North Country's fields and forests, the on-the-ground search, nerve-wracking and potentially deadly, was proving fruitless. During the first week, with the focus still on the area closest to Dannemora, teams of heavily armed officers faced the dangerous challenge of entering and searching unfamiliar buildings. Many of these were dark or only dimly lit. More than 160 abandoned buildings had to be checked within the first dozen days.

This put heavy demands on manpower. One news photo from June 8, the search's third day, showed a State Police search of an abandoned farm near Dannemora. No less than nine heavily armed troopers wearing camouflage uniforms, helmets, and night-vision goggles performed that single sweep.

The possibility of surprising—or being surprised by—one or both of the inmates lurked around every corner. Police also had to guard against accidentally confronting each other during a search. The high potential for injury meant officers routinely wore bullet-proof vests and other protective gear—if it was available.

For many, it wasn't. For the hundreds of Department of Corrections guards deployed on the North Country's roads, the decades of skimpy budgets meant they were put in harm's way poorly equipped and poorly protected.

The first two weeks generated some good news but plenty of

bad. The good news was that none of the searching officers encountered any deadly peril, though they endured more than their share of discomfort. Unseasonably wet, cold weather hampered everything. The bad news was that the search hadn't turned up any sign of the escapees or even clues to where they might be.

Solid leads were few. No vehicles were reported stolen. Daily "welfare checks" of local homes turned up nothing. Within the first few days, law enforcement sources were telling the media the escapees could still be within five or ten miles from the prison.

The first week of searching produced over five hundred leads, each of which had to be either chased down or ruled out. The search perimeter steadily expanded as days passed with no useful leads and no confirmed sightings.

The June 15 *New York Post* reported that the search was still concentrated on the area along Route 374 east of Dannemora, and that the highway would likely be closed at least another day. At that point, more than eight hundred law officers were on the local roads, chased by hundreds of reporters and photographers.

By the tenth day, searchers had covered more than thirteen square miles. That's 8,300 acres surrounding Dannemora. Roadblocks closer to the village were being lifted as the intensive dragnet shifted farther afield and the perimeter widened.

A few days later, on June 19, CNN's headline was about Matt and Sweat being added to the U.S. Marshals' Fifteen Most Wanted List. The feds had also followed the state's lead, offering an additional $25,000 for information that would help catch either fugitive. But the network's story went on to acknowledge that despite intensive searches in the prison's vicinity, no clues had turned up.

By now, two weeks into the search, state police were asking residents and hunting camp owners to check all footage from their surveillance cameras going back to June 6.

Systematic checks of back-woods hunting camps had also begun by the nineteenth. Police were looking for obvious signs of break-ins: splintered doors, broken windows and the like. For reasons that would eventually become clear, there were no such clues to be found.

Over fifty digital billboards displayed Matt's and Sweat's faces across New York, New Jersey, Massachusetts, and Pennsylvania. The billboards told the public who to call if they saw either of the inmates. Plenty of people made those calls, but not one yielded a useful clue. The search went from hours to days. Days turned into weeks. And still no confirmed sightings. The governor was publicly discouraged. "We don't know if they are still in the immediate area," he said, "or if they are in Mexico by now." It was beginning to seem like the media speculations might be true: Matt and Sweat were long gone, maybe even out of the country.

CHAPTER 31
CLINTON STRONG

NORMAL LIFE IN SMALL-TOWN NORTHERN NEW YORK requires an hour for such routine errands as shopping or stopping at the post office. This hour consists of five minutes to get your groceries or mail and then fifty-five minutes to visit with your neighbors, discuss the weather, and catch up on the local gossip.

Clinton County has limited public transportation. So any trip longer than around the corner requires jumping into the car or truck and cruising over what's often a dozen or more miles of rural road. The distance between gas station, post office, and grocery store is often substantial. But the closeness among neighbors helps to mitigate that. If you were to come upon a neighbor with a flat tire, by the time you got the tire changed, two dozen or more people would have stopped to offer some kind of help.

Locals in northern New York seldom lock their homes. Keys are often left in vehicles parked in driveways or garages.

But on that first Saturday in June, life for the residents of this prison town was about to change. The simplest errand—going to the convenience store for bread or milk or the post office for the mail—suddenly became complicated. Within an hour after the escape was reported, roads were blocked by police or corrections officers. Just getting the ten blocks from one end of Dannemora to the other required several mandatory vehicle inspections by heavily armed officers in bulletproof vests. They made sure to keep their weapons visible. At these checkpoints, small talk was discouraged, definitely not the norm.

Among the horde of journalists who had descended on Dannemora were our local news media. They staked their own claims with portable shelters from which they broadcast. WPTZ from Plattsburgh is the local NBC affiliate. From just across the lake, in Burlington, Vermont, we get CBS from WCAX, ABC from WVNY, and the Fox network from WFFF. Public TV also has a presence, in both Plattsburgh and Burlington. Two daily papers are published here: The *Press-Republican* in Plattsburgh, and the *Malone Telegram*. All were covering the story intensely. Within an hour after the story broke, descriptions and mugshots of the fugitive inmates saturated the local morning news. Within a day, the mugshots had made it to the network news for national audiences to see.

Here in the North Country, we try to make the most of our short summers. After the long winter hibernation, warm weekends often bring visits from friends and neighbors. During June 2015, though, most of our visitors were heavily armed corrections officers or police making sure we were all right and searching any buildings on our property. Even though these weren't social calls, we considered them friendly visits. It's typical of our area that everyone welcomed the officers without hesitation.

As the weekend progressed, the North Country's serenity was interrupted by the buzzing of low-flying helicopters, quite a change from the normal buzz of mosquitos in June.

As the work week started, employers ensured that all employees were accounted for on Monday morning. Schools closed and remained empty for the majority of the first week. Before the schools re-opened, buildings and buses were searched, then monitored by law enforcement during the school day. Students were welcomed onto school grounds and into their buildings by heavily armed police officers. Outdoor recreation and field trips were canceled.

Police enlisted residents to help. They asked everyone to turn on all outdoor lights at night, lock doors and windows, and review any video from home or business surveillance systems. Hardware stores reported brisk sales of outdoor light fixtures and bulbs. Many customers also lined up to get new house keys made. If you didn't normally lock your door, you didn't need a key. Until now.

Locals were getting spooked as rumors of sightings began to circulate. Whenever a tipster phoned in a supposed sighting, the result was roads being closed, an influx of hundreds of uniformed officers, and the noise of helicopters hovering overhead.

It was hard to relax. Like most every other family across the region, we hunkered down in our home, on high alert. Considering how well armed and secured many places were, "bunkered" might be a better word. Doors and windows were closed and locked, yards lit up. Nobody got much sleep. Nighttime's normal silence just intensifies the no-longer-normal sounds of a barking dog, vehicles driving by or a low-flying helicopter.

Some areas were completely closed to local traffic. Residents were advised that they could leave their property. Coming back home was another matter. Nobody was allowed to return until the cordoned-off area was cleared. Sometimes that took days!

The old saying about the mail—neither rain, nor snow, nor sleet, nor hail shall keep the postman from his rounds—never accounted for escaped inmates. In some areas locked down during the search, the mail was not delivered for days.

Another ritual that's important to us northern dwellers is the annual opening of the beaches on the mountain lakes and rivers. Those events were canceled in 2015. The little town of Cadyville, just down the road from Dannemora, called off its Fiftieth Annual Field Day. As the days passed, tensions soared as weddings, vacations, and graduation parties were canceled or moved to safer locations.

But amid all the anxiety, something important was happening. On social media, the hashtag "#Clintonstrong" started to appear. It was a grass-roots movement, something bigger than the escape; bigger than the fear. The movement's leaders and participants were all northern New York residents. They emerged from the confines of their homes armed with bug spray, energy bars, apples, desserts, coffee, power drinks, and sandwiches. They handed these useful, comforting items to law officers standing their posts, or just passing by.

Restaurants began delivering free meals and drinks, subs, sandwiches, pizzas, and donuts to police and corrections officers. The Champlain Valley Physicians' Hospital in Plattsburgh supplied fresh linens and towels. Volunteers staffed the region's fire and rescue departments around the clock to address any minor injuries the searchers incurred. They had plenty to do: insect stings, tick bites, cuts, and scratches from bushwhacking through wild park land, and blistered feet were common problems.

A June 15 column by Lois Clermont, editor of Plattsburgh's *Press-Republican,* summed up what her paper's readers were saying. Public support for the officers conducting the search "is sky high," she wrote. On the paper's Facebook page, a reader named Robin Marie said, "Thank you, stay strong, be safe and we hope this ends soon so you can get back to your families. Keep up the great work!"

Caitlin Varano posted, "Thank you for leaving your families to protect our community and catch these criminals. Standing out in the rain searching for them, hungry and tired. I will never be able to thank you enough."

Susan Ashley Drown said, "Thank you and God bless. Such a miserable task they have at hand. We are NOT taking their efforts for granted."

Those are just a handful of the dozens of comments the paper's editor quoted, and those came from a tiny fraction of the people who shared similar feelings.

The North Country showed its true colors through a sea of blue ribbons tied to trees, light poles, mailboxes and house doors. Each ribbon was a token of support and appreciation for the law officers' effort and sacrifice. Wanda Collins lives in Dannemora, on Smith Street. The escapees walked right past her house the night they broke out. As soon as she heard about Clinton Strong, she cut up some blue velvet to hang four ribbons around her property. It was her way of acknowledging the efforts of several corrections officers who live in her neighborhood. Nearby in Cadyville, Becky Stanilka put blue ribbons on her mailbox and flower boxes. "We need to show law enforcement, especially the COs, that we support them," she said. Like so many others, it was personal for her. She's married to a retired corrections officer.

While prison guards and local police were out working, their neighbors were seen mowing their lawns and tending to other needed chores.

In times when people are often isolated from one another, and in a region where plenty of folks value their privacy and like to keep to themselves, it was remarkable how the community came together. Even with heavily armed officers crossing private properties by the hundreds, I never heard a single person balk. I never heard of a single person asking, "Do you have a warrant?" In so many ways, big and little, the North Country's people truly did hold law enforcement in their thoughts and prayers. The message was clear: through this long ordeal, local residents were appreciative and grateful for the law enforcement presence.

Many of those officers would find that they got better support from local volunteers than they did from their own department.

CHAPTER 32
THE PURSUIT
AND THE PURSUED

THE FIRST SEARCH PERIMETER WAS LITTLE BIGGER than the Village of Dannemora, but it quickly expanded as the manhunt went on, reaching deep into the countryside and the foothills of the Adirondack Mountains. Every house, barn, and outbuilding in the villages and rural country and every seasonal home and hunting camp deep in the woods had to be searched and cleared, one road at a time.

Some of the search procedures created a surreal feeling for those of us inside the perimeter. A brilliant glare often blotted out the night sky, normally full of stars like you never see in towns. Generator-powered floodlights by the tractor-trailer load were deployed to illuminate roads and farm fields. The U.S. Department of Homeland Security generated automated robo-calls to all local phone numbers, asking homeowners to turn on their outside lights at night and shelter in place.

While we were keeping a close eye on our own property, the search was pushing deep into the Adirondack Park's thick woods, swamps, and tangled brush. That task was assigned to three groups. New York State's forest rangers and environmental conservation officers, whose duties included searching for lost hikers, were both heavily armed and well equipped for bushwhacking. The third group was one I knew well: the Department of Corrections Emergency Response Team. During my time in Corrections, I was one of six supervisors on the Upstate CERT team. Guards apply to be selected for CERT duty. Successful applicants get specialized training in areas such as using firearms and chemical agents, unarmed defense tactics, and escape and pursuit procedures.

Unfortunately, the CERT members were poorly equipped compared to the rangers and officers with other agencies. The department sent these guards into the field without basic communication equipment or even real handcuffs. While even the tiniest village police departments equip their officers with portable radios, most CERT teams were left to rely on their personal cell phones. In the Adirondacks, cellular towers are few and far between, and the mountains often block what feeble signals there are. That meant these officers were left with no means to report any findings or to call for help or reinforcements.

And if they had come across the escapees, most of the CERT officers would have had to rely on so-called "Flexicuffs" to restrain their captives. Think a "zip tie," like you might use to bundle a tangle of wires under your computer desk. While these might have been OK for mass arrests of mild-mannered environmental protestors—which happened elsewhere in the state around the same time—it's not what I would want to rely on to hold a desperate escaped murderer.

Only the CERT leaders and supervisors were issued standard Smith & Wesson steel handcuffs. They were also the only CERT officers with proper radio equipment.

Within a day, CERT members abandoned their bulky batons after they kept getting snagged on trees and heavy brush. To a pencil-pusher in Albany, sending hundreds of officers into the field on a life-and-death assignment without the most basic equipment may have seemed economical. To me, and anyone who ever wore a law enforcement uniform, it was reprehensible.

Fortunately, the CERT teams had been trained better than they'd been equipped. When I was on that duty, we had regularly practiced formations for such hazardous tasks as retaking control of a prison yard, or finding fugitives in the brush. A typical tactic for these back-woods searches was to deploy a line of officers along a park road, power-line right of way or snowmobile trail. Then a second line of rangers or environmental conservation officers leading CERT officers would sweep through the woods towards them, like beaters flushing game toward a line of hunters, pushing everything in front of them.

Because of the rugged conditions and abrupt changes in the terrain, this could be accomplished only by boots on the ground.

Those boots often proved unserviceable after days in the soggy back woods. One officer wrapped his disintegrating footwear with orange duct tape so he could keep working. Another, whose feet were literally covered with a mass of oozing blisters, accepted medical care but refused to take any time off from the search.

Searchers battled assaults from swarming mosquitos and black flies, a constant torment even when they don't bite. And they do bite, as do ticks, adding another level of misery to duty in the back country. Daily slogs through chest-deep swamps, heavy rain, and bone-chilling temperatures became routine. While enduring lows in the forties and fifties may not seem so bad, combine that with being constantly wet and wind-blown and hypothermia becomes a real danger. Each day, when they returned to wherever they would be sleeping, the searchers fought to dry their equipment and clothing and, most important, their socks and boots. One of the most treasured gifts from the "Clinton Strong" volunteers was dry socks. Some officers were fortunate enough to be able to come home at night. For corrections officers brought in from around the state, the department reopened the mothballed Chateaugay Correctional Facility. It provided a warm bunk, sure, but it couldn't have sat well with a prison guard, assigned far from home, to be sleeping in a prison dorm. For other searchers, New York State provided lodging in motels and in dormitories on the SUNY Plattsburgh campus. The small private Paul Smiths College, deep in the Adirondacks, made its dorms available, too.

Once again, the community rallied to support those searchers. Volunteers helped prepare meals in the Chateaugay prison's reopened mess hall. Others delivered food from restaurants or their own kitchens.

Out along the roadside, searchers had to stand guard for hours or days, often in the rain. Neighbors helped out by delivering firewood and building campfires for warmth. They also provided chairs, food, and hot beverages, and charged cell phones for officers.

Those of us who had become temporary prisoners in our own homes could see that we didn't have it so bad. What was evident to everyone affected by this crisis was the stamina, dedication, and perseverance of the law enforcement officers involved in this mission.

David Sweat knew, from seeing the mountains from the prison tailor shop's windows, that the Adirondacks were not a hospitable place to be traveling on foot. He had also gotten some idea what to expect from watching TV nature shows during his years in prison.

But neither he nor Richard Matt was truly prepared for what they would encounter outside Clinton's thirty-foot wall. Because they had expected to be riding in Joyce Mitchell's Jeep, they assumed that police wouldn't bother to set up roadblocks close to the prison. They quickly learned better. Sweat blamed Mitchell. Not only had she stood them up at their planned midnight rendezvous, he was convinced that she had thoroughly ratted them out.

"She went and told on herself," he concluded, "and told on us, about she was supposed to pick us up." And that, Sweat quickly deduced, meant the authorities knew they were on foot and still nearby.

And so with the roadblocks, motorized patrols, and aerial searches, they had to carefully stay out of sight.

Walking on a road was safe only at night; walking off the roads was possible only in the daytime, when snags, briars, and pitfalls were visible. Even when following roads, their progress was mostly parallel to, not on, the right of way. Diving into underbrush or sticking to the tree line, they managed to avoid being spotted after that first backyard encounter in Dannemora.

And when they decided to head mostly west, they quickly ran

out of road. In that direction from Dannemora, busy Route 374 is the only option—and for Matt and Sweat, it wasn't an option. Between that state highway and the next paved road, far to the south, is Lyon Mountain, which rises to nearly four thousand feet, covered with dense timber and underbrush. On the mountain, temperatures are routinely five degrees colder—or more—than down in town, where our idea of a beautiful June day involves a high of around seventy. A not-so-beautiful June night might have lows down in the forties or even colder.

"We froze our asses off," Sweat admitted later. But because of chronic rainy weather and low cloud cover, the two figured they could get away with building fires to keep warm at night. For the first couple of weeks, they saw and heard search planes and helicopters only during daylight.

Sweat took pride, after his capture, in portraying himself as a resourceful woodsman. Although his partner isn't around to contradict him, much of what he told interrogators jibes with other evidence. Like the food supply he brought through the escape tunnel and carried in his soft guitar case. "I had the foresight to take—you know, planning for the worst—I took like twenty packs of peanuts," he told State Police. He had bought these at the prison commissary, along with forty granola bars and "probably twelve sticks of pepperoni." Savvy backwoods hikers would approve: those rations would keep well and keep a traveler going for a long time.

In other ways, they weren't so well prepared. Frequent rains soaked through their prison-issue clothing. And Matt's feet were quickly a drag on their progress. "He had bought new boots," Sweat said, "And the dumb-ass wore his old ones . . . which fell apart. Which is pretty stupid."

Also falling apart was their improvised luggage. The backpack Matt had sewed illicitly from stolen green prison-uniform fabric didn't survive long after getting soaked by rain and snagged by branches and briars. The seams on Sweat's cloth guitar case also started to fail.

They had only a vague idea of where they were or where they

were going. Sweat said he remembered hearing somewhere that prevailing winds usually come from the west. So as they thrashed their way through the woods and over the mountains, they tried to keep the wind in their faces.

That wind, on top of the rain, made things miserable for them when darkness forced them to stop. The wind-chill factor always worked against them. Their first few nights on the run, Sweat recalled, they took shelter in old deer-hunting blinds, "because it was raining pretty hard."

But despite Sweat's self-proclaimed survival smarts, it was Matt who had the experience in getting by in the woods. The technique he had learned years earlier in another New York State wilderness area as a teenage jail escapee would serve them both well for a time. But it would also be their undoing.

CHAPTER 33
THE POWER OF POLITICS

AS THE DAYS DRAGGED ON, AND THE NATIONAL MEDIA REPORTED no progress in recapturing the two convicted killers, the State Police and Corrections officials started to feel pressure from their bosses in Albany.

If the escapees couldn't be caught, at a minimum the powers that be wanted a scapegoat. The State Police started getting demands for both capture and closure. Under questioning from police interrogators, Joyce Mitchell had quickly revealed her involvement. She admitted having supplied maximum-security prisoners with escape tools, a serious crime. After a week of interviews with police, Albany officials wanted to know, why hadn't she been charged and arrested?

Maybe the governor and his advisors had never watched a police procedural on TV or at the movies. Or maybe they already knew the answer to their question but didn't care about what it implied. That answer, simply put, was that a steady flow of information from a cooperative witness is worth far more than a quick arrest.

Worth more in terms of solving the case and getting a conviction, that is. Not worth so much, though, to a politician who badly needed something, anything, he could announce in front of the TV cameras.

John Donahue of the State Police was the experienced senior

investigator who took the lead in interviewing Joyce Mitchell. He had gained her confidence and was getting a stream of useful information from her. Like any intelligent cop, he knew the well would run dry the minute his source changed from "witness" to "defendant." Facing a criminal charge, even a less-than-brilliant character like Mitchell would immediately hire a lawyer. And once "lawyered up," she would shut up.

Donahue stood firm and defended his position. To his superiors up the chain of command, he made two essential arguments. First was that, in the absence of any other good leads, what Mitchell was confessing in the interview room might be critical to finding Matt and Sweat. Second was that Mitchell wasn't going anywhere. She could be arrested at any time, once she had run out of useful information. Donahue had an excellent success rate in closing cases and securing convictions. He was, and is, highly respected among his peers. But the top officials in Albany were not impressed by either his techniques or his success rate. They demanded Mitchell's immediate arrest.

Donahue then committed the ultimate sin for a state employee. He asked whether the emperor was wearing any clothes. More specifically, he questioned the political motive behind the rush to arrest Mitchell. His punishment was to be removed from the case. But that wasn't enough for his bosses. They charged him with insubordination, putting him through a formal disciplinary process.

And so on June 12, with the inconvenient professional Donahue out of the way, the State Police arrested Joyce Mitchell. She was charged with a felony, promoting prison contraband, and a misdemeanor, criminal facilitation. Mitchell promptly hired a lawyer, and as Donahue had predicted, her free flow of information to the police abruptly ended. Unable to make her $110,000 bail, she remained in the Clinton County Jail.

By this point, Governor Cuomo was starting to let his frustration show. Even with Joyce Mitchell in jail and John Donahue in the State Police dog house, he needed to find others to blame. On the ninth day of the search, he ordered the state's inspector general, Catherine Leahy Scott, to investigate the escape. She and more than a dozen investigators reported to Clinton Correctional Facility to interview the staff and gather documentation for her report. For days, weeks, and months, the prison's guards and other employees were put under a microscope, probed, and examined. Ultimately more than 165 staff members would be interviewed, along with eleven inmates.

New York State brought in outside experts to review the design of Clinton Correctional Facility. One of them was Michael P. Jacobson, now a sociology professor at the City University of New York, who ran the city's probation and jail departments in the 1990s. The investigators also closely scrutinized the facility's operation and security protocols, with help from prison officials from Minnesota, Pennsylvania, and Los Angeles County.

Cuomo talked tough when the investigation was announced. "We have zero tolerance for anyone who aided or abetted these criminals, no matter how minor their role," he said. "Make no mistake: Any individual found to have assisted in this escape will be prosecuted to the fullest extent of the law."

The governor's internal investigation didn't go unchallenged. His announcement of Leahy Scott's assignment drew a critical response from a group of retired rank and file corrections officers who had worked at Clinton. They issued press releases that called attention to Albany's role in making the escape possible. The retired officers alerted the media to the impact of the state's cost-cutting measures, its decades-long history of eliminating jobs and adding duties to the remaining positions' job descriptions, and its tolerance for insufficient staffing.

News reports quickly pointed out that half of the towers that rise above the Clinton prison's wall were not manned on the night of the escape. Some of those wall towers, the local press revealed, had been empty for more than a decade.

The media began connecting the dots. News stories asked that if such highly visible posts were unmanned, what other security positions or jobs had also been considered nonessential and eliminated to save money? The public started to hear the disturbing details: Wall towers unmanned for decades. No inspections of the tunnels under the prison since the mid-1990s. So many job duties added to guards that they were now working without breaks or a lunch period.

In a June 16 story, the *Press-Republican* quoted a recently retired guard who said orders from Albany had stopped regular inspections of the catwalks behind Clinton's cells. The Department of Corrections had responded to inmates unhappy that guards sometimes cut off electricity to their cells, said Jeff Dumas, who retired as a sergeant in November 2014. "They complain, and Albany sides with them, and we are not allowed to do things anymore," he said. For the same reasons, Dumas said, guards weren't permitted to use flashlights while making night-time rounds after the 11 P.M. standing count, and inmates were allowed to hide their heads under their blankets. He put two and two together for the newspaper's readers: with guards kept out of the catwalks and forbidden to make certain each bunk contained a live body, Matt and Sweat would have easily had five to six hours every night to work on their breakout. He didn't want the prison's guards blamed for policies dictated way above their pay grade. "The guys do a good job, but with all the grievances and rule changes they have to deal with, it is tough," Dumas said.

One skeptical outside observer was Kenneth Lovett, a reporter for the *New York Daily News*. In a June 15 column, he said, "Cuomo and his administration might have some explaining to do." The two empty wall towers "were left unmanned because the Cuomo administration was pressing for cuts in overtime," he said. It was also the cost of overtime, he said, that led state officials to deny permission for the preventive lockdown just before the escape.

One way or another, these news stories all asked the big question: who, exactly, had ordered all these cost-saving and inmate-pleasing measures?

This question is still unanswered today.

What these stories seemed to be pointing out, in addition to the effect on public safety, was that New York State's prison inmates were treated better than the staff.

Even while the fugitives were still on the loose, the prisoners behind the walls in Dannemora were free to resume their normal routines. The lockdown of the inmate population at Clinton Correctional Facility was lifted less than two weeks after the escape. Inmates' privileges were restored. Recreation periods resumed. Friends and family returned for regular visits. But while the inmates' lives returned to normal, the prison's staff members were still being summoned to a small room, day after day, for interviews—interrogations would be a better word in some cases—by the inspector general's office.

And while the prison staff was being grilled, life for everyone living outside the prison walls also remained far from normal. Matt and Sweat were still at large, and nobody knew if they were far away—or still in our back yards.

PART VI
THE CHASE

CHAPTER 34
Twisted Horn

John Stockwell is a corrections officer. His friends, and I count myself among them, call him "Stumpy." When the inmates escaped from Clinton, he had just turned forty-seven. On the second Saturday after the escape, he got his marching orders from his wife and best friend, Nancy. "I love you," she said. "And be careful."

On most days, that warning made good sense, when Stumpy went to work at one of the prisons that line Bare Hill Road north of Malone. On June 20, he was off the clock, but just like for all of us, it was not a normal weekend. He was on his way to check on their hunting camp in the Adirondack Park. He and Nancy call the place "Twisted Horn." The name is a private joke that they don't explain, even to friends. He hadn't visited the vacant camp since the first week of May, when he had placed his game cameras, hoping to capture photos of wildlife.

As he headed out from their home in Lyon Mountain, Stumpy made a promise to his wife: the next day, they would celebrate the anniversary of their twenty-eight years together by visiting the Akwesasne Mohawk Casino, a short drive away in the St. Lawrence River valley.

Nancy planned to get some yard work done while it was sunny. June had been very wet so far; the day before had been rainy, and more rain was forecast for Sunday.

Going to check the camp, Stumpy did what many of us had

gotten into the habit of doing: he took his sidearm. He also took Nancy's cell phone and his Labrador retriever, Dolly. Nancy remembered that Stumpy had a smile on his face as he got into his pickup to leave. It would be a beautiful Saturday morning in the Adirondack Park.

Like everyone else, naturally, Stumpy was very aware of the two murderers' escape. Even more so as a prison guard himself. All of us who have worked with inmates were especially alert, knowing what they can be like. By this time, two weeks had elapsed and the news was full of possible sightings pretty much everywhere. At this point, law officers reported, they had pursued something like 1,500 leads. A few hundred of the officers assigned to the search here had been redeployed, but there was still no hard evidence of where the escapees might be. A force of six hundred local, state, and federal officers was still here, still looking.

Stumpy's short trip into the Adirondack back country was uneventful, though slow and bumpy. He had asphalt under his tires until he passed though the little hamlet of Standish. Then, crossing from Clinton into Franklin County, he turned onto unpaved Wolf Pond Road. That uneven, rocky single-lane track twists and climbs up and down through rugged country. Even a four-wheel drive truck like Stumpy's often has to slow to a crawl, and both he and Dolly were bounced around inside the cab. Finally, after almost ten miles of this, Stumpy turned his pick-up onto the path to Twisted Horn. Then the going got really rough.

That 1.7-mile route to his camp is more rock than dirt. A full-sized vehicle, even with four-wheel drive, can't make it all the way. Stumpy stopped the truck at a small clearing in the woods, not far from Wolf Pond Road, to unload his all-terrain vehicle. He would ride the ATV rather than walk up the rocky track to his camp. The last mile and a half is filled with hairpin turns, ups and downs, and an endless supply of loose rocks. Just getting to Twisted Horn offers plenty of opportunities for a twisted ankle or broken leg. The Adirondacks are full of spectacular hiking trails. This isn't one of them.

Stumpy and Dolly had made this trip plenty of times. He easily maneuvered the six-hundred-pound four-wheeler while Dolly trotted alongside, pausing here and there as dogs do to enjoy all the sniffs in the woods.

Just before Stumpy got to Twisted Horn, Dolly bolted ahead of him. When he caught up, he saw she was on alert. The barking Labrador's attention was focused on the camp. The fur on her back was standing up. Clearly, something was wrong.

Before Stumpy could even get off his ATV, he spotted movement in his camp. No wild critter; what he saw through the window of his bunk house's front door was human. Something moved again. This time he could make out a hooded figure scurrying back and forth inside the camp's only building.

Stumpy knew his approach had been well announced by his ATV's powerful engine. He never had the element of surprise. He drew on his training and calculated his best course of action. He knew his only option was to stay out in the open, with no cover, so he could see as much of the camp as possible. Stumpy drew his handgun and shouted a challenge to whoever was in the bunkhouse. He barked an order: come out and show yourself. He heard no response, but saw more movement inside the camp. Again, Stumpy ordered whoever was inside to show himself. By this time, the veteran corrections officer's training and gut instinct for self-preservation had kicked in. He felt the danger.

Stumpy couldn't be sure if he had seen one or two people in the camp.

Suddenly, without warning, he heard the back door slam and the sound of footsteps on the camp's back deck. Then came the crashing sound of movement through the woods.

Stumpy knew he couldn't get cell phone service. Not at the camp; not anywhere nearby. He knew he would have to get back to his truck and then drive to someplace where he could get a signal and call police. He swiveled the ATV around and took off as fast as he could. Racing down the narrow path for a few seconds, he remembered that he had left Dolly behind. Nuts! He waited a few more seconds until, thankfully, she caught up with him. Good dog, he thought. After all, by giving him warning, she had likely just saved his life. Both finally got to the pickup truck, where Stumpy jumped off the ATV.

He couldn't spare the time to load the four-wheeler into the pickup's bed. As quickly as the rocky track permitted, he and Dolly lurched their way toward the Wolf Pond Road. A glance in his mirrors reminded him he'd neglected to release the ramps he'd used to unload the ATV. Exasperated at even a few seconds' delay, he stopped the truck, got out, and tossed the ramps clear. He wouldn't get the chance to retrieve them or the ATV until much later.

Once back on the Wolf Pond Road, he turned west instead of going back the way he'd come. This end of the road has a smooth dirt surface, much easier going, and connects to the Mountain View resort community. He sped toward civilization and a cell phone signal. About a mile and a half from Twisted Horn's gate, meeting a group of ATV riders, Stumpy quickly described his encounter. One of the riders told him they had passed a State Police car just minutes before. Some of the four-wheelers raced off to chase the patrolling troop car.

Others got off their ATVs to try what we call the "cell phone dance" out here in the boondocks. That means walking around aimlessly, phones in their hands and arms stretched toward the sky, hoping by luck or magic to get a signal.

Stumpy couldn't wait. He had vital information and no way to communicate it. Feeling the frustration, he drove his truck farther down the road, searching for that sweet spot where his call could get through. Even though he was less than three miles from his camp, he knew he had lost too much time. Any police who could respond now would find the bunkhouse empty and the intruders long gone. At the Bryant Siding Road, almost into Mountain View, he finally got a cellular signal. Punching in 911, he quickly identified himself to the operator. He described his remote location and started to explain his encounter with the trespassers at his camp. Then suddenly, without warning, the call ended.

* * *

The phone rang at the John Stockwell residence. Nancy answered. The caller identified himself as a 911 operator. He had just been talking with John Stockwell. Nancy's heart sank.

She listened as the operator explained that John had called 911 moments earlier. He was reporting a possible encounter with the prison escapees when his call had abruptly ended. The operator told Nancy that despite trying several times, he couldn't re-connect with John. Now the authorities were wondering if she knew where he was.

Nancy's guts twisted. Her head was spinning. She was feeling a hundred emotions. She wanted to scream but forced herself to hold it together. Meticulously, she answered all the questions the 911 operator asked her. She shoved her emotions aside to provide him the necessary details. To tell the police how to find her husband. John had gone to Camp Twisted Horn. It's off the Wolf Pond Road. South side, between Bryant Siding Road and Black Cat Mountain. Yes. This side of Mountain View. No, they'll have to walk the last mile or more.

When the call with 911 ended, Nancy was all alone to wonder exactly where John was now. And why had the call ended? Just a weak signal? Or something much worse? He was probably in danger, she knew. But how much danger? Picking up the home phone again, she tried to call her own cell phone, the one she had given John less than an hour before. No answer. She kept trying, over and over, to connect with her husband. No answer. Again, no answer.

It wasn't long before Nancy heard sirens approaching. A minute later she saw a line of police cars racing toward Camp Twisted Horn. Minutes later, she heard a noise overhead. Quickly stepping outside, she saw the helicopter was going in the same direction.

What had happened? Where was John?

CHAPTER 35
TIMING IS EVERYTHING

AFTER THE 911 OPERATOR'S TALK WITH NANCY STOCKWELL and his failure to reconnect with John, the State Police command center dispatched a string of officers to Wolf Pond Road. Cell phone communication is sparse at best in this mountainous area but police had gleaned enough information from the Stockwells to send cars precisely to Twisted Horn's vicinity.

Wolf Pond Road is mostly in Franklin County, connecting Malone and Mountain View with Standish, the first place across the line in Clinton County. It can best be described as a two-lane dirt and rock playground, mostly enjoyed by ATV drivers in spring, summer, and fall, then used by snowmobilers for spectacular rides in wintertime. A handful of seasonal camps are sprinkled along this secluded road. The section east of Camp Twisted Horn, toward Standish and Dannemora, is hard going even with four-wheel drive. The occasional splashes of yellow and orange on the trees lining this stretch are "Posted" signs. They warn that the land is owned by various timber companies and leased by hunting clubs. All others are on notice to keep out.

When the flashing red and blue lights got to Mountain View, officers found John Stockwell safe and sound. Talking with him encouraged the police that they had just gotten the break they needed. With help from police, "Stumpy" Stockwell connected with Nancy, dispelling her anxiety and assuring her he was safe.

They would tell the story of his encounter with the intruders at Twisted Horn for years to come.

When police were confident they had enough force on the scene, they commandeered Stockwell's four-wheel drive pick-up. With Stumpy riding shotgun to navigate, a heavily armed force made its way to Camp Twisted Horn. The officer driving didn't know the track was impassible beyond where John had left his ATV. He drove on, past where road vehicles always stopped, onto terrain where no truck had gone before. Well before reaching Twisted Horn, the squad of heavily armed police perched in the pick-up's bed discovered that the rugged, densely forested terrain was not conducive even to four-wheel drive. Stumpy's truck quickly became mired. The team abandoned it and proceeded on foot.

First goal, on arriving at Twisted Horn, was to clear and secure the camp's perimeter. Police, with Stumpy's help, quickly found evidence of a break-in. In the bunkhouse, they saw signs someone had been staying in the camp for several days, literally sleeping in the beds, sitting in the chairs and eating the porridge. It seems the occupants had escaped the recent downpours and cold nights in the shelter of the cabin.

To its owners, the invasion of an Adirondack hunting camp is offensive, wrong, and inexcusable. Hunting camps and their surrounding acreage are considered sacred. Their interior walls often display generations' worth of photographs and mementos from their owners' traditions of trapping, big-game hunting, and other outdoor pursuits. Most camps are left unlocked for months. But in the Adirondacks, the unwritten code is that if you don't own it, you don't enter.

John Stockwell was furious when he saw that some stranger had violated his camp's sanctity, right down to his own bed. Signs that his camp had hosted uninvited guests included rearranged sleeping bags, a coffee pot that showed signs of use, and several empty tanks of propane. The fuel had been burned in the stove and the camp's heater. A thorough inspection found that some of the stored food supply had been consumed. Missing items included oatmeal, spaghetti, protein bars, peanut butter, coffee, and worst of all, Nancy's homemade raspberry jam.

On the kitchen table were dirty coffee cups, plastic spoons, a half-full jug of water, a newly opened jar of peanut butter, duct tape, rags and bloody socks. The trash can held a pair of boot soles, empty oatmeal packets, and wrappers from Pop-Tarts and Sunbelt Bakery granola bars. That's the brand sold in the prison commissary. One clue was especially telling. The camp's radio was tuned to 93.3 FM. That's WSLP, an "adult contemporary" station in Lake Placid, which had been airing regular news updates about the prison escape. It appeared that the occupants had been keeping track of the search.

Investigators asked Stockwell to provide a list of items missing from the camp. The most obvious was a topographic map of the area, which had been removed from a wall. This kind of map shows fine details of terrain, including how steep the slopes are, as well as forest cover, bodies of water, populated areas, roads, railways, trails, and utility lines. Other missing items included a poncho, rain pants, toothbrushes, and boots. The most troubling items Stockwell found missing were two pepper shakers, a large container of garlic pepper, a compass, a Mason jar of Ole Smoky Tennessee Moonshine, and a 20-gauge shotgun. One bit of good news was that no ammunition had been kept in the camp.

While he was taking this inventory, police were searching the surrounding woods and the intruders' apparent escape route, based on Stockwell's description. Trackers quickly found a trail of dropped or discarded items: a pair of boots, Bowie knife, poncho, beard trimmer, toothpaste, toothbrush, razor, and "Corcraft" branded underwear. These and other evidence collected from the camp were rushed to State Police headquarters in Albany. State crime labs got to work on analysis, including DNA testing.

Police dogs picked up a scent, but after hours and miles of tracking, they lost the trail in the soggy back country. Meanwhile, police and prison guards were redeployed to set up roadblocks and stand watch along nearby roadsides and waterways. For the first time, Major Guess surmised exactly where the fugitives had been and when. Suddenly the search had narrowed from nation-wide or even international; the dragnet could now concentrate on just a few square miles.

Not that it would be easy. Unfortunately, those few square miles were mostly roadless wilderness, crisscrossed by streams and punctuated by half-mile-high peaks.

The commander quickly assigned roving patrols to try to establish a perimeter. Aerial surveillance was focused on the area west and south of Wolf Pond Road. However, the dense Adirondack forest and impenetrable underbrush around Camp Twisted Horn made finding the scene by air nearly impossible.

A view of Camp Twisted Horn from the air, if you know precisely where to look, reveals mostly a canopy of mature timber. Underneath the treetops, the camp's roof is completely covered by green moss. Flourishing tree seedlings that sprouted in the moss and leaf litter make the roof hard to tell apart from the forest floor. This natural camouflage is typical of these remote camps. Finding them from the air under the thick timber is a formidable task; finding a person, unless he let himself get caught in a clearing or on a road, is hopeless.

Within a day, the DNA evidence came back. It confirmed that the trespassers at Twisted Horn were indeed David Sweat and Richard Matt. By now, a massive redeployment of personnel was under way. Police and prison guards who had been assigned to Clinton County posts were moved west from staging areas near Dannemora and across the line into Franklin County. Pursuing them was a convoy of national media and their mobile broadcasting trucks. Major Guess set up a new forward operating base at the Owls Head/Mountain View Fire Station, just five miles from where the escapees had last been seen. To provide space for aircraft and ground support vehicles, the nearby Titus Mountain Ski Center was commandeered as a staging area. Titus Mountain's ski lodge became a makeshift command center, where the law enforcement agencies conducted daily briefings. The parking lot at nearby Owl's Head Methodist Church filled up with TV satellite trucks and other news-media vehicles.

Among the early pieces of news was the authorities' praise for John Stockwell. The off-duty corrections officer's report had transformed the search from a wait-and-see game into an urgent, focused manhunt. By now, two weeks into the escape, six hundred officers from all agencies were on the hunt locally. Each of the thousands of leads that had poured in had required time and manpower to check out, often far away. Stockwell's lead, now rock-solid, returned those far-flung assets to the Adirondack Park. Within days, a swarm of law officers brought the total deployed locally to about 1,500, easily outnumbering the few dozen residents who call Mountain View their home all year long.

Mountain View is one of the best kept secrets in the Adirondacks. Only a few tourists, many of them kayakers, make the annual pilgrimage to this secluded area for its rustic charm, quiet lakes, and relaxed atmosphere. This tiny town's only "hot spot" is Belly's Mountain View Inn. As police and reporters discovered, you won't find cell phone or internet service inside this unique bar and restaurant. I call it a "hot spot" because it's the perfect place for both locals and tourists to get cold beer, great conversation, and the best prime rib you'll ever eat. When I'm in the mood for something more than a hot dog in a cardboard box, Belly's is the place to go. Terry Bellinger—that's Belly—and his wife Beth are the best hosts you'll ever meet.

During the time their little village was ground zero for the search, Terry and Beth accommodated the hordes of police and media, and the disruption that came with them, with typical good humor.

During this time, Terry added an important detail to his usual routine after closing the place for the night. It's a short drive home in his pickup. "For ten days, I'd ride home every night with a loaded shotgun on the floor. I'd get stopped by ten troopers, and each one would look in the window, see what I had, and tell me, 'OK. You're good.'"

Homeowners in the area, and tourists who had arrived at their seasonal camps, were instructed to be vigilant, secure all buildings, and report any possible sightings or suspicious activity to police. The normal traffic of locals driving all-terrain vehicles was replaced by armored tactical units driven by police.

On a normal summer night, typical sounds and lights in these hills come from crickets and frogs, campfires and fireflies. In their place now were the roar of generators and the glare of mobile light towers. Folks had to forego their peaceful nightly walks on roads and trails patrolled by heavily armed law enforcement.

Whenever local folks had to go out, they went armed. And just as I was during that time, they were prepared to use their weapons if necessary. One of Terry Bellinger's neighbors got stopped at a roadblock near Mountain View. He had a shotgun in his car. As Terry tells the story, "The trooper looked in and he asked, 'Is it loaded?' 'Yep.' 'How many shells?' 'Three.'" After a moment the trooper added a bit of advice. "'It'll hold five.'"

Soon after Stockwell's discoveries at Twisted Horn, other owners began reporting burglaries at their seasonal camps. Many of these weren't obvious to the casual eye. Nothing was broken to indicate forcible entry; only a few items were stolen at each place. At Camp Stillwater, on the Wolf Pond Road a few miles west of the Clinton-Franklin county line, some food, alcohol, and personal items had been taken. The Doll House, another camp on the Wolf Pond Road, had also been selectively plundered. Plotting these sites and Camp Twisted Horn on the map confirmed that Matt and Sweat had traveled on foot, generally going west, since leaving Dannemora.

The searchers took heart from this. It now appeared that the inmates' eerie disappearance and elaborate escape plan was unraveling. Contrary to what they had intended, the escapees never found transportation. They were undoubtedly struggling through the back woods, somewhere near Mountain View.

John Stockwell's decision to check his camp on a sunny Saturday morning had made all the difference. Timing is everything!

CHAPTER 36
BOUNTY HUNTERS AND MEDIA FOLLIES

IN THE TWO WEEKS LEADING UP TO THE BIG BREAK at Twisted Horn, every lead had come up dry. But the hundreds of officers from a dozen or more different agencies had kept at it, steadily chasing leads, conducting interviews, beating the bushes and looking under every rock. Before it was over, the case would generate more than three thousand leads, all but a handful of which would turn out to be worthless. No doubt the volume of leads owed something to the reward money, a combined $150,000 from state and federal authorities. Supposed sightings of Richard Matt and David Sweat were reported from all over the country.

What that money also brought were bounty hunters. A number of these soldiers of fortune turned up in Dannemora, dazzled by the vision of a six-figure payday. The one with the highest profile, who showed up during the search's final days, was Duane Chapman. On cable TV, he's known as "Dog the Bounty Hunter." He would boast to media that he'd been collecting his own tips about the escape.

Later on, a self-proclaimed psychic from Texas sued the state, claiming he should get the reward money. Why? Because his metaphysical sources had led him to make some vague predictions about the case. Those insights included that Matt and Sweat had separated, that Joyce Mitchell knew more than she was telling, and that one of the escapees was heading for the mountains.

One of the bounty hunters, dressed in full tactical gear, sporting a badge and identification card dangling from a lanyard around his neck, managed to worm his way into the secure law enforcement command post in the small prison town. It didn't take long, though, before he was identified as someone who didn't belong there. Grateful as the cops on duty were for genuine public-spirited help, they weren't impressed by this self-serving character. He wasn't just escorted out; he was arrested.

He wasn't the only outsider drawn to the case who would overstep his bounds and cause unnecessary distractions to the searchers. Among the media hordes who descended on Dannemora and later fanned out across Clinton and Franklin Counties, at least a couple of them leaped when they should have looked more carefully.

During the search's final week, an infrared-triggered camera, placed by federal law enforcement, went off in the country outside Malone. This was in my normally quiet rural neighborhood. The digital image captured two men walking, each carrying a shotgun or rifle. One was fairly burly with dark hair and a round face; he looked something like Richard Matt. The other's face was obscured behind the first man's head.

I first learned about this when a line of State Police cars came screeching up our road, armed troopers established a perimeter that included our property, and two helicopters appeared overhead. One of the troopers explained that they had obtained a photograph of what might have been the escapees. I noticed where the helicopters were hovering and told the trooper that my neighbor, Eric Couture, lived in that area. I also explained that he normally carries his 20-gauge Browning pump shotgun and a pair of binoculars. What the photo showed, in other words, was situation normal. Eric finds his shotgun useful to discourage trespassers on his spread, which he calls "Off the Grid Acres."

The man behind Eric in the photo was another neighbor, Charlie Coutu, who's a retired contractor. And just like most of us did during those weeks, he was carrying his gun, too: a .30-30 deer rifle.

When the State Police realized the photo was just solid citizens, and not a good lead, they shut down the operation. In less than ten minutes, the helicopter turned away and the troopers got back in their cars. And so I figured that would be the end of it.

But then after all the excitement was over, one day in early July, Penny and I were out walking the dogs when a man in a car pulled up and spoke to me. His name was Thomas Palmer—no relation to the compromised prison guard Gene Palmer. He's a professor in the journalism school at the State University at Albany, and editorial design director for the *Albany Times-Union* newspaper. The professor was passing out fliers with the headline "Help Solve Mystery." They included a copy of a photo that had run on page 1 of the *New York Daily News* on June 29, the day after the escape drama ended. Palmer's flier went on to say, "The *New York Daily News* published this trail cam picture, claiming these were the fugitives on the run. Sources have verified they weren't. So who are they?"

As soon as he showed me the picture, I laughed my ass off. Of course, it was my neighbors, Eric and Charlie.

It turns out that the *Daily News* had claimed to have an "exclusive" picture showing the armed and dangerous Matt and Sweat on the loose. It was first published June 28 via Twitter by a reporter-editor named Tina Moore. Who leaked the photo to the paper, I have no idea. Unknown. But I do know that, even after the professor and others called the mistake to the editors' attention, the *Daily News* refused to retract it or issue a correction.

One other incorrect bit of media folly came after the real escapees—not some misidentified neighbors—were flushed out of the Twisted Horn camp. Many of us, including the camp's owner, John Stockwell, were surprised to see a report on NBC news, in which the reporter Stephanie Gosk was broadcasting from Twisted Horn. Now I'll grant that for the reporter and her camera operator to make their way up that rugged track, almost two miles of rocks and mud twisting off an unpaved public road, showed more enterprise than your typical TV crew. But enterprise is no excuse for trespassing, and Stephanie Gosk was no more welcome at Twisted Horn than Richard Matt and David Sweat had been. Not only that, Gosk's report made much of the fact that "Stumpy" Stockwell works for the Department of Corrections, darkly hinting that something was suspicious about prison escapees holing up in a prison guard's camp.

Had the reporter bothered to talk with anyone who actually knew something about the place—such as its owner—she would have learned that most of the camps in the northern Adirondacks belong to prison guards. That's just because prison guards make up such a sizeable chunk of this area's population.

For her trouble, Gosk earned a criminal citation for trespassing.

One other public folly didn't originate with the media, which distributed it nevertheless. It's unclear who got the bright idea to have the State Police make a video recording, with a miniature Go-Pro camera, reconstructing the escape from the inmates' point of view. It ended up in the custody of Clinton County D.A. Andrew Wylie, from whom the press obtained it. Just in case anybody in the state's prisons needed a step-by-step tutorial in how to burrow, hammer, and cut your way out of a maximum-security lock-up, making this re-enactment public did the trick.

CHAPTER 37
ESCAPE ROUTE

SO HOW HAD THE FUGITIVES MADE IT AS FAR AS TWISTED HORN?

Two weeks before, as dawn approached on June 6, Richard Matt and David Sweat reached a sign that told them they were just one mile from the unincorporated crossroads of Saranac—not to be confused with much bigger Saranac Lake, another thirty miles south. This was less than a mile from Pickett's Corners Road, where a roadblock would soon be set up. For now, though, nobody was looking for them, but the escapees knew that couldn't last much longer. To avoid being seen and not to get too deep into the mountains, they took the first opportunity to turn west.

Based on what Sweat would tell investigators, their new route was Clark Hill Road, which eventually dwindles into an ATV path as it rises into thick woods. They had been walking a good six hours, and the sun was well up. After a short distance on that trail, they took shelter in the woods after hearing an approaching helicopter.

The day had started off cool, and it turned rainy. Sweat's recollections of their first few days in the wilderness were vague, possibly because he had no map to orient himself. Besides some hunters' blinds and tree stands they found, one night they took refuge in an abandoned cabin. They had to improvise a patch for the floor and clean it enough to make a suitable shelter.

The fugitives' first full night was the coldest, with temperatures approaching the freezing point. But their second day, Sunday the seventh, dawned clear and stayed pleasant, with just a few
clouds interrupting the sun.

A due westward track would have taken the escapees across Lyon
Mountain's southern flank, at least six challenging cross-country
miles. They would have had to cross half a dozen streams, all of
them overflowing from the frequent rains. Walking into the wind,
they stayed between the nearest highways, Route 374 to the north
and State Route 3 to the south.

They didn't choose an easy route. To the contrary, they tried to
follow the path of most resistance, intentionally choosing terrain
where they thought they would be least likely to be pursued. This
is where the inmates' fascination with spices came into play. They
used the pepper that Joyce Mitchell had gotten for them to satu-
rate their clothing, boots and the ground whenever they changed
direction. The idea was to confuse the tracking dogs.

Did it work? Most likely not. The pepper trick has showed up
in the movies at least since Paul Newman tried it in *Cool Hand
Luke*. And State Police Superintendent Joseph D'Amico did say
the pepper might have thrown off his department's dogs. But re-
searchers, including the *Mythbusters* crew from cable TV, have
shown that bloodhounds and other trained tracking dogs can follow a human scent despite distracting odors. What gave the dogs
real trouble was the rain, which more than once washed away
promising scent trails.

On Sunday the fourteenth, while on the run somewhere in the
backwoods, Sweat celebrated his thirty-fifth birthday. But if he
made any special note of the day, he didn't say anything about it
when questioned later.

After several rainy days and chilly nights, the escapees emerged
from the woods on Standish Road, on Clinton County's far western
edge. The road is miles of tree-lined monotony, broken only by a
few tracks that lead to hunting camps. Matt and Sweat may have
used one of these to help them on their next cross-country leg, a
short hop of a mile or so to Wolf Pond Road. By now they were

thoroughly cold and damp—and suffering from insect bites. But their luck was soon to change for the better.

This eastern half of Wolf Pond Road is rough-going for vehicles—just a twisting single lane of loose rocks—but a much easier path for footsore hikers than the raw mountain slopes. It's narrow enough that the tree canopy will hide walkers from overhead aircraft. And here and there along the road are seasonal camps, hunters' tree stands, and other secluded structures, useful for shelter, as supply depots, or both.

The first burglary was at Camp Stillwater, sandwiched between Wolf Pond Road and the abandoned right of way of an old railroad. The dates are uncertain, but it probably was a week or more after the escape. They found an unlocked window, which let them slip in without causing any damage. The two stole only as much food, alcohol, and personal items as they hoped would go unnoticed.

But the alcohol would almost immediately start creating a new problem. Sweat didn't turn down a chance to drink liquor, and admitted that he got drunk during one of their hunting camp layovers. But Matt couldn't seem to stop drinking. "Every chance he gets," Sweat would complain, "he finds liquor and he keeps it and he keeps drinking; and we're trying to walk and go places." The drinking didn't help Matt's mood, either. When his compatriot was drinking heavily, Sweat said, "He's just becoming whatever he was before he got in jail. And it wasn't good."

The tension Matt's drinking created just got worse as the days went on. "He was getting out of control," Sweat recalled. "He would say, 'It's all we do, is just keep drinking.'"

But that would come later. For now, they kept going west along the Wolf Pond Road until they came upon The Doll House, another hunting camp. Sweat picked the lock to get them temporary shelter from the elements, small amounts of food and alcohol, and some needed gear. They didn't stay there long, but Sweat remembered that he liked the place, thought the owner must have been a pretty cool guy. He later mentioned seeing a photograph of a man with an owl on his shoulder. When they left The Doll

House, they left no footprints or other obvious signs they had been there.

At a third camp, the fugitives stumbled upon a marijuana patch. It was guarded by a game camera that the growers apparently used for surveillance. To be sure no record of their presence remained, Matt pulled the SD memory card from the camera. Not long afterward, a truck pulled into the camp and three people got out, an older man and a young couple. From a hiding place, Sweat said, he saw the older man checking the camera. He racked his shotgun and yelled that someone had stolen the memory card. The younger man jumped on an ATV and hurried up a trail, probably to the pot patch. He came back a little while later and reported, "No, they didn't touch anything. We're OK."

Sweat and Matt thought that was funny. They were confident that, even if the pot growers suspected who had tampered with their camera, they weren't about to file a police report.

So far, the escapees had not stayed in any of the camps they burglarized. For shelter from the persistent rains, they spent several days huddled in elevated tree stands erected by big game hunters. The second week they were on the run, it rained most days. And the days with little or no rain were usually colder.

As the days passed, Matt became morose and suicidal as he drank. "He's talking dumb shit about 'I'd rather die than go back to prison,'" Sweat remembered. "I'm like, 'Dude, what are you talking about? I'm not dying, and I'm not going back to prison. Just keep going.'"

Sweat was able to calm Matt down, but only for a little while. Soon the crazy talk would resume, about hijacking cars and taking hostages instead of following their original intention. But that plan was moot. Joyce Mitchell had ruined it.

The escape plan, known in detail only to Sweat and Matt, had been for Joyce Mitchell to pick them up in Dannemora and drive straight to West Virginia, seven or eight hours away. Using the camping gear Joyce had obtained for them, they would hide for a week or two in the mountains there. They assumed that things would cool down in that time, making it safer to move on. From

West Virginia, they would head south to Mexico, where Matt said he had connections.

That much is plausible; we know Matt had once rubbed elbows with drug cartel figures, and he had done hard time with plenty of Mexican felons. Of course, their fantasy that they'd be home free once across the border did contain one or two flaws. As they should have known from Matt's prompt arrest and quick conviction on his earlier visit to Mexico, foreign countries also have police, courts, and prisons. But Matt and Sweat may not have taken the trouble to think this through. It's a common failing among convicted criminals. Later on, Sweat would be guilty of the same self-delusion when it came to crossing a different border.

Once in Mexico, according to their plan, they would take on assumed names. Sweat would have become "James Tuttle." Matt would have gone by "Tony Goya." The two murderers didn't assign a new name to Joyce—if they actually intended for her to stay with them any farther than the first convenient patch of woods outside Dannemora.

At least one investigator was convinced that Joyce's usefulness to the escapees wouldn't have gone any further than supplying them with a getaway car. Interviewed by the *New York Post*, Clinton County Sheriff David Favro said she would have just slowed them down. "If she went with them, I believe she would have been killed," he said. "I mean, why keep her? It makes no sense."

But now, instead of riding comfortably in Joyce's Jeep—whether they intended to travel with or without their gullible accomplice, we may never know for sure—the two fugitives were hiking around the Adirondacks, trying to remain invisible, but continuing on a steady westward track.

Why did they decide to head west? Maybe it was because their original plan called for getting to Interstate 81, first leg in a leisurely motor trip to Mexico. Or maybe not. Sweat claimed later that, for the first part of their cross-country trek, he bucked Matt up with the idea of getting into the open farm country west of Malone, along U.S. Route 11. There, he assured his companion, they were sure to find some old car stashed away in some old barn, which they would be able to start right up and drive south. Whether this is true, and if so whether Matt bought it, we'll also never know. For that matter, we can't be certain whether Matt had his own more sinister plans. If he did, Sweat said nothing about it during his many hours of interrogations.

None of the official reports addresses this, exactly. But I have my idea. Could the escapees—or one of them, anyway—have been trying to get to the Mitchells' home? A pair of escaped murderers are probably not the people you would want to leave hanging by the side of a road. The price of not giving those two their expected ride might have been a house call—from people with a well-known urge for revenge. By the time Matt and Sweat got to Camp Twisted Horn, they had already covered half the distance to the Mitchell home in Dickinson Center. What's another twenty miles or so?

Richard Matt was known to have threatened dire consequences to anyone who crossed him. While in the midst of the horrific crime that brought him to New York's prison system, he issued a chilling threat to a fellow criminal. Lee E. Bates, who did a long prison stint for his role in the Rickerson kidnapping, robbery and murder, said Matt had no tolerance for betrayal. "You rat me out," Bates recalled Matt telling him, and "I'll kill you. I'll kill your entire family."

I have no reason to think that this vengeful attitude, which Matt displayed so frighteningly in 1997, had mellowed by the time Joyce Mitchell failed to turn up—and then started talking to police.

CHAPTER 38
THE CHASE IS ON

IF REVENGE REALLY WAS ON MATT'S MIND, even he had to be patient. Steady rain and cold had been brutal for him and Sweat, just like for the army of law officers beating the bushes for them. They had to take a break, and Twisted Horn provided the perfect spot. It might have been as early as Tuesday, the sixteenth, an especially rainy day, or as late as Thursday. Sweat's later recollections are hazy on that point.

Whenever it was, they found that Twisted Horn gave them a snug shelter, complete with propane heat, a cook stove, alcohol, and a radio. The detailed topographic map pinned to a wall let Sweat carefully study their surroundings, get the lay of the land, and plot out which way they would go next. He decided that he'd better not take the map, which would instantly be missed. The squatters also had a bag of marijuana, most likely taken from the pot-growers' camp up the road. So as they settled in to get drunk and high, cook themselves pasta and eat peanut butter and home-made jam, the radio let them catch up on the news. "A guy in the morning," Sweat recalled, "He'd do regular updates, every hour." That guy in the morning probably never had two such devoted listeners.

From the radio, they learned where searchers were concentrated—and what areas to avoid. The map, Sweat would brag, let him "estimate exactly where I was at all times." He later qualified that to say he could get "Pretty close. Close enough to know how far I was from the searchers."

Radio reports also told them that citizens had sighted them in Clinton and Essex counties, far behind or entirely off their track. That was worth a laugh, Sweat said later, and gave them a sense of relief. The searchers were all apparently off on wild-goose chases. They were also amused by clues that told them they were hiding in a prison guard's camp. Even so, both felt comfortable enough to rest, relax, warm up, and dry out for two or three days. But then came another piece of news, more worrisome. The radio told them Joyce Mitchell had been arrested. "It was a shock," Sweat would admit. And it made up his mind that they should get on the move again.

Matt resisted the idea. The last few nights had been wet out, with temperatures down in the 40s, and the cabin was toasty warm. He was comfortable and enjoying the break from foot travel. Early on June 20, with the morning sun visible through the trees, Sweat again urged his companion to pack up and get ready to leave. It was a Saturday, he pointed out, the first nice weekend since they'd broken out. Very likely somebody would be coming today to check on their cozy hideout.

Sweat was proved right when they heard the ATV approaching. They had no idea its operator was Stumpy Stockwell, an armed off-duty corrections officer. But this did provoke a heated argument. Matt wanted to kidnap or kill whoever was on the ATV. They should "take him," Matt argued.

And how would they do that, Sweat wanted to know, when they had no ammunition for the 20-gauge shotgun they'd found?

When they saw Stockwell dismount from his ATV and draw his handgun, the argument ended. They snatched up their backpacks with whatever was in them and ran out the back door. Sweat was wearing a pair of boots he'd found; he left his old pair behind. And while cargo spilled willy-nilly from Matt's carelessly packed bag, Sweat was carrying something he hadn't originally intended to take: the topographic map.

As they crashed through the leaves and underbrush, the two

fugitives heard an engine revving behind them. Before they could be sure that Stumpy's four-wheeler was retreating back down the mountain and not pursuing them, Sweat was already well ahead of overweight, out-of-shape Matt. "By the time we got down the hill," he told investigators, "I was quite a ways in front of him, running up the creek already." As the noise behind them faded, Matt struggled to follow Sweat, splashing through the rain-swollen Barnes Brook and back into the wilderness.

The escapees continued west, making the effort to climb "this massive mountain," as Sweat called it, to look for signs of pursuit. From the top, he remembered, they could see the sign welcoming visitors to Mountain View. "We ended up right on top, looking right over the lake; absolutely beautiful, too," he recalled. "Completely glad that I got to see that, because it was quite a picture."

His companion wasn't sharing in these esthetic pleasures. At this stage, Matt was drunk all the time and seriously slowing their pace. Sweat was starting to think of alternatives: a different destination and maybe different destinies.

What neither one could see, just hours after being flushed from their hiding place, was the massive influx of searchers who were already on their way to Mountain View, ready to throw out new perimeter lines, inexorably tightening the noose.

But in the meantime, as Major Guess was rallying his forces, his targets kept moving. They didn't find any shelter from the thunderstorms that drenched the Mountain View area Sunday night, June 21. When they emerged from the mountains again, the Goldsmith and Plumadore ranges were behind them and a two-lane blacktop, County Route 27, was ahead. They crossed cautiously, waded across Duane Stream and negotiated another mile and a half of insect-filled woods before coming to Ayers Road and Charlie Champagne's Camp.

Again being careful not to leave any visible signs of their illegal entry, Sweat picked the lock; he and Matt searched it for anything useful. As at the other cabins they had plundered, they found food, liquor, and gear that filled several important gaps in their equipment inventory.

That included a rain jacket, a compass, a flask and 20-gauge solid-slug-load shotgun shells. Now the weapon they'd found at Twisted Horn would have a lethal kick.

Matt immediately found his way to a bottle of what Sweat remembered as Jack Daniel's whiskey. While he stood at the sink pouring the liquor from its bottle into the flask, Sweat later said, Matt again started talking "dumb shit" about his death wish.

Matt returned to that theme as they left the Champagne camp and resumed their cross-country hike. Within a few miles, this dialogue was starting to wear thin. As was Sweat's patience with his companion's sluggish pace and drunkenness. But for now the going was easier. Ayers Road merges into Studley Hill Road, a mostly dirt byway that they followed north. It was as if they still planned to reach Highway 11 and find that mystical car in some mystical barn. When they had roads to follow, they mostly walked at night, hiding out in woods during the day and sleeping an hour or two at a time. That was yet another irritant in the two convicts' unraveling bromance. Sweat complained that Matt "wanted to sleep for half of the day" instead of keep moving.

During those days, Mother Nature was harsh for both the fugitives and the searchers. Heavy rains kept washing away scents, letting the escapees get a jump on police tracking dogs. Extreme weather grounded search aircraft. Flooded streams posed another hazard for law officers, who sometimes had to wade chest-deep through bone-chilling water.

Franklin County's mountains and foothills threw up yet another obstacle: they blocked radio communication. Cell phone towers are scarce, as Stumpy Stockwell knew only too well when he flushed the fugitives out of his cabin. And police radios, which rely on line-of-sight transmissions, often proved useless in the deep valleys. To restore modern communication capabilities, the state called for help from the feds. High-tech relay units with telescoping radio towers were eventually dispatched to pick up signals from hand-held and car-mounted radios. These would be amplified and passed on to command centers. At least one airborne radio link was deployed, too.

For the rest of this third week of the search, national media continued to chase the story, reporting on the frenzy of activity in Franklin County and on the arrests of prison employees back in Dannemora. By this time, the number of leads had reached about 2,200. Almost all of them were false.

When one legitimate lead did turn up, it had already become stale. Because the Champagne Camp was used only sporadically, and mostly in hunting season, its owner Charlie Champagne didn't discover the burglary there until days later. Even then, he almost overlooked the evidence that somebody had been there. Charlie works at Upstate Correctional Facility, one of the three prisons right outside Malone. Checking the camp, he peeked into the storage compartment of his ATV and found a couple of wrappers from Nature Valley granola bars, something he never kept in his camp. His first thought was that one of his buddies on a CERT team was playing a prank on him. But then, despite seeing no sign of breaking and entering, he started to notice some things were missing from his cabin. Most alarming, a box of solid-slug loads for a 20-gauge shotgun was gone.

CHAPTER 39
THE BROMANCE ENDS

WITHIN A DAY AFTER STEALING SUPPLIES from Charlie Champagne's hunting camp, Matt and Sweat had covered six miles on secluded Studley Hill Road. That got them to another east-west route, Fayette Road. Also known as County Route 41, this let them resume their westward course.

By this point, Sweat was starting to wonder if he'd be better off without Matt. But as they turned west again, he proposed a change of plans. With every day that passed, Mexico was seeming more like an impossible dream. But he'd studied his map, and he knew they were tantalizingly close to another border. "We can't go the way we want, we'll go up to Canada; we can stay in Canada for a year or two." Sweat, with his methodical planner's habits, had worked out a new scheme, in detail. He had the notion of finding someone north of the border who would give him food for work. "I figured I'd get up around people, like country folk, and, 'Hey, listen, I'm down and out, I need a place to live . . . I'm a hard worker. I learn fast. I just need a warm place to sleep and a little bit of food.'"

He assured Matt that they could lie low in Canada and get new identities. Then, after enough time had passed, he told him, "Change our ID and take our ass down to Mexico."

Privately, though, Sweat was fuming. "He was slowing me down so bad it wasn't funny," he would tell investigators. "I knew if I stayed with him, I knew I would get caught. Because, you know, I'd walk ten, fifteen feet and have to stop and wait a second for him to catch up. He's kind of lumbering on; he keeps drinking, just talking dumb shit. About getting a car, and how I should just hijack a car." Sweat said he retorted, " 'What is wrong with you? You can't do that.' "

As the day progressed, they reached a "T" intersection. Branching off to the north was Webster Street Road, which led toward Malone, U.S. 11, and Canada.

This would be a decision point. Go straight, continuing their westward track, with many miles of wilderness ahead of them, or veer to the right and head north and closer to civilization. For now, anyway, they would stay on County Route 41. Another mile down that road, and off in the woods, is a hunting camp owned by the Whitacre family. Once again, Matt and Sweat burglarized the cabin.

Clues found there make me believe this is where they sawed off the stock from the 20-gauge shotgun and wrapped its cut end with black electrical tape. A roll of that tape would later be found in Sweat's backpack. Matt, however, would keep the gun.

After this break-in, the two backtracked, returning to the Webster Street Road intersection. Whether they were in full agreement on their plan at this point isn't clear. But soon a decision would be forced on them.

Hiding in woods along the Webster Street Road, they spotted a white SUV with a police light bar on top. Sweat thought it was a deputy sheriff's vehicle. The police car stopped suddenly and its occupants got out. To Sweat, it looked like they were examining tracks in the unpaved road. Seeing this might have spooked Matt, who stumbled backward and made some noise. Sweat concluded that the officers had heard this, knew where they were hiding, and were trying to circle around them.

He took off running, leaving Matt behind. He never looked back.

"So I ended up leaving there and started heading north. Myself," Sweat told his interrogators. Though the passing encounter with the police SUV was the trigger, he had already been preparing to split from Matt. "I'd been thinking about it for a couple days," he said, "because he was getting really bad; because they were searching so intense."

It was about to get even more intense.

From what Sweat later said, we know he had a rational plan. Delusional, maybe; a fantasy of freedom that had almost no chance of succeeding. But even "one in a million" means there is some slim chance. But Sweat seems never to have considered that even if he reached his goal, the Canadian border, he wouldn't be home free. From the day he poked his head out of the manhole at Bouck and Barker streets, authorities in Canada had been on the alert, intensively patrolling their jurisdiction, just as their U.S. colleagues were. Quebec's provincial police force, the Sûreté du Québec, works closely with the Royal Canadian Mounted Police to cover the rural territory north of the border. Solid history justifies that old slogan: "The Mounties always get their man."

But before he'd have to worry about dodging the Mounties, Sweat would have to get to the border. For that far, anyway, he did have a plan.

About what Matt was thinking after his partner ditched him, we can't know. But looking back at his movements and his actions after the two split we can draw a couple of conclusions.

One is that, as his ex-partner said many times, he was "talking crazy shit" about dying. A twisted interpretation, maybe, of the motto on one of his many tattoos: "Death before dishonor." The second conclusion, based on Matt's criminal history, is that he was likely planning revenge on Joyce Mitchell, the ultimate punishment for her betraying him.

Maybe we can add a third conclusion. It's that at some point, alone, drunk, exhausted, and with no plausible way out, Richard Matt had decided to die, but not without taking as many other people with him as he could.

Late in the afternoon of Wednesday, June 24, Robert Whitacre went to check on his family's camp, in deep woods about a mile south of Fayette Road. He noticed one of the cabin's windows had been damaged. A screen was cut and the window frame bent. This was the first discovery of a brute-force break-in, very different from the lock-picking finesse in the earlier burglaries. Inside Whitacre saw a chair, out of its usual place, under the damaged window. The window shade was lying on a bed. Whitacre also found a pillow case, dirty Corcraft underwear, a blue sweatshirt, and a gold colored T-shirt: size triple-XL, bloodstained. A further search showed that a tool had been moved from its proper spot; it turned up in the camp's outhouse.

That tool would prove to be a calling card for one of the burglars. It was a hacksaw.

Whitacre reported the break-in to the State Police. Officers processing the crime scene sent the shit-stained drawers and blood-stained shirt to the state lab, which found Matt's DNA. Sweat's DNA would also be found at the scene. This latest hard evidence shifted the search area another few miles west.

While State Police were documenting the latest crime scene in Franklin County, Corrections Officer Gene Palmer was arrested in neighboring Clinton County. He was willing to cooperate.

For the previous week, Palmer had been on administrative leave from his job at Clinton Correctional Facility. One of his first acts after learning he was under suspicion had been to get rid of some incriminating artwork. He took the paintings he'd bartered from Matt and Sweat and tried to hide them by burying them in the woods near his house. He didn't hide them very well; police quickly found them.

After hours of interrogation, investigators concluded that Palmer had not known anything about the escape. He was never accused of helping Matt and Sweat to break out.

What he was charged with was official misconduct, tampering with evidence, and promoting prison contraband. All those charges stemmed from Palmer's interactions with Sweat and Matt—and their artwork.

Before those of us living in Franklin County learned about these developments, we got warnings that something was up, much closer to us than before. Like all other residents in the area around Malone, we heard our phone ring that Wednesday evening, June 24. It was a police robo-call. The automated message notified us that we should "expect a strong police presence." We were instructed to "shelter in place" and report any unusual activity. It was that now all-too-familiar slogan: If you see something, say something.

By this time, hundreds of CERT officers had been redeployed across a broad swath of Franklin County, stretching from Mountain View to Malone. These corrections officers were clearly visible as they established line formations along roadsides, preparing to search private properties. Their tactics were simple but relentless. A line of CERT officers would walk abreast off the roadside and across lawns and fields, into tangled underbrush, finally vanishing into thick timber.

Tense, on high alert, these specially trained prison guards were keeping their eyes and ears open for anything that didn't belong in our peaceful countryside. But the first who would spot something significantly out of the ordinary would be several of their off-the-clock colleagues.

PART VII
THE RECKONING

CHAPTER 40
GIN AND POTSHOTS
AT HUMBUG MOUNTAIN

WHEN THAT LATEST AUTOMATED CALL WOKE US UP on Friday, June 26, we didn't know the drama would soon be approaching its climax. One of our Franklin County neighbors who got that call was Bob Willett Jr., thirty-two years old, a corrections officer. He and some of his friends, also off-duty prison employees, started noticing things that just weren't right.

Every day, during his off-the-clock hours, he had been checking his family's hunting camp. Named for a nearby mountain, Camp Humbug is just off State Route 30, south of Malone, not far from Willett's home. Like all of us, he'd been following the reports of the shifting search, and knew the escapees had to be somewhere close.

It was around noon on Friday that Bob Junior knew something was wrong. Opening the door of Camp Humbug, he noticed a sickly-sweet alcohol smell filling the air. He immediately spotted an opened bottle of Seagram's grape-flavored gin on the counter. The bottle was half empty and the clear liquid had been spilled on the counter. Lying in the puddle of gin was a Northern Tool and Equipment catalog. He knew this mess hadn't been there when he checked the camp the day before.

He took a quick look around and didn't see anything else out of place. Satisfied that his camp was safe, Bob drove out to The

Blarney Stone, a roadside convenience store on Route 30, pondering what he'd just seen.

He used his cell phone to call his father, describing what he'd found inside their camp. After a few minutes discussion, Bob Senior decided this was serious enough to come see for himself. His car-repair shop is just a few miles up Route 30, so it didn't take him long to reach the camp.

Meanwhile, his son had called another member of Camp Humbug, Paul Marlow, a forty-eight-year-old nurse with the Department of Corrections. After hearing what young Bob had seen, Marlow strapped on his pistol and drove to the camp, too. He got there first, sending Bob Junior a text message before he got out of his truck. With his pistol drawn, Paul walked the camp's perimeter, scanning the woods and then looking into each of the cabin's windows as he passed. He waited for Bob Junior to arrive before entering. They found no one inside, but neither could miss the smell of grape gin.

Within minutes, Bob Senior arrived, shotgun in hand. All three did a more thorough search. They found the cap from the gin bottle under a frying pan on the counter. Bob Senior noticed that a bottle of much better liquor—Tanqueray gin—was out of place and a box of toothpicks had been spilled. Nothing appeared to be missing. Paul snapped a picture of the open grape gin bottle and the mess on the countertop.

"That grape gin bottle had been in the camp for years," Paul explained. "Somebody brought it two or three years ago but no one liked it, and no one drank it."

Until today. Obviously, somebody with a powerful thirst for liquor had not been so particular as the hunting camp's members, but even he couldn't manage to finish the stuff. Bob Junior thought to check the liquor cabinet, where he noticed something else peculiar. Two bottles of rum—Captain Morgan and Admiral Nelson brands—had been drained, and the empties put back in the cabinet.

Bob Senior had to get back to his garage, but told his son he ought to call the police tip line. When Bob Junior reported what he'd discovered, the dispatcher asked him to have someone wait by the road so police could find the place. Like so many of these cabins, Camp Humbug is remote enough that it doesn't have an address in Franklin County's 911 database.

Leaving Bob Junior at the camp, Paul Marlow drove out to Route 30 to meet the police. Waiting along the highway, he got a cell phone signal and decided to call his neighbor Jason Pelkey, a State Police investigator. Like most police in this part of the state, Pelkey was working the fugitive detail, assigned to the Tactical Operations Center in Clinton County. Paul texted him his picture of the uncapped Seagram's gin bottle.

Pelkey reported the Camp Humbug burglary to his command post. Officers there relayed a message back to Paul, confirming that he should wait by the roadside to direct troopers to the camp's unmarked driveway. Sitting in the driver's seat on the shoulder of Route 30, just yards from the tree line, he kept an eye out for arriving police. His vantage point also gave him a clear view of passing locals and tourists.

Suddenly he was startled by a gunshot. He knew it was close by, maybe just a few hundred yards away. Close. Too close. Paul put his truck in reverse, backed up and turned into Camp Humbug's driveway. He called Bob Junior at the camp, asking if he had heard the shot. Yes, his friend confirmed. He had heard it, too.

Paul started to call 911, but changed his mind and hung up. First, he wanted to call his neighbor Jason Pelkey, the State Police investigator, to see what he thought about the gunshot. But before he could complete that call, his phone rang. It was 911, calling him back. He reported hearing the gunshot and asked the dispatcher to patch him through to Pelkey. The 911 dispatcher was unable to make the connection. Paul hung up and tried another tactic. He punched the words "GUN SHOT" into his phone's keyboard and sent it as a text message. The time was 1:11 P.M.

Just a few minutes had passed since Paul Marlow had first told his neighbor Jason Pelkey about the burglary at the camp. And now he was texting him about a gunshot.

One minute later Pelkey texted, "Call me now."

Paul called Pelkey, who asked him to get a nearby 911 address to help police respond quickly. Drive to the nearest house, the investigator instructed him, and call back with the precise address. Paul drove the short distance to what turned out to be his friend Marvin Raville's house, and phoned in the address visible on the mailbox. What he didn't know was that on his short drive, he had passed an armed man lurking in the woods. That armed man was Richard Matt.

As Paul turned his truck around, he saw a State Police troop car pulling off the highway. Two plainclothes investigators stepped out, both wearing bulletproof vests over their dress shirts and ties, and both carrying semiautomatic M-4 tactical rifles. Paul told the investigators about the camp burglary and the shot he'd heard.

While they were talking, all three heard another gunshot. They also saw a caravan of three trucks heading toward them, two of them pulling campers and the third towing a boat trailer. For some reason, all three trucks then pulled off the road and stopped. Two of the drivers stepped out onto the shoulder.

The little caravan of vehicles was carrying the Brown and Gokey families, local folks from the Moira area west of Malone. They were headed to Meacham Lake Campground, another ten miles south on Route 30. Brett Gokey was in the lead, driving his Super Duty Ford F-250 pickup with his wife Dottie in the seat beside him. Next in the procession was Tim Brown, a forty-nine-year-old prison guard at the Bare Hill Correctional Facility, taking a day off. In his Dodge pickup with Brown were his daughter Amber and granddaughter Ainsley. Both trucks were towing campers. In the third truck, towing the boat, were Brett's seventeen-year-old son Neil Gokey and Neil's girlfriend Cheyenne Burdo.

It was Tim Brown who first pulled off the road. He had heard a loud noise. The others stopped with him, one in front and one behind. Brown thought his Gulf Stream camper had blown a tire, and he walked back to take a look. But the tires were all fine. No sooner had the three trucks pulled back onto the highway, though, the State Police investigators stopped them. Brown told the troopers he had been checking for a bad tire, but that everything was fine. They waved him on.

It was only after the group had gotten to Lake Meacham, that Brown discovered things weren't so fine after all. At the camp-site, Brown parked the trailer and pulled out a garden hose to fill its water tank. That's when he discovered a hole in the Gulf Steam camper. Two holes, in fact, which he immediately recognized as bullet holes. Something had pierced the camper's wall on the driver's side, at exactly the height his head had been as he drove the truck. The projectile had punctured the camper's opposite wall as it exited. He knew he had to report this to the State Police. But once again, he couldn't get a cell-phone signal anywhere in the Meacham Lake campground. Without disconnecting the camper, he drove back to the main gate. He used the ranger station's land line to call 911. The dispatcher said he would send someone to talk to him.

Meanwhile, soon after the caravan drove off, Paul Marlow and the two State Police investigators were still waiting along Route 30. A third gunshot rang out. It sounded like it had come from the northeast. All three headed toward Camp Humbug; Bob Willett Jr. met Paul at the end of the camp's driveway. The investigators were having trouble pinpointing where the gunshot had come from. The uneven terrain created echoes. By this time, police had thoroughly searched Camp Humbug and determined that the shots had not come from there or other hunting camps nearby. They wouldn't have long to wait, though, before they got additional evidence.

Within minutes, a fourth and fifth shot pealed through the air.

The search perimeter instantly narrowed to a matter of just a few hundred yards.

At Meacham Lake, twenty minutes had passed since Tim Brown's 911 call. No police had arrived, so he and Brett Gokey decided to drive back to where they had heard the noise. There they found a trooper and explained what they had heard on the road and about finding the bullet holes. They were directed to return to the campsite and assured that someone would be sent to interview them.

By this time, police from many different agencies were flooding the area. They closed Route 30 to all traffic. Minutes later, two A-Star helicopters would land on the pavement carrying heavily armed federal officers. Five men, wearing camouflage fatigues and bristling with high-tech combat gear, leaped out and hustled into the woods, primed for a deadly confrontation.

CHAPTER 41
CLOSING THE BOX

As the echoes of the latest shots were fading into the trees, troopers by the dozens were deploying along Route 30 and the Camp Humbug driveway. One team, armed with state-issued patrol rifles, went to secure the crime scene and establish a perimeter at Camp Humbug. Others extended that perimeter to the south along the highway.

Among the troopers arriving were three from State Police Troop B, local men, including a captain and a sergeant. They were assigned to a stretch of road about a hundred yards south of Camp Humbug's driveway. Directly in front of them was a break in the trees: a grassy path, just wide enough for one car, rising from the road and into the woods. They drove their troop car about sixty feet into this narrow passage. Getting out, they noticed a small metal storage shed, a rusty little camper trailer—and a strange odor in the air.

Three more uniformed troopers quickly joined them. They had walked in from the road. Armed with patrol rifles, the six troopers opened the shed and found nobody there. As they moved closer to the camper, the odor got stronger. Coming from the little trailer's doorway was a thin stream of smoke. "State Troopers" they shouted. No response. "Exit the camper," they commanded. Still no answer. Several times, they shouted, "Exit the camper." Hearing nothing, the troopers pressed forward to clear the camper but found it empty.

Except for a burning stick of incense and a two-liter Pepsi bottle, one-third full of a clear liquid. They had discovered the source of the odor. Closer observation revealed a black T-shirt outside the camper's door and a small knife under its step.

Troopers also found what looked like two different sets of tracks heading in two different directions. Both sets of tracks led to a ridge just yards away from the camper. On the far side, the ground dropped about forty feet into a swamp. From the top of the ridge, the troopers following the first set of tracks spotted a pair of boots placed against a tree about halfway down the slope. The second set of tracks led troopers to an empty whiskey bottle, also visible from the ridge.

As troopers were satisfying themselves that the immediate area was clear, reinforcements arrived. This was a federal Border Patrol Tactical Unit, known as "BORTAC," from the sector headquartered in Swanton, Vermont. BORTAC teams are the elite among the forces protecting the nation's borders. Their specialized training includes rapid-response tactics and advanced weapon skills. BORTAC's basic training course is considered one of the most difficult in civilian law enforcement. It mirrors aspects of the selection courses used by the military's Special Operations Forces.

Working with the Swanton BORTAC team was a Hostage Rescue Team of FBI agents. This unit functions as the FBI's SWAT team, called in for the most dangerous missions. Its members are detailed to capture armed subjects who have barricaded themselves. They make high-risk arrests and coordinate manhunts, especially in rural areas. Soon after these two federal agencies reached the scene, a third was on its way by air. These were the men who arrived by helicopter from the command post at the Cadyville School on the far side of Dannemora, a twenty-minute flight.

The airborne reinforcements were the National BORTAC Team, an elite squad normally based along the Mexican border. It was commanded by Team Leader Christopher Voss. Leaping out of their copters onto the pavement of Route 30, the five-man National BORTAC Team hurried up the driveway to Camp Humbug. Their search of the woods behind the camp turned up nothing. Passing more troopers moving in to set up the perimeter on the camp driveway, the BORTAC Team returned to the highway.

By now, the state troopers had established a two-legged line, shaped like an upside-down "L" along Route 30 and the camp drive. The federal officers had turned up a few clues, but no fugitives. It was beginning to seem like yet another promising lead had gone up in smoke.

Jason Lewis is a state trooper who's normally assigned to patrol Interstate 86 around Corning and Elmira. Today, though, he was more than two hundred miles from home, deployed along the shoulder of State Route 30. "I ended up near a swamp," he said. "I heard a little bit of movement," and listened more carefully. His partner, Trooper Jeff Grebleski, asked him to bring their patrol car closer to where they were standing. "When I returned, he told me he heard someone crashing through the woods." Lewis heard it, too. "For about ten seconds, I heard rustling and then it became obvious that branches were breaking and someone was walking through." A moment later, "I heard a cough that was obviously, clearly human. There was no doubt someone was in there." Grebleski used hand gestures to signal that he'd heard it, too. Lewis drew his pistol and pointed it toward the tree line. His partner did, too. Others up and down the line noticed, and aimed their patrol rifles and sidearms toward the trees. In a matter of seconds, dozens of troopers were on high alert, guns out and ready.

Police radios came to life with a warning that somebody might be just inside the woods. Christopher Voss directed his National BORTAC Team to push back toward this area. Again, troopers along the highway heard signs of movement and another cough from the woods. Just then, one of the state's A-Star helicopters flew directly overhead. The rotor and engine noise drowned out the faint sounds from the woods; the troopers lost their bearings toward the movements they'd just heard.

Major Guess, the State Police commander, had experience with aviation and knew its value. But he also knew when aircraft were a hindrance, and this was one of those times. He promptly got on the radio and ordered all aviation units out of the area. As the copters' rotor noise faded, troopers once again heard movement in the woods. State Police were ordered to hold their lines, but not to enter the woods. That was the job for the feds; the BORTAC and FBI Hostage Rescue teams pushed off from the Camp Humbug driveway, moving southeast into the trees. This track would clear a swath through the woods, adding a third line to the two rows of state troopers. If anyone was in the woods, they would either find them or box them in from the east, just as the State Police had already done to the north and west.

The National BORTAC Team, HRT and Swanton BORTAC Team worked parallel to each other. This type of formation allowed any of the teams to flank anyone who might engage one of the others. They found it tough going through extremely dense underbrush. Holding a consistent formation while navigating the overgrown, hilly terrain proved difficult. The three parallel teams forged their way up steep hillsides and down into chest-deep swamps. On some hillsides, the federal officers had to pull themselves up by trees, roots, and rocks. Keeping in formation became impossible. Team members would later report visibility ranging from fifteen yards to as little as three to five feet. Eventually they reached the swamp that bordered the search area to the south. The wetlands thinned out, becoming an open marsh, which nobody could cross without being seen. It was time to narrow the box.

CHAPTER 42
MATT'S FINAL STAND

AT THE SWAMP'S EDGE, THE FEDS REDEPLOYED. They turned to face west and resumed their sweep through the woods, this time toward the highway. After resuming their struggle through the dense underbrush, the National BORTAC Team came to a steep ridge. Climbing this rise, they struggled to maintain a "V" formation, with Agent Eric Cavazos "on point." Close to the top, Cavazos dropped to one knee and assumed a defensive position, leveling his rifle. He whispered, just loud enough for the agents on either side to hear: "I got one."

Voss, the team leader, was just to Cavazos' right. He stopped. Speaking softly, he asked, "What do you have?"

"Friendlies?" Cavazos called out, to be certain he hadn't encountered other law officers. He got no response. His training and experience told him he was facing a likely threat. "Let me see your hands. Let me see your hands," he commanded. Still no response. He hollered again, louder: "Let me see your hands; let me see your hands." Nothing. By this time, all five members of the team had taken defensive positions, their weapons leveled in front of them, scanning left and right, searching for the threat.

Voss had quietly moved ahead to flank whoever was in front of Cavazos. "As I rounded to my left," he said, "I saw a log on the ground in front of Eric. There was a man lying prone against it." All he could see was a head, with eyes, nose, and mouth visible.

Voss took aim with his M-4 semi-automatic rifle—a law enforcement variant of the U.S. military's standard infantry carbine, designed to fire only one bullet for each squeeze of the trigger. With the gun's high-tech LED and laser sights on his target, Voss shouted a forceful echo of Cavazos' words:

"Let me see your fucking hands! Let me see your fucking hands!"

It's not quite accurate to say he got no response. But the response he got wasn't spoken, or the show of hands he'd demanded. Instead, Voss saw something moving. It was the barrel of a long gun, swinging in his direction, now pointed directly at him.

Before joining the Border Patrol, Christopher Voss had been an Army Ranger. His training in the elite Rangers had included hostage rescue. During the 2003 invasion of Iraq, he had been part of the rescue of Army Private Jessica Lynch, that war's most celebrated P.O.W., who had been captured by the Iraqi army. Voss had also taken what he described as "high-value target training, which included differentiating between 'shoot' and 'no-shoot' situations."

In Afghanistan and Iraq, Voss explained, "High-value targets needed to be taken alive for intelligence purposes." He and his Ranger comrades "could not engage them unless they had a weapon system pointed directly at us."

Now, in these New York State woods, a decade later and half a world away from those hot, dusty combat zones, Christopher Voss had to make a split-second decision. Was he facing a "high-value target" who should be taken alive and interrogated? Probably. But was he in immediate danger to his own life? Definitely. He was looking right up the barrel of a gun aimed squarely at him.

Witnesses later reported hearing "multiple" gunshots. They came so quickly nobody was able to say for sure how many, just that they were in two distinct clusters. Then silence.

Out on the road, Trooper Lewis heard someone say, "He's down, he's down," and "Get law enforcement down here for a perimeter." State Police supervisors radioed in an urgent "Shots fired" report, then ordered radio silence.

When Voss fired, he was about fifteen yards from his target. His judgment, after years of training and combat experience, was that this was a "shoot" situation. He was certain the man behind the log meant to kill him with the gun. But now, with only eight of his thirty-round clip's shells gone, the threat to himself and his other team members had been neutralized. Voss ordered Cavazos, "Move up." When the point man did so, he discovered he'd been less than ten yards down-range.

The dead man's head was a bloody mess. An autopsy would later confirm that two bullets had hit him there, plus another in the shoulder.

Voss removed a sawed-off 20-gauge shotgun from the man's hands. Its stock had been sawed off and the stump wrapped in electrical tape. "I thought he could be dead," Voss said, "but I needed to make sure he wouldn't be able to fire the weapon." Taking no chances, Voss pulled it away, about two feet out of reach. Broken sunglasses, a camouflaged backpack and a green flask were scattered around the body. Cavazos rolled the corpse to one side and checked for other weapons. Nothing.

To avoid contaminating the crime scene with fingerprints or DNA, one of the BORTAC team used a stick to pull up the dead man's jacket and shirt. He was covered in tattoos from stem to stern. As ultimately documented in the morgue, they included a cartoon character with the words "Death Before Dishonor." The only one the BORTAC team was interested in, though, said "Mexico Forever" on his back. This was what they needed to confirm that Christopher Voss had, in fact, killed Richard Matt. One day after his forty-ninth birthday, Matt was confirmed dead. It was 3:50 P.M.

From the death scene just off State Route 30, it was just a dozen miles cross-country to Joyce and Lyle Mitchell's front door. If, as I suspect, Matt had been on his way there, he had chosen the most efficient route. His detour south on Route 30 was the best way to reach the only road that could get him to Dickinson Center. The alternative would have been another cross-country slog, through ten miles or more of forest, lakes, and hills. But it's also likely that Matt had finally given up any hopes of either a clean get-away or of revenge on Joyce Mitchell. Otherwise, why take pot-shots at highway traffic? Maybe he was trying to hijack a vehicle. But why choose one traveling in a group? Other than to kill strangers out of sheer meanness—which was totally in character for Matt—he had to know this would tell the searchers exactly where to find him. As it did.

Finding Matt, of course, had accomplished only half of the searchers' mission.

As soon as he'd identified Matt, Voss and his men turned their focus to finding David Sweat. He ordered the National BORTAC Team to form a perimeter around Matt's body, weapons aimed outward. Within seconds, they formed a circle, took a knee, leveled their rifles, and scanned the woods for threats.

Voss's next act was a transmission through his helmet-mounted microphone. "Shots fired, one down hard." Hard meaning "dead." State Police commanders ordered the troopers on the Route 30 line to "push." Side by side, they moved into the woods, hoping to flush out the other escapee, while BORTAC held its own small defensive perimeter.

Everyone was on high alert, knowing they were on the hunt for a man who had already murdered one police officer. The last information police had was that the escapees were together. The state troopers and feds were acutely aware that Sweat might be nearby. And if nearby, he could seriously injure or kill any of them as they tried to flush him out of the brush.

CHAPTER 43
PRESS CONFERENCE, THE LAW, AND THE LOCALS

ONCE CERTAIN ANY IMMEDIATE DANGER WAS OVER, the BORTAC team turned the shooting scene over to State Police. Investigators secured the scene, logged the time—3:50 P.M., Friday, June 26—and began collecting evidence. They found eight shell casings about twenty-four feet from Matt's body, confirming that Voss had fired fewer than a third of the bullets in his M-4's clip.

Meanwhile, State Police officials in Albany were notified that Richard Matt had been killed. Within an hour, State Police Superintendent Joseph D'Amico was on a small jet with Governor Andrew Cuomo and his staffers flying to Malone.

Governor Cuomo had been briefed on the day's events as they unfolded. He had been informed of where Matt had been cornered and killed, and the fact that he had challenged law enforcement with a weapon. The governor was advised that a massive force of state, local, and federal officers had been deployed in an intensifying hunt for David Sweat. While the governor and his entourage were en route, Cuomo's staffers announced that he would hold a press conference later that evening upon arriving in Malone.

As the long mid-summer day wore on, Route 30 remained closed and barricaded. National and local news media broadcast from just outside the roadblocks. The evening news reports said Richard Matt had been killed but that David Sweat was still on the run.

Those two essential facts had promised a splendid media opportunity for the governor—and then ruined it. As he boarded his jet in Albany, Cuomo had every reason to think that by the time he landed, he could announce to a waiting world—and to New York State's voters—that both escapees had been captured, dead or alive. The intended message was to have been a satisfactory end to the state's long ordeal.

When he stepped off the jet at Malone's modest airport, though, not a single reporter was there to greet him. In fact, the runway apron was entirely vacant, except for one retired prison guard carrying a camera. It was me. As of this writing, the governor's office has still not asked me for any of my pictures. I guess they wouldn't look as flattering as the ones they'd posted on Flickr.com from three weeks earlier.

Just up U.S. Route 11 from Malone's airport is State Police Troop B Barracks. It's the same police outpost that Joyce Mitchell had stared at, then ignored, the night before her prison buddies' escape. Now, twenty days later, it was the spot Cuomo's aides had chosen for the governor's press conference. The news media scrambled to relocate their reporters from the shooting scene on Route 30. As strobe lights flashed, the governor addressed the killing of the escaped murderer he referred to as "Mr. Matt" just outside Malone. And he updated the public on the continuing pursuit of the cop killer David Sweat. "Mr. Sweat," in the governor's words.

Meanwhile, out on Route 30, as daylight slipped away, the search for Sweat went on. By now certain he had not been with Matt, the police again expanded their perimeter. It now ran along State Route 30; County Route 26, the Port Kent-Hopkinton Turnpike; County Route 41, the Fayette Road; and the Studley Hill Road. Inside those lines were close to twenty square miles of steep wooded emptiness, cut up by swollen streams and dotted with wetlands.

Again, over and over, police were deployed into thick timber, dense underbrush and deep swamps. Tracking dogs, Swanton BORTAC, National BORTAC, and FBI Hostage Rescue Team members spent endless hours searching the wet, rugged terrain.

Meanwhile, hundreds of federal, state, county, and local law officers joined to form a solid perimeter. But by day's end, when full darkness had fallen, David Sweat had not been found.

When Governor Cuomo arrived at the Troop B Barracks, he brushed past representatives from over a dozen of the law enforcement agencies tasked with capturing the escapees. On his way to the podium and the massed cameras, Cuomo offered no acknowledgment to any of these police officials, all of whom had been awaiting his arrival.

Cuomo stepped into the spotlight, stood behind a lectern and spoke into the microphones, addressing the local and national media as well as the dozens of local residents. And for reasons that defy understanding, he spoke about the confrontation with "Mr. Matt" and the ongoing search for "Mr. Sweat." I still cannot wrap my head around his motive for this. What possible political advantage did this veteran politician think he might gain by showing such courtesy toward a pair of cold-blooded killers?

"There are several leads that are being tracked down as we speak about Mr. Sweat and his possible whereabouts," the governor said, "but we don't have anything to confirm where Mr. Sweat is at this time." His choice of words was no accident; he used the title "Mister" consistently. "We have no reason to believe that Mr. Sweat was not with Mr. Matt at the time, but we don't have any confirming evidence that he was either." It got even worse. After describing both escapees as "dangerous, dangerous men," Cuomo concluded, "That's why you see law enforcement from across this country arrayed before you today, cooperating with one mission: to bring these gentlemen to justice."

Joseph D'Amico was assertive and direct when it came his time to speak. And to his credit, he never referred to the two inmate escapees, convicted killers, murderers of an elderly widower and a police officer, as "Mister." Much less as "gentlemen."

The State Police superintendent commended the residents of Clinton and Franklin counties for their understanding, support, and patience. "I would like to extend my personal thanks to the people of the communities where we have been searching," he said. "We do understand it is very intrusive to have the level of law enforcement we have maintained over the last three weeks." To everyone watching on TV, and those clustered around the TV cameras, he made it clear that the pursuit was still on.

That fact—that one of the killers was still on the loose—may have explained the grim look on Cuomo's face when the press conference ended. Once again, on his way out, he snubbed the supervisors, team leaders, and chiefs of local law enforcement agencies, sweeping past them without any acknowledgment. Perhaps he was so peeved because he had flown all the way up from Albany only to discover he had only half of what he'd hoped to announce in front of all the cameras. He wouldn't be able to bask in the glory of a successful finish.

When a cool, cloudy Saturday dawned on the twenty-seventh, the locals inside the new search perimeter realized what they had been watching on television for the past three weeks had now become their reality. For all of us anywhere near those twenty-some square miles, the manhunt was now directly outside our front doors.

We had been advised just a day earlier that all roads inside the perimeter had been closed. Just like it had been earlier in Clinton County, those in that area were warned that they wouldn't be allowed back in if they had to leave. Until searchers were certain the area was clear, no one would be allowed to enter; all vehicles were turned away.

Many homes were sandwiched between roadblocks staffed by heavily armed officers. Most of the homes themselves were guarded by armed police officers standing post in their front yards. Residents were no longer able to walk their dogs, exercise, work outdoors, or send their children out to play. Everyone who chose to stay in their homes within the search perimeter stayed vigilant behind locked doors.

That was our routine, too, in our Malone home. We were a few miles outside that day's official search perimeter, but we were taking no chances. While Penny took the dogs out for their morning exercise, I stood watch with my 9mm pistol.

Throughout the entire manhunt, no one that I heard about minded the intrusion. In fact, in "North Country" fashion, everyone enthusiastically supported law enforcement. Just as our neighbors over in Clinton County had done during the search's first weeks, the residents of Franklin County also unlocked their doors every morning to offer fresh-brewed coffee to the officers out front. They opened their homes for warmth and bathroom necessities. They passed out sandwiches, granola bars, fruit, and other snacks to those standing sentry in their yards.

The county's volunteer fire departments provided first aid and began serving breakfast, lunch, and dinner to the many searchers. Both businesses and residents provided homemade meals, dry socks, clean T-shirts, and toothpaste. Food, snacks, water, and supplies poured in for the searchers.

The "Clinton Strong" movement that had started in Clinton County had moved to Franklin County. The message was always the same: we're proud to support law enforcement; and we hope the pursuit ends soon.

We wouldn't have to wait much longer.

CHAPTER 44
SWEAT RUNS
FOR THE BORDER

AFTER DAYS OF ENDURING what he called Matt's "dumb shit," his drinking, slow pace, and rants about dying in the woods, David Sweat had had enough. Or so he claimed when interrogated later. Whatever the reason, shortly after leaving the Whitacre Camp and encountering the white police SUV, Sweat left Matt behind. And doing so, he changed direction, heading north by northeast toward Canada. That left his former companion to continue, alone, the westward track they had been following since day one.

Going north, on or parallel to Webster Street Road, Sweat eventually came to a power line. Its cleared right of way gave him an alternative to trying to penetrate Malone's relatively crowded streets. Now, for the first time since that first night on the Hugh Herron Road, he was moving through populated country. The south end of Webster Street Road has a few permanent residences; they sit on patches of dry ground separated by numerous marshes and streams. People living there reported several suspicious incidents that hint, in retrospect, at the escapee's progress.

A woman who lives in a house that backs up to thick woods said motion detectors turned on the lights that shine into her back yard.

Police concluded that this quiet, unpaved road was a very likely escape route. They moved in personnel and equipment, but as in the weeks past, probably about a day too late.

A ways farther north where the road is paved, a doctor returned home after being informed that his alarm system had been tripped, also by motion detectors. On white carpeting in his upstairs bedroom, he told police, he found muddy footprints. If those tracks had belonged to Sweat, he'd once again demonstrated his lock-picking skills. The doctor's house showed no sign of forced entry.

The night after Matt was killed, I woke up and saw brilliant lights just a couple of miles away, across the valley of the Salmon River, which runs due north into Malone village. At two o'clock in the morning, Webster Street Road was all lit up like a Christmas tree. The generator-powered light towers that had been used since the search's early days were illuminating a perimeter that extended into view from our house.

CERT searchers, combing the marshy woods along that road, found an empty pepper shaker, another confirmation that their prey was still ahead of them. By the time the lights went on, though, Sweat was almost certainly miles away.

The power line he followed angles east, with a few northwardly jogs, just outside the Adirondack Park's boundaries. While its right-of-way crosses plenty of deep ditches, marshes, and the Salmon River, none of those would have been serious obstacles.

On Friday night, he holed up "in a high deer blind, it was like in the middle of a swamp, so I could see where the searchers were, just below Malone." His description matches the area where the power line crosses the shallow Salmon River, sandwiched between the Malone Golf Club and the town's Rotary Memorial Recreation Park. Only later would Sweat learn his former partner had been killed that afternoon. During the night, hidden in the deer stand, he watched helicopters flying overhead.

When Saturday morning came, it was chilly, only in the high forties, with more clouds than sunshine. By then Sweat had probably made at least several miles from his overnight hiding place. For a change, there was no rain that day, but on his route along the power line he couldn't help slogging through stretches of marsh and water-filled ditches and across endless soggy ground. Even with the stolen raingear he was wearing, his feet and legs would have been soaked.

Less than a mile east of where he waded through the Salmon River, Sweat would have crossed our road, just down the hill from our house. By then he was in farm country, well clear of Malone village. Grazing cows might have seen him, but no humans did—not right away. At some point it surely occurred to him, convenient as this route was, that it was taking him east. To get to Canada, he would have to turn north again. What may have forced the matter for him was a natural feature he couldn't cross easily: the Little Trout River. Lower down, this stream trickles less than a foot deep over a wide, stony bed. But near the little village of Burke, it roars and tumbles over rapids and a waterfall. Crossing there could be fatal.

Sweat discovered this for himself. Making his way along the river's western bank, he got to the waterfall, a favorite spot for hikers, dog-walkers, and romantic teenagers. Looking over the falls to find a way across, Sweat had a chance encounter with a man and his dog who had strolled down to the river's opposite bank. For the first time since encountering Leslie Lewis in his Dannemora back yard, Sweat had been clearly seen. But he put on a convincing act, pretending to be a bird watcher. He scanned the trees with a pair of stolen binoculars, then reached into his stolen backpack for a notebook. He pretended to write something, as if documenting a bird sighting. The man never imagined that he himself had scored a rare jailbird sighting. He didn't give Sweat another look. Neither one spoke.

Aside from his clever ruse at the waterfall, Sweat's wits were starting to fail him.

His position in Burke, New York, placed him just six miles from the Canadian border. But for some reason, maybe fatigue or hypothermia, or both, Sweat found himself disoriented. Despite the topographic map he had stolen, he confessed later, he was confused about his best route north. He needed to avoid the few houses in Burke village, where he'd be spotted. That ruled out the only bridge over the Little Trout River, which flows through

Burke and then northwest into Canada. The river would be dangerous if not impossible to cross anywhere else nearby. Instead of taking the most direct crow-flight route north, which would have required picking his way into a steep ravine and across the swift-flowing river, he turned west once more. From County Route 23, Burke County Road, he walked west parallel to Finney Road, through farmland and scattered woodlots. That got him away from the river, which he wouldn't encounter again. Then resuming a northerly track, he followed Fleury Road to his next major landmark, U.S. Route 11. That's the main east-west highway closest to the border. Watching carefully for a gap in traffic, he hurried across the two lanes, continuing cross country through the cover of woods. He came out on another east-west road, State Route 122. After about four indirect miles, he had gotten a couple of miles closer to the border. He was now just four miles from Canada.

The farm country here was very different from the tangled wilderness he'd struggled through in The Park. He realized he needed to change how he was moving. He was feeling the pressure of pursuit, the danger of being spotted, and the need to keep going.

A tree stand he chose as a shelter, shortly after crossing Route 122, started to feel too close to people. He moved on during the night, improvising a lean-to after finding what seemed like a safer place. But he couldn't relax. When Sunday morning arrived, the twenty-eighth of June, he heard talking and dogs barking. He used the binoculars to scan the area, barely making out something white in the distance. Was it a roadblock or checkpoint? Maybe a Border Patrol vehicle?

This country is a patchwork of woods and fields, more open ground than cover. Rough walls of stones, which farmers have been pulling out of the soil for the past two hundred years, run between the fields. Trees growing out of these piles make ragged hedgerows, often running north and south, that gave Sweat cover as he resumed his hike. Up here, you'll see plenty of dirt roads, the occasional Amish farmer driving a horse-drawn buggy, and frequent appearances by deer and wild turkeys. In the distance, on the ridges east of Burke, Sweat would have seen dozens of wind turbines calmly rotating above the cloudy eastern horizon. The day had turned out cool, with occasional spells of rain.

Sweat abandoned his plan to move only at night. Quickly dismantling his lean-to, he started moving north. He came to a field and saw a road. He also spotted a Border Patrol unit with an enclosed trailer carrying ATV's. He became convinced that a dog was tracking him so he stripped off the noisy rain gear and doused himself with pepper. He climbed over several barbed-wire fences, crossed a couple more open fields and another road. Another mile closer to Canada.

When Sweat got close to Coveytown Road, his topographic map would have shown him he had just three more roads to cross before reaching the border. He could follow an abandoned railroad right of way through mostly wooded land and across the unfenced border, right into rural Quebec. But first, of course, he had to get across the road, and a freshly planted field of alfalfa on its north side. From his hiding place in a patch of woods, he watched a State Police car go by. Following a hedgerow for cover, he moved up toward the road and sat down. He heard a second State Police car before he saw it, the tires hissing on the wet road as it approached and went past. He had timed the cars and was now confident he knew how long he had before the next one would pass. Inching closer to the road, he took cover again and waited. All he had to do now was get across the road and through the field to the next tree line. Then he's a ghost. Gone. Disappeared into Canada. Sweat was now less than three miles from freedom—at least as he imagined it.

CHAPTER 45
SWEAT GOES DOWN

FOR NORTH COUNTRY RESIDENTS, JUNE IS FILLED with the opening of seasonal summer camps, commencement ceremonies, graduation parties and Father's Day celebrations. And, of course, children stay out late playing outdoor games like "hide and seek" on warm summer nights. Summer comes suddenly, and we all dive enthusiastically into it. Lots of memories are being made.

Unsettlingly, a couple of things were very different this June. For the past three weeks, North Country residents had lived with the nightmare of escaped murderers on the loose, now known to be skulking around seasonal camps. On top of that, the weather was unusually cold and wet. Instead of occasional summer showers, we coped with torrential rainstorms. Children weren't playing outside games.

Commencement ceremonies, celebrations, and parties were protected by armed guards. Supplementing the heavily armed police were property owners, also armed. In this wild country, gun ownership is almost universal. One reality hung over every one of these events. That was that 1,500 people had descended on our quiet corner of the world with the sole mission of hunting down two murderous escapees. Among the crowds of corrections officers, State Police, and federal officers from literally the far corners of the United States were some of our own.

One of those was New York State Police Sergeant Jay Cook.

During the past three weeks, the veteran forty-seven-year-old sergeant had been assigned almost every day to the Troop B manhunt detail. During the daily morning briefing on June 28, Sgt. Cook was assigned as the sergeant in charge of a roving detail. Unlike most of the officers in his detail, who had come from all over the state to help in the manhunt, Cook is a local man. He lives in the area he was patrolling. He knows all the rural roads. He knows who lives along those roads.

It had rained off and on all of that third Sunday of the search. Yet another wet, sloppy day. Most of the troopers patrolling the rural roads along the border worked in pairs: one driving, one riding shotgun and on the lookout. But as a supervisor, Sgt. Cook was patrolling solo.

That day, June 28, his assigned area was the town of Constable, the same rural expanse Penny, Mom, and I had crossed three weeks earlier between Malone and the Trout River border crossing. While zigzagging along the network of farm roads, Cook frequently met and passed other troop cars. Around 3:15 that afternoon, he was eastbound on Coveytown Road toward the town of Burke. That was another forty square miles of territory to cover.

After timing the intervals between police patrols, David Sweat concluded that it was safe to cross the road. To his right, he had a clear view down almost three miles of straightaway through open fields. In the other direction, a couple stands of trees masked a curve on his side of the road. But he saw no cars in either direction when he jumped up, hurried across the road, and clambered over a tangle of dead branches and brambles that filled the roadside ditch. Just a couple of hundred yards of alfalfa separated him from the welcoming tree line.

As Sgt. Cook rounded a blind curve and got a clear look straight east, the first thing he saw was the wind turbines off on the horizon. Then he noticed something more down to earth. Somebody was walking north, parallel to a hedgerow, in a field on Coveytown Road's left side.

He couldn't tell if it was a man or a woman. The person was dressed in camouflage, carrying a large camouflaged backpack, and quickly approaching a wall of thick underbrush under mature trees. Cook braked to a halt, his patrol car angled to the left across both lanes. Through his open window, he hollered to the figure retreating through the alfalfa. "Come here! Come here for a minute."

The camouflaged person turned around, removed a baseball cap and yelled back, "No, no, I'm good, I'm good."

The voice told Cook he was looking at a man. And the man's face, clean-shaven except for a mustache, told him he was looking at David Sweat, standing just thirty yards away. "I instantly recognized the man," Cook said, from the mug shot that had been in everyone's face for weeks. It was a photo "I had seen countless times over the course of the manhunt detail," he remembered.

Sweat turned away and resumed his quick-time walk toward the tree line. Cook hollered again. "Get back here!" That's when Sweat broke into a run.

Cook jumped out of the car, leaving the motor running and the door open. It took him a moment to get over the bramble-choked brush pile and the ditch and into the field.

Shouting as he ran, Cook ordered Sweat to halt. "STOP! STOP! Get on the ground. Get on the ground!" Sweat looked back long enough to confirm that the state policeman was chasing him. He shed his backpack and picked up speed. Just a few dozen more yards separated Sweat from the woods, and from there, Cook knew, he could easily reach the border. It was time for deadly force.

"STOP OR I'LL SHOOT!" Sweat kept running. "STOP OR I'LL SHOOT!" Sweat was almost to the tree line.

Now it was time for Cook to make the same "shoot" or "no shoot" decision that Christopher Voss had made two days before. Just a few more steps and Sweat would be in the trees. "I knew that if Sweat made it," Cook said, "I was going to lose sight of him."

Cook made his decision. He stopped, drew his Glock .45 pistol and assumed a shooting stance. He fired once. Sweat stumbled but kept running. Cook took a second shot. Sweat tumbled to the ground. His run had ended. It may have been Sweat's bad luck that Cook's lengthy law enforcement resume included service as a gunnery range instructor. Even though, like most police, he had never fired his gun at a human target, his aim was perfect. At a range of seventy-five yards, both his rounds had hit home. His sprinting, moving target was down.

Cook followed standard tactics as he approached Sweat, placing himself between the escapee and the trees. "I can't breathe," Sweat gurgled, blood coming from his mouth. To minimize his captive's discomfort, Cook let him sit up. One of the bullets had pierced Sweat's lung; the other had hit muscle in his shoulder. Cook reported in on his portable radio: "Shots fired, suspect shot."

Cook asked for backup and emergency medical services to be sent to Coveytown Road.

Within seconds the State Police frequencies were full of reports: "Shots fired . . . Coveytown Road . . . Any rovers respond for assistance." Within minutes, troopers were rushing to the scene. The first to arrive found what looked to be an abandoned State Police cruiser in the road with nobody in sight. But after a moment of panic, they spotted Sgt. Cook, far out in the field with a prisoner in his custody.

Troopers ran through the alfalfa to reach Sgt. Cook and Sweat, who was sitting on the ground dressed in camouflage. Troopers clamped a pair of Smith & Wesson handcuffs on Sweat's wrists and searched him. An officer ran back to his car to get a first aid kit and began to tend to Sweat's wounds while waiting for EMS.

A quick search of the prisoner was next. Sweat had an empty knife sheath on his belt, $36.00 in U.S. currency in his pants pocket, a compass attached to his shirt, and a Ziploc bag of pepper in his jacket pocket. As more troopers arrived, they secured the entire scene to preserve and collect evidence. Troopers stood next to Sweat's dropped backpack. Others stood where two empty .45 caliber shell casings marked Sgt. Cook's shooting location. These troopers' job was to protect all the physical evidence until forensics specialists could catalogue and collect it.

Sweat asked the troopers how close he was to the border. The map shows about three miles. The troopers told him two. Mighty close either way. Between gasps for breath, Sweat told his captors, "I just wanted to get away. I just wanted to disappear."

The next few days would give him plenty of time to think about his exploits, and his ultimate failure. Outnumbered as he was, hundreds to one, he reflected that his pursuers could make plenty of mistakes and still get him. He had no margin for error, though. "You have to be right a hundred percent of the time," Sweat would say. "That day, that cop was right; I fucked up."

Rehashing his decisions, he wished that he'd chosen to stay in cover, "move a little bit" and wait for the police cars to go by. Instead, to his regret, "For whatever fucking reason, I thought I could make the distance."

In those last seconds, when Sgt. Cook was chasing him and the trees were just yards ahead, he made one final decision: to drop the backpack with his carefully selected provisions and meticulously chosen stolen gear. They say time slows down in a crisis, so maybe these thoughts really did go through his head out there in the alfalfa field. Or maybe he was just rationalizing after the fact. Either way, he said he figured he could survive awhile without his supplies, if that was the price of outrunning the trooper. "It was no big deal. I could go a couple of days, you know, on stream water, whatever I could forage . . . eat worms and grubs and beetles or anything like that."

But now he sat handcuffed in the alfalfa, bleeding and wheezing through his punctured lung. The notion of finding his food under rocks, just like finding freedom in Canada, had proved to be just another delusion.

Within a few minutes, the Constable Fire Department and EMS arrived to treat Sweat for his gunshot wounds and punctured lung. He was conscious and talking as they loaded him into an ambulance and raced off to the Alice Hyde Medical Center.

Word of Sweat's capture began to spread almost instantly via social media. Some people turned up at the hospital just to watch the ambulance bring him to the emergency room door. Near the command center at Titus Mountain, small children stood in their yard holding signs thanking police. Along Main Street in Malone, people cheered passing police cars.

In Dannemora, a sizable crowd turned out in a cold rain, lining Highway 374 for a spontaneous "thank-you" to passing law enforcement officers. Whenever a police vehicle came by, people cheered and waved signs and flags. Whenever police stopped to talk, they faced a forest of hands reaching out to shake.

Some people drove to Dannemora from twenty or more miles away to join in the celebration. Among the crowd, the papers reported, were two sisters from Cadyville, holding a home-made sign commending the searchers. Cheyenne Roe said, "We want to support all the hard work they've done in our community. It's the least we can do."

Her sister Shelby added, "It makes us feel like part of what is happening."

Cheyenne concluded, "It shows our strength."

Clinton strength.

PART VIII
THE AFTERMATH

CHAPTER 46
ASSIGNING THE BLAME

THE PURSUIT OF THE ESCAPED CONVICTED MURDERERS David Sweat and Richard Matt captured the nation's attention. This manhunt was documented as the largest in New York State Police history. As it concluded, the nation had become aware of the sacrifices made by the men and women, and even the dogs, of law enforcement.

Within hours of the convicted murderer Sweat's capture, Governor Cuomo returned to Malone for yet another press conference. He wore a beaming smile as he addressed the local and national media. To make a photo backdrop, his aides had lined up over a dozen law enforcement representatives behind him. The governor outlined the particulars of the legal and authorized shooting and capture of the man he still called "Mr. Sweat."

While the press conference was going on, arrangements were made to move Sweat from Malone's local hospital to the Albany Medical Center. During the days that followed, Sweat's condition was officially stable. Which meant he could be interviewed by both the New York State Police and the New York State Inspector General's Office. The questions covered everything leading up to and during the escape.

These bedside interviews started by restating the obvious. Sweat identified his co-conspirators, inmate Richard Matt and their civilian supervisor, Joyce Mitchell. He described in detail the contraband items the eager Mitchell had smuggled into their maximum-security prison. Sweat also told what he knew about the conspiracy Matt and Joyce Mitchell allegedly cooked up to kill her husband. He confirmed what investigators had already concluded: that Corrections Officer Gene Palmer was never aware of the escape plan. Even so, Palmer would have to answer for his misdeeds and bad judgment.

Others were under the spotlight, too. While Sweat was still being interviewed by the state authorities, twelve members of the Clinton Correctional Facility staff were administratively suspended with pay. Three of the staff members were the prison's top administrators. The superintendent, first deputy superintendent, and the deputy superintendent for security would become the sacrificial lambs for the Albany leadership.

Superintendent Steve Racette, a rock-solid pillar of the prison, with a stellar thirty-seven year career, was forced to retire. Stephen Brown, the deputy superintendent for security, with over three decades of unblemished service, also retired. Donald Quinn, the first deputy superintendent, kept his rank but was reassigned to a prison in Malone after weeks of being suspended.

Racette did as he was told, but not happily. After the inspector general's report was issued, he told the *Adirondack Daily Enterprise* in Saranac Lake, "The report says I retired, which is true, but it fails to say that I was told to do so, ordered to do so, almost before the investigation even started." He and the other Clinton administrators were suspended on June 30, 2015, just days after the escape concluded. He was ordered to retire a month later. "I think it gives the impression that I ran away from it all, which is far from the truth."

Catherine Leahy Scott, the state inspector general, brushed aside Racette's defenses. "Leadership is always responsible," she told the Plattsburgh newspaper. But while the leadership her report held responsible included unnamed "DOCCS executive management," no heads rolled in Albany. None of the actual consequences for the escape went any higher than Racette's office.

This didn't sit well with North Country folks who know how things work in the prisons. One of them was Richard Gonyea, a retired corrections officer. He said his friend Racette was being punished for things he had little power over, things that had been dictated by his superiors in Albany. "He has to refer to Albany and then do what Albany says," Gonyea said. It's the departmental brass, he argued, who should have been held responsible. "The people that run the facility—that are on the front lines—can't make the decisions. They come from someone sitting behind a desk. They're the ones that are cutting back."

Gonyea had been inspired by the blue ribbons of the Clinton Strong movement. And so he started an orange-ribbon campaign to show solidarity with the prison's administrators. But even though plenty of his friends and neighbors wrapped orange ribbons around trees and utility poles, it didn't change the outcome. Racette and his top assistants were still out.

There was also talk among rank-and-file corrections officers about staging a slowdown. This is called "working to rule." The idea is simple: follow every departmental order, mandate, and procedure absolutely to the letter, to demonstrate just how impossible strict compliance would be.

The union that represents prison guards, the New York State Correction Officers and Police Benevolent Association, said it didn't support the slowdown. But its Northern Zone vice president, Chris Hansen, took issue with how the state blamed the Clinton prison's leadership. "I don't believe that the top three administrators are responsible for this," he said. "That's ludicrous."

For the lower-ranking nine prison employees who'd been suspended, the outcomes varied. Significantly, none of the twelve faced any criminal charges.

One of the more damaging conclusions from the state's investigation was that on April 7, 2015, the Department of Corrections had sent out a warning, after an escape attempt at another prison, about the importance of going by the book in such areas as gate checks, daily counts, and tunnel inspections. The inspector general's report said Clinton's leadership failed to respond.

In his own defense, Racette said his marching orders when he was made Clinton's superintendent in 2014 were about improving relationships with inmates and among the staff, not about security. In a 2016 interview with the *Press-Republican,* he said, "It was more that the staff had absolutely lost confidence in the administration, and they felt that nobody was listening to them on any topic, including security."

State investigators said, despite the inside help from Mitchell and Palmer, that the escape could not have succeeded without "executive management's failure" to correct serious security problems.

One of those problems, the report said, is that "There are no cameras in place to monitor night counts in any housing block." True enough. Of course, cameras cost money. About how that issue fit into the Department of Corrections' budget, the report had nothing to say. Installing—and paying for—cameras would have required a decision from leadership in Albany, not by the prison's superintendent.

Another problem the report mentioned was that employees weren't thoroughly searched as they entered and left the prison. That, too, was a direct consequence of budget and staff cuts. Racette said it would have been impossible to search every worker every day and that no state prison required it. "You would only frisk employees as a rarity," he said.

I can attest to the impossibility. The Clinton prison's huge steel gate leads into a little room, with locked doors at both ends, that holds maybe twenty people at a time. A single guard is responsible for everybody going in and out. Now consider this. At the start and finish of each of the prison's three shifts, hundreds of employees have to pass through this little room in just a few minutes. Compare that to how the Transportation Security Administration processes airline passengers. At any busy airport, a dozen or more TSA officers will be searching passengers, often using multiple lines, to avoid intolerable bottlenecks. Even so, we've all been advised to get to the airport a couple of hours early to be sure we can get through security on time.

Now picture one prison guard, responsible for getting hundreds of people through the gate in time to start their shifts, three times a day, every day. How is that staff member, working alone, going to inspect hundreds of bags in a matter of a few minutes? Or, put another way: How could any workplace function if the entire staff had to wait hours every day for a mandatory frisk?

Much of what the inspector general's report says makes perfect sense—from the outside. Each of these requirements is a good idea—taken by itself. But they require manpower, and that costs money. Money that the State of New York is still unwilling to invest in the security of its prison system.

Maybe you've heard the cynical management motto: "Nothing is impossible . . . if you don't have to do it yourself."

As to the state's own responsibility for the escape, the official blame flowed downhill. The inspector general's investigation, which began while the escapees were still loose, found plenty of fault. But, curiously, it never named any officials in the highest levels of the Department of Corrections, the governor who appointed those officials, or the Legislature that set the department's budgets. Governor Cuomo's mandate to Inspector General Catherine Leahy Scott was "to conduct a thorough investigation to determine all factors potentially involved in the escape" and "recommend any potential reforms and best practices to prevent future incidents." After a year, Leahy Scott released her findings and recommendations in June 2016. Her report included a few general statements about the department as a whole. "Systemic failures," one of these comments noted, "raise fundamental questions about the ability of DOCCS to oversee itself." But when it came time to name names, only lower-level managers were singled out. The report listed a number of security concerns and blamed the Clinton prison's administration and staff for all of them. Other than dancing around the question of why the pre-escape lockdown had been rejected, the report did not directly address the role anyone in Albany played.

When the report came out, the governor talked tough about what needed to be done, but kept his focus squarely at the individual prison level. "I said there were no holds barred," he told the *Press-Republican.* By his own words, he then admitted that some holds might have been barred: in Albany. Leahy Scott's mandate, the governor said, was to "Take a microscope and go find out how the place works"—the prison, not the department, and certainly not his own budget office—"see how the culture works and what needs to be changed."

But if anything has changed in Albany, I haven't heard about it.

When the report first came out, an editorial in the Plattsburgh paper took aim at state-level officials. "Fault carries on to Department of Corrections and Community Supervision for not being responsive—sometimes for the sake of money—to suggestions from the people actually working amid all the danger and friction posed by close contact with convicted criminals."

So who was to blame for the escape? Well, certainly David Sweat, Richard Matt, and Joyce Mitchell deserve the most blame. The two inmates planned and executed the escape. Could they have escaped without Joyce? I say no. She supplied the tools they needed. Without those tools, they wouldn't have succeeded.

The IG report is highly critical of the staff at Clinton Correctional Facility. Were mistakes made there? Probably, but those mistakes didn't directly affect the escape. But what about mistakes made at higher levels? What if sufficient manpower had been provided to inspect the tunnels? What if the staff hadn't been steadily cut and the "do more with less" ethic never imposed? What if the wall towers hadn't been closed? What if Corcraft had placed a higher priority on security instead of income? What if Albany had approved the lockdown the prison administration proposed?

There's plenty of blame to go around. But the people in Albany who made the decisions to cut staff, close wall towers, and deny lockdowns never accepted any of the blame, or even responsibility. Policies and procedures ordered by Department of Corrections leaders in Albany failed. And yet nobody in Albany was held accountable.

Since the escape, tunnel inspections have resumed at Clinton prison. All the wall towers are now manned twenty-four hours a day, seven days a week. Many policies and procedures have also been modified. Too little, too late.

Around $23 million of New York State taxpayer money was spent on this escape, a direct consequence of failed policies and procedures the Albany leadership imposed. Federal taxpayers were on the hook for another $60 million.

Amid all this waste of public resources, though, some bright lights would shine through.

CHAPTER 47
FINAL ACCOUNTING

RICHARD MATT'S AUTOPSY RESULTS REVEALED that he died of two gunshot wounds to the head. His body was covered with insect bites and his feet with blisters. And to confirm what Sweat said about his former partner, his blood alcohol content was 0.18 percent when he died. A point of comparison: in New York, a level of 0.08 will get you arrested for driving while intoxicated. Matt's body was released to his family.

Paul Marlow, who had helped police zero in on Matt after the break-in at Camp Humbug, would eventually collect a $25,000 federal reward. But because he was a state employee, he wasn't eligible for the $50,000 state reward. Neither was Corrections Officer John Stockwell or Trooper Jay Cook, for the same reason. In 2017, after collecting the reward, Marlow quit his job with the Department of Corrections. At last report, nobody has collected the reward Governor Cuomo first promised in the first few days of the search.

Joyce Mitchell pled guilty to both of the charges against her: promoting prison contraband and criminal facilitation. On September 27, just three months after the escape came to its bloody end, she stood before Judge Kevin K. Ryan in Clinton County Court. "You did terrible things," the judge told her. "At any time, you could have stopped the escape from happening." He lectured Mitchell about the consequences of her actions. The State of New

York had incurred expenses in the millions, he said, and "incalculable" non-economic costs. "A large portion of the local population was terrorized. Many residents did not sleep for many nights." The law enforcement officers hunting for Matt and Sweat never knew, the judge said, "if the next step they took in deeply wooded areas would be their last."

Ryan also told Mitchell that he didn't buy her story, the one she'd used in her defense. She'd claimed that she helped the inmates escape only out of fear that they would hurt her husband or her son.

But when it came time to pass sentence, Ryan said, he was bound by a plea bargain Mitchell's lawyers had worked out with Clinton County District Attorney Andrew Wylie. The D.A. concluded he would have trouble making other charges stick. Such as the murder plot against Joyce's husband, or sex offenses involving her encounters with Matt and Sweat in the tailor shops. The judge OK'd the deal, which sent her to prison for at least two years and four months, possibly as much as seven years. She was fined $6,000 and ordered to pay $79,841 to the State of New York to repair the damage the inmates did to the prison.

As of this writing, two years later, Mitchell had just reached the minimum term of her sentence, which potentially made her eligible for parole. But the state parole board said no. Her good behavior behind bars wasn't enough to grant her early release, which would have been "incompatible with the welfare of society," the board ruled. The next time her case comes up for review, the decision will again depend largely on public comments. Between the state's corrections officers and their families, the state's law enforcement community, and the residents of the northern Adirondack region, those comments are likely to be numerous and vehement. And negative.

Joyce Mitchell is now known as inmate 15G0834, serving her sentence at Bedford Hills Correctional Facility, New York State's only maximum-security prison for women. If she serves just a couple more years beyond her minimum sentence, she could start collecting her New York State pension while still behind bars.

Despite having betrayed every trust as a state employee, her years on the state payroll automatically entitle her to that retirement income when she turns fifty-five. Let's hope she uses it to pay what she owes to the state.

Lyle Mitchell was never criminally charged, and despite evidence that his wife plotted to have him killed, still publicly stands by her. He'd been suspended from his job without pay right after the escape was discovered; he never returned to work at Clinton Correctional Facility. Like the wife to whom he remains loyal, he will also be eligible for state retirement when he turns fifty-five.

Corrections Officer Gene Palmer pled guilty to promoting prison contraband and official misconduct. Palmer resigned from his job, was sentenced to six months in Clinton County Jail, and was fined $5,000.

Inmate David Sweat, also known as 03B2297, was sent to Five Points Correctional Facility in the Finger Lakes region after his gunshot wounds healed. He's serving his life sentence for the murder of Broome County Deputy Sheriff Kevin Tarsia and a new sentence resulting from the escape. After pleading guilty to escape and promoting prison contraband, he was sentenced to another three and a half to seven years, fined $5,000, and ordered to pay the same amount of restitution as Mitchell: $79,841.

At Five Points, instead of a relatively cushy "Honor Block" cell, Sweat earned himself a place in the Special Housing Unit, where especially disruptive or dangerous inmates are sent. In the SHU, he spent twenty-three hours a day in his cell. But ingenious as ever, he put that time to good use, studying the cell's construction and looking for weak points. He found some, and some ways to exploit them. As *The New York Times* reported in December 2017, he believed he'd come up with a way out.

Instead of trying another escape, though, Sweat had what he thought was a better idea: offer his services to DOCCS. As an in-house security consultant. Through a new girlfriend on the outside, he made a proposition to prison officials. He'd tell them about his escape idea in exchange for privileges including extra visits and food packages.

Officials from both Corrections and the Inspector General's Office interviewed Sweat, the *Times* reported. They were not impressed. Instead of upgrading his living conditions, they immediately transferred him to Attica Correctional Facility, where he's still doing hard time. At last report, he's in the SHU at Attica.

During the three-week search, twenty Correction Emergency Response Teams were brought in from prisons around the state. Weeks later, some of these CERT members returned to the North Country bearing gifts. With help from the New York State Correction Officers and Police Benevolent Association, they brought donations for schools in the search areas. The gifts included school supplies, backpacks, and money. Eight members of a CERT team based in the Mohawk Valley town of Rome came back to the Malone Central School and the Chateaugay Central Elementary School to express their appreciation. After sleeping in makeshift accommodations in Dannemora, they had been housed in the mothballed Chateaugay prison during the search's final days. During their time here, the CERT members had gotten thank-you letters from elementary school children.

Back at home, "We told people what we went through while we were here," Corrections Officer Tom Achen said, "because we feel the real story was this and not the escape at all."

Lt. Todd Worden added, "The kindness and support shown to us during our deployment was amazing." According to a report in the *Press-Republican,* Worden teared up and his voice cracked as he thanked Chateaugay's people "for treating us like one of your own. We felt like the people here were proud of us and the job we do daily, and we'll always remember how nice everyone treated us here."

This story could have ended in many ways. How it did end was what I'd call the best-case scenario, with one man shot and killed and the other one captured. The worst case, what we all feared, was that one of the civilians, law officers, or both might have been abducted, injured, or murdered by these two sadistic killers. Almost as bad would have been that they would never be found;

the peace and serenity we've come to love and expect would have been replaced by a lingering dread, never knowing when or where these escaped felons might show up.

Any way it might have turned out, it would have changed our lives forever. The sacrifices made by many are huge and too many to mention.

It's no accident that this ordeal ended with "the best-case scenario." It's necessary for me, just like everyone else in the North Country, to thank the 1,500 prison guards, police, and federal agents who joined in the search. They are all heroes. Absolutely deserving special mention are the three men who were essential to ending this nightmare: New York State Corrections Officer John Stockwell, New York State Trooper Jay Cook and U.S. Border Patrol Agent Christopher Voss.

ACKNOWLEDGMENTS

I would like to take this opportunity to acknowledge the persons behind the scenes who made my dream of writing this book become a reality.

Dr. Calvin Martin, who advised, encouraged, and mentored me along the way. You believed in me!

John Meyer with Cape Fear Publishers in Wilmington, North Carolina. You certainly were the right developmental editor for me! From the time we first spoke on the phone and I shared my idea with you, you were as excited as I was. Your willingness to visit the North Country and your fresh set of eyes proved to be so incredibly valuable. Your experience, hard work, and talent helped me to achieve my goal. There is a part of you in this book. Additionally, your contacts with fellow editors provided me with a chance to pitch my idea to a great agent. I will be forever grateful.

To my agent, Kevin O'Connor, of O'Connor Literary Agency in New York. From our first conversation until now has been a whirlwind. There has been a barrage of phone calls, emails, and deadlines. You secured a publisher for me before we really had time to get to know each other. Somehow, I don't think that's the way this normally works. Thank you for your guidance, assistance, advice, and making my dream a reality. I know I am truly lucky to have this opportunity.

To Michaela Hamilton, my editor at Citadel Press, Kensington

Publishing. Thank you for believing in this project and allowing me to tell this story.

To my beautiful wife, Penny, who was my computer IT consultant, typist, proofreader, and biggest supporter. Thank you for your patience in putting our life on hold so that I could achieve this goal. I never could have accomplished this without you and I promise you that your "honey-do" list will get done. Thank you for the endless days and nights of hard work. Love you.

INDEX